TEXAS AGGIES IN VIETNAM

NUMBER 152

Williams-Ford Texas A&M University Military History Series

Texas Aggies in Vietnam

WAR STORIES

Edited by Michael Lee Lanning

TEXAS A&M UNIVERSITY PRESS   COLLEGE STATION

First edition

This paper meets the requirements
of ANSI/NISO Z39.48–1992 (Permanence of Paper).
Binding materials have been chosen for durability.
Manufactured in the United States of America

Library of Congress Cataloging-in-Publication Data

Names: Lanning, Michael Lee, editor.
Title: Texas Aggies in Vietnam: war stories / edited by Michael Lee Lanning.
Other titles: Williams-Ford Texas A&M University military history series; no. 152.
Description: First edition. | College Station: Texas A&M University Press, [2016] | Series: Williams-Ford Texas A&M University military history series; number 152 | Includes index.
Identifiers: LCCN 2016030146 (print) | LCCN 2016032207 (ebook) | ISBN 9781623494704 (cloth: alk. paper) | ISBN 9781623494711 (ebook)
Subjects: LCSH: Vietnam War, 1961–1975—Personal narratives, American. | Texas A & M University. Corps of Cadets—History—20th century. | Agricultural and Mechanical College of Texas. Corps of Cadets—History—20th century.
Classification: LCC DS559.5 .T48 2016 (print) | LCC DS559.5 (ebook) | DDC 959.704/340922764—dc23
LC record available at https://lccn.loc.gov/2016030146

To the Texas A&M University Corps of Cadets:

past, present, and future—

and for all those who come forward to serve

when lesser men call for peace

and there is none.

Contents

Editor's Note

This book began in the fall of 1964 when I stepped onto the quad to join the Class of 1968 in the Texas A&M Corps of Cadets. In those first days as an Aggie, when I made friends and solidified beliefs and values that would last me a lifetime, Vietnam was in the distant future. By the time we pulled on our senior boots, though, we had seen wounded Aggies on the front covers of national magazines and had answered "here" at Musters for those fallen in the war. By the time we graduated, Vietnam was the present.

Less than a year after crossing the stage at G. Rollie White to receive my diploma and commission, I stepped off a contract commercial airliner in Vietnam to pick up an M-16 rifle and the responsibilities of an infantry platoon leader. After the war, having survived, I found that I enjoyed both being a soldier and feeling that I was participating in something important.

Remaining in uniform, I experienced even more fun, travel, and adventure than the army had promised. Like most Vietnam veterans, I placed my Southeast Asia memories and mementos in an old green duffel bag that remained in closets as I moved from assignment to assignment. The idea of writing about the war was always in the back of my mind, but work, family, and other obligations always took priority. Finally, in the mid-1980s, the glut of negative stories, books, and movies about the war and its warriors made me take up pen and paper. I knew that we Vietnam veterans had done well under extremely difficult circumstances—both geographical and political. I also knew that history is not what actually happened but what gets written about what happened.

I had nothing to apologize for and no regrets to express. I was not broken; I did not need to heal. Writing for a year produced a 250,000-word manuscript. After many phone calls, I determined that an editor at Random House in New York was the most likely person to be interested. He was. With his guidance I divided the lengthy work into two books—*The Only War We Had: A Platoon Leader's Journal* and *Vietnam 1969–1970: A Company Commander's Journal*—that were released in 1987 and 1988. Then, after they had remained in print for twenty years, in 2007 the Texas A&M University Press acquired the rights to the books and released them under its imprint.

Although I wrote the introduction to *The Only War We Had* nearly thirty years ago, my words remain appropriate in regards to my thoughts then and to this book today. I wrote:

> A war is a major event in a man's life. It was popular among many who fought to say that Vietnam "wasn't much of a war, but it was the only war we had." I can only add that it was enough of a war for me, for I am neither old nor young enough to want to experience another one.
>
> I am proud to have served in Vietnam. I feel no guilt, have no regrets, harbor no memories I cannot cope with, and—except for a few terrifying moments and the many young men resting for eternity under neat rows of military headstones—I would change nothing.
>
> What I do feel is satisfaction and pride in doing what had to be done, in standing up when called upon by my country, and in being prepared to die if necessary.
>
> I may have been naive in my love for and feeling of obligation to my country. My attitude was that the USA had been good to me; now it was time to pay a little back. The elected officials said the war was right and I had a duty to fight. That was enough for me.
>
> However, I went to Vietnam not only because of the obligation I felt to do my duty but also because I did not want to miss the chance to experience the major significant event of my generation. I wondered, of course, what it would be like to go to war, and I dreaded the prospects of hardship, discipline, family separation, and the possibility of death or debilitating injury. Yet I knew I did not want to let pass the opportunity to challenge myself and to experience the adventure. I felt it would be an irreversible mistake to avoid the war for I knew if I did, I would never know myself to the fullest.

In the years since those first books, I transitioned from professional soldier to full- time writer. The majority of my books focus on the military, especially on the war in Southeast Asia. Over the decades my Aggie buddies have encouraged me to write about A&M, but I have long been convinced that only Aggies understand the Spirit of Aggieland. Trying to reveal this unique esprit de corps is impossible to explain adequately to outsiders.

In 2014 Stackpole Books released my *Tours of Duty: Vietnam War Stories* that included narrations by warriors I had met over the years. In the introduction I wrote,

> Any time Vietnam veterans get together—whether two or twenty—war stories follow. The tales they relate about the paddies, the jungles, the highlands, the waterways, and the airways provide the vets themselves with an even greater understanding of the war they survived and allow the nonparticipants glimpses into the frequent dangers of intense firefights, often hilarious responses to inexplicable situations, and strong bonds that only they can share. All too often, these individual stories from soldiers, airmen, marines, and sailors remain only oral, are never captured or compiled in any meaningful way that would more fully complete the whole of the Vietnam War. This is but a small effort to record some of our stories.

After the book's release, the staff at the A&M Press encouraged me to do a similar book on Texas Aggies in Vietnam. I finally realized there might be a way to show rather than tell the Aggie character. Soon a contract was signed and I began my efforts to record the Aggies' story of the war in Southeast Asia in their own words.

My initial queries went out to more than eighty Aggies who had attended the dedication of the Texas Capitol Vietnam Veterans Monument in Austin on March 29, 2014. Their email addresses were provided by Ed Kainer, Class of 1965, who put together a fellowship at Scholz Garten following the ceremony. I added the addresses of Aggies with whom I had maintained contact. And I contacted class agents to help solicit stories. Each email request for firsthand stories also asked that the recipient forward the correspondence to other Aggie veterans. Another source of names was John A. Adams's books *Keepers of the Spirit* and *Texas Aggies Go to War* (written with Henry C. Dethloff). I found addresses and phone numbers through the Association of Former Students website Aggie Network.

The nearly five hundred emails that I sent out multiplied via the net so that in the end about a thousand Aggie veterans were contacted. Not all, or even the majority, responded. Some surely lacked interest. Some had no time to write down their experiences. Others did not want to revisit memories that they preferred remain in the back of their mind, if not forgotten altogether. One Aggie veteran responded, "After considerable thought, I have decided not to participate. Some things are best left alone."

Another wrote that because much of his tour was classified, he did not know if he could discuss it even after the passage of time. A common reply was that the respondent did not think he had done anything really noteworthy—he had only done his duty. An Air Force pilot said that he had one tour as a combat controller in Laos and another flying fighters over North and South Vietnam but that he had "nothing much to share regarding either tour."

An infantry veteran wrote, "I never write or discuss my personal combat actions or stories with those who've never been there. I'm not eloquent enough to describe my role in active combat situations for fear of sounding self-promoting. For those who have 'been there,' it's not necessary anyway. They know how difficult it is to make courage overcome gut-wrenching fear to do what needs to be done. Some of us were lucky, some were not. I know you've been there and will understand."

Fortunately many Aggies chose to share their stories. Some required more editing than others. As one veteran explained, "Aggies are better fighters than writers." I was not surprised that, in addition to telling their own stories, many Aggies mentioned assistance they had received from fellow Aggies and the importance of impromptu reunions in the war zone. The cover letter to one story contained a note from the wife of an Aggie veteran. She said, "My husband has poured out a lot of his heart in the attached. I want you to read it and know he 'did the best he could.'" No one could ask for more.

MICHAEL LEE LANNING
Bolivar Peninsula, Texas
September 2015

Introduction

For more than one hundred fifty years, Texas Aggies have answered their country's call in time of war. From the Spanish American War of 1898 to the conflicts in Iraq and Afghanistan, Aggies have stepped forward. Vietnam was no different.

Wars topple thrones, replace leaders, change borders, and leave death and havoc in their wake. Throughout history, the results of warfare have determined the future. The outcome of war has been the single greatest factor in determining what choices were available to peoples. Religion, politics, and philosophy have contributed to the twist and turns of history, but they exert their influence only when tribes, kingdoms, or nations unite behind a strong military force to win battles and thereby ensure a way of life.

With the passage of time, politicians and policy makers often become staunch allies and valuable trading partners with once sworn and hated enemies. For those who fight the wars and make the sacrifices, however, time does not necessarily change their opinion of those they faced on the battlefield. Warriors may forgive, but they never forget. Their stories are memories that do not fade.

History generally is written by gray-bearded academics and scholars. Their classroom education and teaching experience may be impressive, but few have experienced the exhilaration and smells of ground combat or felt the adrenaline rush when taking evasive measures to keep a telephone-pole-sized SAM rocket from knocking you out of the sky. The historians may accurately relate political, economic, and social events leading up to and following warfare, but they rarely, if ever, capture the fear, misery, hardship, and visceral reactions of those who actually fight the wars.

This book is not a history of the war in Southeast Asia; rather it is a series of snapshots revealing the inner truths of Texas Aggies who served there. Their words echo the pride, passion, fear, fatigue, and frustration that only veterans can truly comprehend. Many of the stories are those shared by veterans when they get together at reunions or over cold drinks in each other's homes. Other stories have remained untold for nearly a half-century. These stories may not capture the whole of the war, but they do chronicle the thoughts of those who fought. They reveal the war as seen through the eyes of and as recorded from the memories of Aggie grunts, cannon cockers, jet-jockeys, peter pilots, REMFs, and other service and support personnel.

Few of these Aggie war stories highlight great victories, huge body counts, or near annihilation of the enemy. Instead they are the stories that remain in the remote parts of our minds—about wounds suffered, friends lost, hardships endured, and often just a great wonderment about how we survived.

Some Aggies answered the call for service in Vietnam with enthusiasm and vigor and, as Army and Marine cadets, volunteered for the infantry and airborne and ranger training. Aggressive Air Force cadets sought to join the ranks of fighter pilots. Some cadets were not so enthusiastic about enduring the hardships of direct combat and the dangers of fighting in the air or on the ground. Still, they stepped forward to do their duty in rear and support positions.

There are no exact figures on just how many Aggies, graduates and non-graduates, served in Vietnam or in other duties during the war. Between 1962 and 1973, the Corps of Cadets commissioned nearly four thousand officers. Considering the fact that some of these officers did not go to Vietnam and that other Aggies, who were not in the Corps, ended up on active duty through the draft, as volunteers, or as already active-duty members, four thousand is a good estimate of the number who actually served in Southeast Asia.

Those fortunate enough to survive the war came home to a changed world—to new babies born, children a year older, wives a year wiser, hunting seasons missed (deer, upland birds, waterfowl—but not men), and sports events not attended. Those who did not remain in uniform returned to civilian life and a work force in which they were two or more years behind those who had avoided service.

In recent years a much-overused statement about Vietnam veterans says, "All gave some, some gave all." When it comes to the support of the war by America's highest institutes of learning, the adage might better be, "Some gave much more than others." Texas A&M lost at least 106 (Appendix A) in Vietnam and its surrounding countries and waterways. More than 80 additional Aggies (Appendix B) died in training or as a result of other accidents, disease, or other hazards during the long conflict. The only institutions to exceed those numbers in losses are the

United States Military Academy, which lost 273, the United States Air Force Academy, with 205, and the United States Naval Academy, with 130.

Other traditional military schools across the country also made sacrifices. The Citadel suffered 76 deaths, Virginia Military Institute 43, North Georgia 27, Virginia Polytechnical 26, and Norwich 19.

This service and loss did not extend equally to other institutions across the country or even in Texas. (Universities were more often incubators of dissent than centers of support for the war and its warriors.) Harvard, Princeton, and MIT lost a combined total of twenty graduates. As for the schools closer to home: few have records of who served or died. Requests to communications directors and public-relations personnel at Texas Tech University and Texas Christian University revealed that each lost about seven graduates. The history of the ROTC program at the University of Texas at Austin shows that four Longhorn graduates fell in Vietnam.

The Aggies who served in Vietnam and survived have become local, state, and national leaders. We are proud of our service and of each other. We laugh at our youthful follies, but we draw strength and wisdom from our experience.

There really is only one story to come out of the Vietnam War—we each just tell it differently. The following are our efforts.

TEXAS AGGIES IN VIETNAM

Michael Beggs (1968, Squadron 1) 1st Marine Division, 1971

My story about Vietnam includes a fellow Aggie. Charlie Rodenberg, from Old Ocean, Texas, was raised by a mother and father who both had been Marines in World War II. I first met Charlie when we were students at Texas A&M and fellow cadets in the same unit in the Cadet Corps. Squadron 1 was made up primarily of Air Force ROTC cadets, but Charlie and I were two of the three Marines in the unit. After we had graduated and received our commissions, Charlie became a pilot and I became an infantry officer. We were in the Marines together, but because we were in different specialty "communities," we rarely saw each other. However, we did have one momentous meeting in Vietnam, one I wasn't even aware of until almost forty years after it occurred.

It was a warm day in January of 1971—every day in Vietnam seemed warm—when Charlie and I met. Just two days earlier I had returned from a five-day R&R in Hawaii with my wife. Wars continue after R&Rs are finished, so two days after kissing my wife goodbye, I was leading a combat mission against enemy forces as the commander of the Combined Unit Pacification Program of the 3rd Battalion, 5th Marine Regiment.

Our operation had been uneventful until we began taking sniper fire from a small hill. I deployed my Marines and started doing all the things Marines are supposed to do in such situations, but then one of my men became isolated in a minefield. I tried to talk my guy out of the lethal area by getting him to retrace his steps—but he was too scared to move. So, I ran up the hill to get him myself, and that's when I stepped on it.

"It" was a landmine. When it exploded, it not only filled me with holes, but also nearly tore my leg off as I was blown into the air. When I came back down I landed on my head, which pinched some nerves in my spine. So there I was, with the memory of my wife's last kiss fresh in my mind, lying in the red dirt of a hill in Vietnam, rapidly losing blood. I was blinded and temporarily (but I did not know that at the time) paralyzed from the waist down. All I knew then and there was that I was badly hurt and that I might never see my wife and children again.

One of my sergeants immediately called for a Medivac for me. I couldn't move my legs or see, but I could hear all of what was going on around me. I heard the radio operator acknowledge the Medivac helicopter pilot's "inbound" call by saying "Roger, Peachbush 1–7 inbound five mikes." In five minutes, I would be on a helicopter being flown to the nearest medical facility.

However, there was a problem. The area where I lay was in a tree line, and there was no place nearby suitable for a helicopter to land. A piece of equipment called the "jungle penetrator" had been designed just for situations such as this, but recently its use had been suspended for safety reasons. Three things could happen if a JP was used, and two of them were bad: the JP could snag on a tree as it was being brought back up into the helicopter, tethering the helicopter to the ground, or it could break, and the wounded Marine attached to the other end could fall to his death. Because of these liabilities, an order had gone out to all aircrews that use of the JP was suspended.

As I lay there listening to the radio operator talk with the helicopter pilot, it became obvious to me that the only way off that hill for my bleeding body was for the pilot to use the JP. It was that or I would bleed to death before I could be moved to a place where a helicopter could land to pick me up. That would be difficult because we were still under fire. Then I heard the magic words spoken by my radio operator: "Roger, standing by for the JP."

The helicopter hovered directly overhead, and over the noise of the blades, I heard the JP coming down through the trees. The enemy sniper shifted his fire to the hovering helicopter, but the pilot held station, even though he was being hit, so that he could try to save the life of a wounded Marine. My Marines tied me to the JP, and I was winched up into the helicopter without incident, although I don't remember much of it. I lost consciousness as I was being pulled up into that beautiful, ugly old CH-46 helicopter. Had the pilot of that helicopter, call sign Peachbush 1–7, not ignored orders and deployed the JP, I would surely have died that January day. That pilot's courage and willingness to take a risk to save another Marine's life did just that—saved my life. It would take me almost four decades to learn his identity.

As time went by, I regained my sight and the use of my legs and ultimately became as near physically normal as is possible for someone who had suffered such an injury. Many years went by, and all us boys from the A&M Class of 1968 became the old men of the A&M Class of 1968, but we stayed connected through phone calls and emails. During one of those exchanges, our classmate Dan Wimberly sent out an email that marked the passing away of an Army helicopter pilot, Ed Freeman, who had braved enemy fire countless times during the Battle of Ia Drang to rescue wounded soldiers. I replied to Dan's email by recounting the incident where a courageous Marine helicopter pilot had risked his own life, the lives of his crew, and a court-martial by choosing to do what was needed rather than what was permissible. I ended my reply by writing "I do not know who the pilot of Peachbush 1–7 was, but I will be eternally grateful to that unknown helicopter pilot who saved my life."

That email was sent out to my circle of A&M classmates. Among them, of course, was Charlie Rodenberg. And Charlie answered that email simply with the following words: "Mike, Peachbush 1–7 was yours truly."

John Blevins (1961, Band) 357th Tactical Fighter Squadron, 1966–73

I graduated from Texas A&M in 1961 and by the time I arrived in Vietnam, in 1966, was an experienced fighter pilot. Combat flying was difficult in Southeast Asia because of the rules of engagement. We were not allowed to go after SAM sites in North Vietnam until they were fully operational. We could bomb a collection of 55-gallon fuel drums in the jungle, but we could not attack major fuel facilities such as 50,000-gallon storage tanks at seaports. Enemy fighter planes were not to be engaged on the ground, nor could we destroy their airfields. We lost some good men because of these and other rules of engagement.

Despite the frustrations and dangers, we fighter pilots believed we were the world's greatest and invincible. We could not possibly be shot down! Just like the proverbial cat, we felt that we had been issued nine lives. Unfortunately we had ample opportunity to use all nine.

My first came on Mission #25. The target was a military-training complex approximately eighty nautical miles northwest of Hanoi. I was number four in my flight of F-105s that day. My job was flak suppression, and I had six CBU canisters on the center-line station. I selected the gun site that appeared to be firing the most rounds at us and released the six canisters at about 6,000 feet altitude. During my dive recovery, my aircraft became very sluggish and would not accelerate above 350 nautical miles per hour. Other members of my flight told me I had a large hole in my horizontal stabilizer that was acting as a speed brake. Fortunately I was able to land at Udorn AFB, Thailand, without further problems. I figured that was Life #1. Eight to go.

On Mission #45 I led a flight of four against a collection of 55-gallon fuel drums approximately thirty nautical miles northeast of Hanoi. We hit the target, and on the way home I spotted a lone vehicle on a road in a small valley between two large hills near the Laos border. Telling the flight to stay high, I rolled in on the road and was about to open fire when the whole side of the hill lit up with small-arms fire. It looked like a thousand flash bulbs. The next thing I knew the cockpit filled with smoke, it was very noisy, and my visor was cracked and broken, leaving a jagged edge across my line of sight. When I recovered, I saw that a round had penetrated the left side of my windscreen, hit my mirror, and blown out the left side of my canopy. My sun visor had saved my eyesight, and I had earned my first purple heart. So ended Life #2.

Mission #85 took place on a date I will never forget—September 9, 1966. The target was a bridge on the railroad leading northeast out of Hanoi. The structure was approximately thirty-five nautical miles from the edge of Hanoi, and the mission called for the flight to ingress from the Gulf of Tonkin. That day we had four flights of four aircraft, each with a separate target along the rail line. The flight I was leading was the last of the four inbound, and the weather was very marginal. A cloud layer about 2,500 feet above ground level and 2,000 feet thick obstructed my view of the ground. This was important, because I needed to see if SAMs were launched at the flight.

I called the lead of one of the other flights, and he indicated that the weather broke open over the target area. I kicked the speed up to 540 nautical miles per hour and lowered the altitude to just above the treetops because my instruments indicated we were being painted by enemy radar. Just as we passed the railroad track I cracked the afterburner and started a pitch-up maneuver to gain altitude, acquire the target, and start the bomb run. As the burner lit, I felt a small bump and got a fire-warning light. A quick check of my instruments indicated that I had a fire and zero pressure on one of my two hydraulic systems. I believe I was hit by an antiaircraft gun, like a 37-mm or 57-mm cannon.

Combat reports had shown that with a hydraulic fire the F-105 normally would fly only about one minute before it became uncontrollable, pitching either up or down completely out of control. I called my flight, told them I was hit, and started a rollback to head for the coast. My roommate, the number three in the flight, indicated my aircraft was burning quite heavily. True to form, about sixty seconds after I was hit, the aircraft started to pitch up, and I lost all control. As I approached vertical, the aircraft yawed violently, and at zero air speed I ejected. I had broken one of the airman's cardinal rules: "The number of landings should match the number of takeoffs." Thus ended Life #3.

The seat-and-lap belt worked just as advertised, and I found myself in the layer of clouds that I had flown beneath on my ingress. I had no sensation of what was up or down, and I had not felt my chute open because the opening shock was so mild. This was probably due to the fact I ejected at close to zero air speed. I was feeling confident until I came out of the clouds. Directly beneath me the burning remains of my aircraft and its 20-mm ammunition were cooking off, signaling my position to all enemy forces in close proximity. Looking around, I saw that I was receiving enemy fire from three separate automatic-gun emplacements to my west. I was very, very happy that apparently none of these gunners knew how to lead a falling object. There went Life #4.

To the east and slightly north I could see two small hills covered with what I thought were tall trees. My plan was to head for these hills once I reached the ground. I hoped I could evade capture and move toward the coast for possible rescue. I deployed my survival seat pack and was prepared to move quickly to the location I had seen from the air. Well, as the saying goes, "The best-laid plans of mice and men . . ." When my feet touched the grass, I pulled the quick-release lanyards on my chute and to my dismay dropped about twelve feet to the ground. While I was descending in my chute I didn't know the grass was that high. As I hit the ground, I remember hearing a sound that reminded me of a tree limb breaking during a Texas ice storm. I jumped to my feet, intending to move quickly from the area, but fell flat on my face. It was then I realized that the sound I had heard was my left leg breaking. I had a compound fracture with my bones extending over my boot. Not a good start for evading capture. Not good at all.

It was time to reassess my position and decide on my next move. Escape to the hills was no longer possible, shoot it out and hope for rescue was not really practical or smart. No rescues had been made from my location, and no rescap were in the area. Surrender was my only viable option. It was about 2:00 p.m., and I could hear the enemy approaching. I took my .45 Colt out of my holster and waited to be captured. At this point I made what might have been a fatal mistake, but luck was with me. Instead of emptying my gun, I handed it over to the old man who found me. He was so excited to capture an "air pirate," as the Vietnamese called us, that he kept waving the gun in my face—and there was a live round in the chamber. If he pulled the trigger I was a dead man. There went Life #5.

When the rest of the capture party (about ten people, none of whom were regular army) arrived, they took my boots, watch, and flight suit. Seeing that I was not able to walk, they found a pole and netting and began carrying me like a wounded animal toward their village. My next mode of transportation, for approximately one mile, was an ox cart. We arrived at the village about sunset, and loudspeakers in the trees were blasting out the news that a captured "air pirate" was entering the village. Of course the voice was speaking in Vietnamese, but I could tell that it was designed to work the crowd into a frenzy. Angry men and women with stones and clubs soon surrounded the cart and proceeded to beat me about my head and shoulders, ending Life #6.

Finally we stopped in front of what I assumed was the house of the

French overseers before the Vietnamese kicked the French out. The apparent leader of the group that had captured me was a young female who was looking to claim a reward for a live American "air pirate." It was well known that Ho Chi Minh had placed a price on our heads. Somehow she managed to part the crowd and move me into the house. An hour or so later a flight of two F-4s flew directly over the house. I assume they were looking to contact me had I been successful in evading capture. Shortly thereafter a member of the group who had captured me came into the room and had me open my mouth. He looked in my mouth and left. I thought this was strange at the time, but later I realized that they probably thought I had been able to contact the F-4s and direct them to the house. They obviously thought we had very high tech capabilities. Some time later, about midnight I think, a jeep arrived. Two soldiers loaded me into the back, and we headed for Hanoi.

We arrived at the infamous Hanoi Hilton about sunrise. I was moved into what the POWs had coined the purple interrogation room. This part of the prison was known as Heart Break Hotel. A small stool was in front of a ten-foot-long table covered by a purple tablecloth, and behind the table were four or five straight chairs for the interrogators. Unable to sit on the stool because of my broken leg, I was placed on the floor next to the stool. After a few minutes an interrogator, an officer I assumed, entered the room and sat down behind the table. He asked for my name, rank, serial number, and date of birth. I replied with the information requested. He next asked for my squadron number and the aircraft type I was flying. I refused to answer based on the rights of a POW according to the Geneva Convention. He said I was an "air pirate" and not a POW and therefore had no right to refuse to answer his questions. After several hours of asking questions that I refused to answer, the interrogator left the room and a stoic guard entered with a length of nylon parachute cord and introduced me to what we referred to as the rope trick. This consisted of tying your hands behind your back and bringing your elbows together to a point at which your shoulders were near being dislocated. After several hours the interrogator would return and ask if you were ready to answer his questions. Each time the ropes would be loosened and then, when I refused to answer, retied.

After a while your arms and hands would become numb but would be more painful each time they were retied. After three days of this treatment, the guard started to include my legs, including my broken leg, in this process. At that point I felt compelled to go beyond name, rank, and so on. But I gave false information about my squadron and other misleading info about the F-105 and personnel. I said my squadron commander was named Col. "Flip" Corkin (from the Terry and the Pirates comic-strip character of the 1950s and 1960s). It was important to remember what I said so that I could repeat the lies if necessary.

The night of the third day I was taken to a local hospital, and my leg was set. I was very fortunate that no major veins had been severed during my landing and that I had lost very little blood. After setting my leg, the hospital personnel strapped it to a board, loaded me into a truck, and took me to the POW camp we called the Zoo in a residential area in the southwest suburbs of Hanoi. The Zoo got its name from the small trap opening in the cell door the guards used to check on prisoners.

The North Vietnamese kept most of the recent shoot-downs in solitary confinement, but because I was unable to care for myself, they moved me in with another POW. As it turned out, he was John Wendell, an F-105 pilot I had known in a squadron at Bitburg, Germany. John had been shot down the month before on a steel-mill target. It is not possible for me to express how much I owe him for the help and support he provided.

My next four years as a resident of the Zoo were characterized by moves to buildings we named Barn, Pig Sty, Garage, Stable, and Pool House, and by changes in cellmates. There were also constant bouts of diarrhea and heat rash.

Despite two small openings at the top of the ceiling for circulation, cell temperatures rose to about 100 or 110 degrees in the summer months. In the winter they were as low as 35 or 40 degrees.

The guards tried to stop all communication between POWs, but they never succeeded for long. To communicate important information, as well as just to B.S., we used a simple tap code. Communications were always initiated with the "shave and a haircut six bits" and would continue once a response of two taps was given. The first sequence of taps was for the row number of the desired letter, and the second was for the column number of the desired letter. For example the letter Z would be 5 taps pause and 5 taps. (To reduce the alphabet to twenty-five letters, the letter C was used for both C and K.) An example of the B.S. was make-believe holiday dinner menus that we passed from cell to cell for Christmas and Thanksgiving.

Our diet consisted primarily of rice and cabbage or pumpkin or greens soup served twice a day and two teapots of water that was boiled, thank goodness. I lost approximately thirty-five pounds before bread replaced the rice diet in late 1967.

Long, sometimes heated, discussions with my roommate(s) about every topic from fruit to nuts helped pass the time. Unending bets were made on when the war would end. For the optimist it was next week or next year; for the pessimist it was many, many years in the future.

Our captors continued multiple attempts to get us to confess our crimes and to condemn our government. We referred to these as quizzes. One that we called the Cuban program was led by a Cuban national who frequently applied torture as a part of his interrogation. He spoke excellent English and claimed to have attended school in the USA.

Ho Chi Minh died in September 1969, and our treatment and food soon improved. It was also my first opportunity to write a letter home—and I received my first letter a year later, four years after my capture. The term letter is a bit misleading. The allotted seven lines didn't allow much space for expressing deep thoughts—or any thoughts for that matter.

We learned of Neil Armstrong's moonwalk from an offhand comment made by Hanoi Hanna on her radio program. She broadcast daily programs to the GIs in South Vietnam and to us POWs. She made a comment about a minor Soviet accomplishment and concluded that it was much more significant than putting a man on the moon.

We also heard about the Paris peace talks—and that it took a year to decide to use a round table versus a square table so that neither the north nor the south would be seen as more important. This was not a morale boost for us POWs! Also about this time several POWs attempted to escape from the Zoo Annex. After recapture, many were tortured.

Although the Son Tay Raid in November 1970 was unsuccessful, it greatly concerned the Vietnamese. As a result they moved POWs from all the camps to the Hanoi Hilton in December, and I remained there until May of 1972. For the first time we were in cells of fifty-plus POWs, allowing us freedom to play cards, teach or take classes in languages taught by fellow POWs, and conduct church services. Guards disrupted some religious services because they thought we were planning a riot or some other insubordination.

The bombing raids around Hanoi during this time frame worried the Vietnamese. We believed they had plans to trade our release for money or other considerations. In May 1972 they decided to move some POWs who had been in prison more than three or four years to the Dog Patch POW Camp, approximately 115 nautical miles north of Hanoi. Then, if a stray bomb were to hit the Hilton, they would still have some POWs to trade.

I joined the group transferred to Dog Patch, which consisted of about ten buildings that housed twenty POWs each. The cells had no electricity, very thick walls, and a water well. The distance between buildings made communication difficult, but we overcame this problem. We could hear the B-52 raids on Hanoi area and believed the war would end soon.

In December 1972 I was moved back to the Hilton. In mid-February 1973 the Camp Commander announced that a peace agreement had been reached in Paris and that we would be going home soon. On March 4, 1973, we were transported by bus from the Hilton to the Hanoi Airport, where we boarded a US Air Force transport plane and flew to Clark Air Force Base in the Philippines—and freedom!

On March 7, 1973, we flew on to San Antonio. Just as I was to board the aircraft, a woman in the crowd gave me a bouquet of flowers and a big kiss and hug. I had completely forgotten about this kiss and hug until years later when I received a film clip of the day. I don't remember how I explained that to my wife. As it turned out, the 7th of March was my thirty-fourth birthday. I had fun celebrating as we crossed the International Date Line and the Pacific Ocean.

There were lessons I learned in captivity. I learned that war is Hell and that if you go to war, you should go to win. I learned that others can imprison your body but not your mind. And I learned to keep faith in my fellow airmen and in God and Country. There were also regrets. I regret that I lost seven years of seeing my children grow up. I regret the pain my wife endured not knowing my status for four years. And I regret the loss of my friends and fellow F-105 pilots.

However, by my count, I still have three lives remaining.

Jim Lanning (1964, D-1) 25th Infantry Division, 1966

The most challenging time of my life was fish year in the Corps of Cadets assigned to Company D-1 (Spider D) at Texas A&M. This includes combat-duty assignments in Vietnam as a Rifle Platoon Leader and a Rifle Company Commander. Fish year instilled the substance to serve as a soldier and as a leader in combat.

This is how my journey played out. The summer of 1963 found me at Fort Sill, Oklahoma, attending ROTC Summer Camp. During this intense six weeks of training I did not go on pass one time. I was focused on mastering the skills of basic soldiering. In order not to miss instruction when KP was assigned during weekdays, I traded for a weekend duty slot.

The evening before graduation, another cadet, Edward B. Herndon Jr., from Texas Tech, a neighbor from back home, stopped by my bunk and said, "Jim, let's go down to the Blade & Wing" (a watering hole a few blocks distant). I thought, "Graduation is tomorrow, and all training is completed. What would it hurt?" The last thing in my mind was the stack of form letters titled, "Recommendation: Tentative Distinguished Military Graduate" waiting for action on the desk of our commanding officer, Maj. James L. Stone.

The evening began—pouring cold beer from a pitcher into my dehydrated body. Every hour the crowd of drinkers grew smaller, but the pitchers kept coming. Finally. When the Blade & Wing closed, I was the last man standing. As I entered the darkness of the night. I made a quick guess as to the general direction to my bunk, and a nearby drainage ditch provided a path to my goal. At that point memory fails.

The next morning, graduation day, I found myself in my bunk fully clothed. My J. C. Penney suit was a mess. I called to my bunkmate, James M. Leatherwood, from Tarleton State College, "What happened?"

"Jim, you missed bed check." Terror entered my spirit—that is another term for AWOL! Bad, bad. And as he continued, it got worse. "Major Stone was called, and he went looking for you. Finding you in the drainage ditch, he picked you up and carried you in his arms to your bunk."

What bad timing! The TDMG letter with my name on it was waiting Maj. Stone's signature. He had two clear choices: "Yes" or "No." His decision would affect the balance of my life. A "Yes" would pave the way for a Regular Army Commission. Major Stone never addressed me about the incident, but he checked "Yes" and signed his name, Maj. James L. Stone, Infantry. Later I learned that he was an ROTC graduate from the University of Arkansas and had served in the Korean Conflict.

Along the Imjin River near Sokkogae, Korea, on November 21–22, 1951, Stone had led the defense against a much larger force of Chinese. Despite being wounded, he continued to lead the fight and then volunteered to stay behind to cover the retreat of his fellow soldiers. Captured by the Chinese, he spent twenty-two months in a POW camp. On his return home he was awarded the Medal of Honor for his bravery.

I praise the Lord to this day for Stone's leadership decision that fateful day at Fort Sill. Another commander might have eliminated Cadet James W. Lanning, 1964, from the running for a Regular Army Commission. His action the night before graduation day reinforced my determination to become a combat leader.

In 1978 I tracked down now-retired Colonel Stone in Arlington, Texas. In his return letter, Stone wrote, "If in some small way I contributed to your success, I feel grateful," and he concluded, "I noticed during my career that the officers from the ROTC program at Texas A&M have far more leadership qualities than those of similar institutions, which includes West Point. They have the ability to make things happen without rubbing their men the wrong way."

In 1966, a short three years after ROTC Summer Camp, I was in Vietnam near the Cambodian border as a rifle platoon leader in Company C, 2nd Battalion, 35th Infantry Regiment, 3rd Brigade, 25th Infantry Division. In an intense battle (chronicled by S. L. A. Marshall in his book *West to Cambodia*) our unit was outnumbered and nearly overrun by a battle-hardened NVA unit. PFC Glen Young, a draftee from Brodhead, Wisconsin, and an M 60 machine-gunner had the critical task of securing the most dangerous avenue of enemy approach. The enemy was determined to eliminate his deadly automatic fire. I heard a shout that Young had been hit bad, suffering a painful and life-threatening sucking chest wound to both lungs. In the dark chaos of the action, I crawled down the incline of the hill to his foxhole, picked him up in my arms, and carried him up the hill for medical attention. Later I connected the two actions, Major Stone had rescued two soldiers that long-ago night at Fort Sill—me and PFC Young. Sadly the rescue was to no avail. PFC Young died quickly of his wounds—but he did so in the arms of his comrades rather than alone in a dark foxhole.

During the same action I was assessing the status of casualties for evacuation. The fight was very intense. I will never forget when one member of the platoon, PFC John Mucci, actually broke an Army-issue machete in the rib cage of a NVA soldier in hand-to-hand combat. During my assessment, a young soldier came seeking attention for a small-arms wound just above his ankle. Seeing there was no hemorrhaging, I ordered him to return to his fighting defensive position on the perimeter. "We'll get you out tomorrow morning," I told him. There were men with more serious wounds who should go first, and I needed every rifleman possible to remain on the defense. With many other more important things to handle—redistributing ammo and offering encouragement—I moved on.

The battle continued with our calling in more than thirteen hundred artillery rounds to break the enemy attack. Despite the ongoing fight, Dustoffs arrived to remove our wounded while still under fire. This included an Air Force medical evacuation helicopter that arrived to extract wounded with a cable/basket lift through the sixty-foot canopy. This ordeal of evacuating the most seriously was complicated as we were now operating in the dark.

As the helicopter continued to hover, I became anxious and commented to my radio operator, "This evacuation is taking too long."

In that instant we heard an RPG fired and saw it strike the vulnerable bird. It began to burn and fall in pieces through the dark, dense canopy of the trees. Our perimeter was small, and soldiers began to scramble from the impact area directly below the doomed helicopter. One of my soldiers, who, moments before the rocket impacted, had positioned himself in the wire basket but had not yet secured the first belt, jumped and ran for safety. Suffering a fragmentation wound to his scrotum, with his testicles hanging out and bouncing from leg to leg, the soldier ran for his life. Still fighting the enemy, we listened to the screams of the men burning to their deaths. Of the five men from my platoon killed in the battle, three died in this burning inferno.

Quietness and daylight finally came. I began to check what remained of the platoon sector. I could not locate the soldier with the ankle-area wound. Nothing coming from his squad leader, I turned to the platoon sergeant. When pressed on his status, the sergeant motioned to the pile of smoking debris of the helicopter and the badly charred bodies. I concluded that during the heat of the battle, without permission, the soldier with the ankle wound had crawled up to the basket extraction site and got in line—

in reality taking another wounded man's place. Somewhere in the State of Illinois today the man who was supposed to be in the basket for evacuation and later was lifted safely from the jungle is likely watching television with his grandchildren. Another, who disobeyed orders, has been in his grave far longer than he ever lived.

Jeffery Murray (1970 and 1973, Squadron 6 and H-2)
281st Aviation Company 1968–69

I entered A&M in 1966 as a fish in Squadron 6. Fifty-two of us began, seventeen finished our fish year, and only twelve returned as sophomores. I was one of those who finished but did not return. My second semester I earned three grade points—in ROTC and PE. On the plus side we were on the three-point system back then. The university said I could return but not in the Corps. So I dropped out, joined the Army, and volunteered for the Warrant Officer Rotary Wing Aviator course at Fort Wolters, Mineral Wells, Texas, and at Fort Rucker, Alabama.

I graduated from flight school in October 1968 and took a few weeks' leave before heading for Vietnam via Seattle. A few of my classmates and I traveled together, landed in Cam Ranh Bay, then were bussed to barracks where we were issued a few standard items and shown a bunk. Later I was directed to a bus that somehow got me to Dong Ba Thin, the 10th Combined Aviation Brigade headquarters, where I was further assigned to the 281st Assault Helicopter Company. Being the PFC of the officer corps I immediately complied and then began to wonder who and where they were. I was eager to fly, a desire I needn't have worried about.

The warrant office pilot who picked me up for transport to the company told me I needed to move from my "window" seat to the aircraft's interior because they had been having trouble with a sniper using a .50-cal to pick off troops in the back of 281st Hueys. Because I was an FNG and didn't know better, I moved. But I never forgot who took the opportunity to harass us new guys.

On arrival at the 281st I was assigned a room and then started making the rounds of the company. I got a lecture from the Ops Officer, who told me that flying in Vietnam was mission-dependent, that sometimes the book goes out the window. He told me about a pilot who over-torqued a Huey getting out of a hover hole with too many passengers, but because it was mission-critical, the over-torque was forgiven. I later found out that the ops officer was that pilot. The maintenance guys, who had to repair the damage, were not his best friends. It was a noncombat extraction, and there had been no need to overload the aircraft. But I was the FNG, so I nodded solemnly.

The company commander, a major, then imparted the party line: follow the rules, work hard, get along with everyone, and things would be just peachy. He then told me about one pilot who liked to horse around with the aircraft, flying insertions out of trim, flying on the edge, and the like. The commander made sure I noted that he did not agree with this at all. I, of course, just looked serious and nodded a lot, saluted, and went on my merry way.

The next day I was given an in-country check ride that I botched every which way outside of crashing. But I was already in Vietnam; what were they going to do? Then I went on a ride with a CW2 with red hair and a loud demeanor. Nice guy. I recognized right away that he knew what he was doing—and he made sure I knew that I didn't know squat. We got up to about 2,000 feet, and he demoed a high-overhead approach by dumping the aircraft on its right side and kicking a boot full of right pedal as we fell out of the sky like an anvil. When we got to about 150 feet he started recovering and we actually settled in right on the intended touchdown point in one piece without any major parts falling off. I thought to myself, "This must be the guy the major was talking about."

As the year wore on, I found my flying experiences leaning more toward those of the redheaded warrant than of the STRAC Army major. It was about to be a great year, I could tell.

On the 17th of November 1968 I reported to the flight line for a mission with a short, round little guy known as Fat Albert who had been in Vietnam forever—and he was frowning. "I had better be on my best behavior," I said to myself. It ended up being an uneventful flight up to An Khe and back, I don't know what we went for, but I had read about An Khe back in the States, and I was half expecting to get shot at any moment. Fat Albert was not only fun to fly with but also a pleasant guy. It was plain that he knew everything about flying—and I could at best start the aircraft two out of three times. He told me stories and put me at ease. He even let me land once or twice.

In the coming weeks I flew with Fat Albert only a few more times, but I got to fly to that hill across the rice paddies from our hooch, and out to Hon Tre Island. I also flew convoy cover with another pilot, who must have called me FNG about 249 times. And it was only a ten-and-a-half-minute flight.

The peak (or perhaps the pit) of my early flights was when we were detailed to transport a body. The dead Vietnamese in a simple wooden box must have been important: he had two US field-grade officer escorts. And this guy was ripe. He had been dead for a while and stunk to high heaven. I had my head out the window. When the primary pilot told me to fly, I immediately took FNG liberty and crammed in a crab to get the wind going from my window to the left so I could breathe. The pilot immediately crammed in the opposite pedal. We played pedal tag for a minute or two—until I glanced back at the crew chief. He was gagging. One of the field-grade officers had tried to barf out the door but had splattered the crew chief full frontal. That started a chain reaction. Soon everyone in the back was throwing up everywhere. We pilots had our heads out our windows, and we managed to get the mission accomplished without barfing. We offloaded the nonspeaking passenger and his escorts, and it was well over an hour before the ship began to smell remotely close to normal. Welcome to Vietnam.

After my tour I returned to A&M and joined Company H-2 in the Corps of Cadets. I graduated in 1973 with a commission as a second lieutenant. I am pretty sure that I am the only ex-Army Warrant Officer to gain a commission via ROTC at A&M.

Ed McDaniel (1965, D-1) Naval Intelligence Liaison Officer —Quang Ngai, 1969–70

The time I spent in the Texas A&M ROTC program convinced me that I probably was ill-fitted for the Army, and perhaps even military life. However, Vietnam and the specter of the draft persuaded me to volunteer for the Navy, and I went on active duty in mid-1966. Motivated by a series of unanticipated circumstances, and knowing that many of my A&M classmates were serving in country, I volunteered for Vietnam duty. From March 1969 to March 1970, I served as Naval Intelligence Liaison Officer Quang Ngai—the southernmost province in I Corps.

The NILO program, which involved only about 250 officers during the entire Vietnam conflict, was unique. Operationally assigned to COMNAVFORV on independent duty, I was to liaison with sister-service intelligence units to collect and report information relevant to the Navy's mission in my operational area. My twelve-month assignment thrust me into contact with elements of all the US services and many of the RVN commands, including conducting air and ground ops with various units. Events also led to work with MACV SOG and the Phoenix Program. I spent considerable time in the field, exactly the thing I had expected to avoid by joining the Navy.

My most memorable time in country occurred as a part of Operation Market Time, the US Navy program to secure the South Vietnamese coastline and adjacent waters by deploying a variety of different platforms in a layered defense. The Coastal Patrol bases, the first line of defense, usually had three or four Americans advising the Vietnamese Navy, who used junks to patrol the coastline and river estuaries.

The next barrier in the Market Time operation was Swift Boats. The boats carried a crew of four or five US Navy sailors with a lieutenant as the CO and were armed with twin .50-caliber machine-guns in turrets topside and an 81-mm mortar and a single .50-caliber machine gun mounted aft. In addition the crew carried whatever personal weapons they desired.

Also patrolling the coast were US Coast Guard cutters. They could operate farther from shore than the Swift Boats. For the next parameter, a variety of destroyers patrolled the Tonkin Gulf and the South China Sea. The efforts of this mini-armada were augmented by shore-based maritime patrol aircraft (P-3s) and electronic-warfare platforms.

The Market Time mission was multifaceted. Shore-based naval guns were on call to provide bombardment when needed, and the small boats were constantly checking Vietnamese fishing boats—looking for contraband, draft dodgers, and deserters. But their primary concern was to detect seaborne infiltration of VC/NVA personnel, munitions, and particularly supplies from the north.

Also involved in this effort was CAP, the US Marine Corps Civic Action Patrol program, which assigned a squad of Marines, usually under the command of a mid-level enlisted man such as a staff sergeant, to live and work in a South Vietnamese village. Their mission was to help provide security and to train a village self-defense force. This involved patrolling a defined area of operations in an effort to detect and/or deter enemy activity.

Within this context, I have a story. Early one morning the phone rang in my combined billet/office (a former French horse stable) in Quang Ngai city. The First Coastal Zone Intelligence Officer in Da Nang, my boss, identified himself and immediately passed me the phone. The Commander of the First Coastal Zone said an unidentified boat had been discovered beached on the coast of the Batangan Peninsula (where the infamous My Lai village incident had taken place a little over a year earlier) and told me, in no uncertain terms, to go investigate and file a report ASAP. Apparently senior Navy personnel in the Market Time HQ were spinning over the reported landing. I quickly gathered up my field gear and went to schedule a helicopter. Fortunately the beached boat had made news in a number of local command posts, and in short order I was in a helo over the Batangan Peninsula. There were only a couple of places where I could be dropped off. One was an Army Fire Support Base that contained a few artillery pieces and mortars. A fixed site, it provided fire support for elements of the US Americal Division patrolling the area. The other site was a CAP site in a village near the coast. I had no influence with Americal but felt comfortable among the Marines, so I opted for the CAP team.

The helo dropped me off, and I scrambled to see the CAP NCOIC, a Marine staff sergeant. I explained the situation, and he said, “I’ll give you a patrol.”

A few minutes later I stepped through the compound perimeter into the bush with three Marines, a Navy Corpsman, and four or five of the Vietnamese village self-defense force. Both the Marine radioman and the Corpsman told me to keep a good interval from them as they were usually the first to be shot. Welcome to reality outside the wire in a war zone.

It took us about fifteen or twenty minutes to get to the coastline and another fifteen or twenty minutes walking along the beach to reach the boat. There it was, fifty or sixty feet long and with a deck seven or eight feet high. I pulled myself up onto the deck and started stumbling around taking pictures, writing notes, and trying to figure out how and why the boat had found its way to this place. The ideograms on its side suggested it was Chinese.

The investigation didn't take long, and soon we headed back. Luck was on my side that day: a helo came in shortly after we returned to the CAP base. I was back in Quang Ngai for dinner and had dispatched a lengthy report well before the bar closed. The report contained a detailed description of what I had observed and ended with the observation that I suspected the boat was of Chinese origin but could not determine what its mission was based on the available evidence.

Bright and early the next morning my phone rang and an irate Navy Captain (o–6) from the Market Time HQ launched into a lengthy diatribe about my report. I kept saying yes sir, yes sir, and he kept yelling. He felt the report was inconclusive and demanded that I provide additional information. We signed off with my saying, "Yes sir, I'll get right on it."

I really wasn't worried, because I knew he was sitting in a nice air-conditioned office in a compound guarded by multiple layers of security far to the south in Cam Ranh Bay, and there was very little probability he would venture into the bush to find me. We couldn't even get a USO show to come to the compound in Quang Ngai City. But I called my boss in Da Nang and learned that the same captain had also been yelling at him. To alleviate the situation, I volunteered (better than being ordered) to go back to the boat and collect additional information. I also knew that once I got back into the bush, none of my superiors would be able to contact me.

Because it was the Marine Corps birthday (November 10), I grabbed a case of beer and went to find another helo. Luck was again on my side, and I was soon disembarking at the CAP site. The Marines were surprised to see me again so soon. (They didn't get a lot of visitors, except for periodic night probes from the VC.) However, the case of beer ensured a warm reception.

Within an hour we were on our way back to the boat. Again I did a quick investigation, and again I had absolutely no idea what that boat was doing there. It could have brought Ho Chi Minh himself down, except that Uncle Ho had died earlier that year.

On the way back we encountered a scene that has stayed with me until this day. There were nine or ten of us, the same mix of Marines and Vietnamese self-defense personnel as on the previous patrol. As we rounded a bend in the coastline below a very high cliff, an older Vietnamese man was standing beside the trail with a five- or six-year-old boy. They had not been there on our outbound leg, and we were a bit surprised to find them there on our return.

The man had his palms together in front of his chest and was continually bowing from the waist to 35 or 45 degrees. The kid also had his palms together and was standing very still beside the old man. As each of us in the patrol passed—Marine, Vietnamese, and me—we held our M-16 level with his chest until we were well past him and his son. I've retained the memory because my son was growing up, and I wondered what the old man must have felt standing there with his kid as a group of strangers walked by training automatic weapons on him, knowing that if he screwed up, they would not hesitate to shoot, that even on a whim, one of them might pull his trigger—just because he thought you flinched or blinked—or because he was scared to death himself.

Back at the CAP base I attempted to get a helo to Quang Ngai City. But my luck had run out. No choppers were scheduled in that area for the rest of that day or the next day. I was screwed. There was no way I was going to get off that hill that night, and being the ranking officer (the only officer) in the camp was not a reassuring thought.

Just after sunset we received word that an Army patrol from the Americal Division was coming in through the perimeter wire. Lacking much else to do, I wandered over and started talking to the 2nd lieutenant in charge of the patrol. After we chatted a bit and I explained my situation, the lieutenant contacted his superiors and requested a helo for the next morning. Trying to be helpful and, I guess, to increase the priority of his request, he blurted out that the helo was needed to pick up a Navy 03 Intelligence Officer. This went out in the clear. My immediate thought was that the VC 48th Main Force Battalion, which operated in the area, would intercept the transmission and come after me during the night, a feeling heightened by the rumor that the VC/NVA had a standing bounty on intelligence officers.

I hastily retreated to the Marine Command Post and informed the sergeant, who shrugged and indicated I should stay with him in the CP bunker (a space about the size of a college dorm room). Within ten minutes I had inflated an air mattress and positioned it on top of a large stack of mortar crates, with the mortar rounds still inside. If the bunker took a hit, the end would be quick.

Sometime later there arose the damnedest noise imaginable. It sounded like every person in the village was beating on something. The Marine sergeant let me know that the noise was our security blanket. Seems that the village self-defense force personnel kept watch along the entire village perimeter at night, and each individual almost continuously hit a large piece of bamboo with a stick. The object was not so much to let the VC know they were there as to let each self-defense force member know the others were still there. The Marines told me that if the noise stopped and things got quiet it was, in his words, time to, "Stand the fuck by, Sir," because it would indicate that the villagers probably had deserted their posts in the face of an enemy attack.

It was a long night. The light in the CP bunker never went out, and the radio was squawking constantly. Sometime around midnight all hell broke loose at the Army's fire-support base a couple thousand meters away. We got ready to heighten our alert when the radio informed us that the Army had decided to hold a "Mad Minute"—everyone in the camp goes to the perimeter and fires his weapon for a full minute. Makes a hell of a racket, but it is a wonderful psychological tool. Scares any enemy troops in the area and relieves tension for the folks inside the camp. Normally it only killed enemy insects, vegetation, and dirt.

And the night wore on. Finally came the dawn, which brought a C-ration breakfast and a cold-water shave. But luck returned. A helo soon arrived to pluck me off that red dirt hilltop. Maybe the lieutenant's use of my rank and specialty had helped. Who knows? I just knew I had survived another night in the bush and was en route Quang Ngai city.

There I composed my second report about the beached Chinese boat. I didn't know anything more about it than after my first visit, but I had become more politically savvy. I composed this report suggesting that the beached vessel appeared to be a Chinese fishing boat, perhaps one that had broken loose from some port on Hainan Island and drifted across the South China Sea to the beach on the Batangan Peninsula. Not long after dispatching the report, I received a phone call from the First Coastal Zone Commander commending me on my second effort. It seemed that the Market Time leaders were placated.

For the past forty plus years I've contemplated the logic behind that incident. It remains a conundrum. The first report contained a factual description of the boat and offered no speculation (what intelligence personnel call "analyses"). The Market Time headquarters went bonkers over that. The second report provided a factual description and an unsupported opinion crafted to suggest there had been no seaborne infiltration of enemy personnel, equipment, or munitions.

So there it was. The Market Time headquarters could accept the scenario of an unmanned Chinese fishing boat breaking loose from its moorings in some unidentified port on Hainan Island and languidly drifting for days across the South China Sea, undetected and unsighted by the ever-increasing layers of the Market Time's overlapping and integrated air- and sea-surveillance units, finally washing ashore on the beach in South Viet Nam . . . and on the Batangan Peninsula, the site of previous seaborne-infiltration attempts. What was not acceptable was the possibility that a manned enemy boat had used cunning, stealth, deception, and other evasive measures to work past those same US maritime-surveillance units.

I ultimately concluded that if something really simple and serendipitous makes you look incompetent, that is okay. But if talent, wit, guile, and determination best you, that is not okay. Maybe there is such a thing as "military logic."

Clarence Sasser (1973, Civilian) 9th Infantry Division, 1968

On March 7, 1969, President Richard Nixon awarded the Medal of Honor to a future Texas Aggie in a White House ceremony. The medal's citation stated the following:

> For conspicuous gallantry and intrepidity in action at the risk of his life above and beyond the call of duty. Sp5c. Sasser distinguished himself while assigned to Headquarters and Headquarters Company, 3d Battalion. He was serving as a medical aid man with Company A, 3d Battalion, on a reconnaissance in force operation. His company was making an air assault when suddenly it was taken under heavy small arms, recoilless rifle, machine gun and rocket fire from well fortified enemy positions on 3 sides of the landing zone. During the first few minutes, over 30 casualties were sustained. Without hesitation, Sp5c. Sasser ran across an open rice paddy through a hail of fire to assist the wounded. After helping 1 man to safety, he was painfully wounded in the left shoulder by fragments of an exploding rocket. Refusing medical attention, he ran through a barrage of rocket and automatic weapons fire to aid casualties of the initial attack and, after giving them urgently needed treatment, continued to search for other wounded. Despite two additional wounds immobilizing his legs he dragged himself through the mud toward another soldier 100 meters away. Although in agonizing pain and faint from loss of blood, Sp5c. Sasser reached the man, treated him, and proceeded on to encourage another group of soldiers to crawl 200 meters to relative safety. There he attended their wounds for 5 hours until they were evacuated. Sp5c. Sasser's extraordinary heroism is in keeping with the highest traditions of the military service and reflects great credit upon himself, his unit, and the U.S. Army.

I was born and raised in Chenango, Texas, south of Houston. After high school I enrolled in the University of Houston as a chemistry major. I did pretty well there but, because of a lack of funds, had to drop to half-time so I could work. That ended my student deferment, and I was drafted. After basic training and a series of tests, the Army trained me as a combat medic. By the fall of 1967 I was in Vietnam and assigned to the Headquarters Company of the 3rd Battalion, 60th Infantry Regiment of the 9th Infantry Division. I was then attached to the battalion's Company A, where I became the medic for the 1st Platoon.

Our area of operations was in the Mekong Delta southwest of Saigon. It was covered in rice paddies full of water as well as irrigation canals and wood lines of nipa palm and vines. We went on a lot of search-and-destroy and reconnaissance missions in the daytime and set up ambushes at night. The entire region was so wet and muddy that jungle rot and other skin disorders were a constant problem. There were also many Viet Cong in the area who set up booby traps and engaged us directly with snipers. I was kept busy treating the soldiers for their skin problems and for wounds from rifle and machine gun fire and from booby-trap shrapnel. It was a hard, dangerous life, but it was also enjoyable and fulfilling because of the camaraderie of the men and the experience of doing something that I thought was important.

By the time I had been in the field for a couple of months, I had pretty much gotten used to the routine. All that changed on January 10, 1968. On my fifty-first day with A Company, at about ten in the morning, we airmobiled into a landing zone of rice paddies flanked on three sides by wood lines in Ding Tuong Province. That day is probably the worst, or the best—depending on what perspective you put on it—in my life. Certainly it was the longest.

Our helicopters began taking fire from small arms and machine guns just before we were to set down. The second helicopter that went in was shot down. The rest of the helicopters, including mine, went in to support the crash survivors. I was on was the fourth or fifth helicopter. Just as I was getting out of the door, I was shot through the leg. It was a superficial wound, but it pitched me into the rice-paddy mud and water that was about two and a half feet deep. The door gunners on the choppers were firing their weapons, trying to provide cover for us and to cover their own extraction. They made it off the ground, but we on the ground continued to receive fire from three sides. We spent the remainder of the day in that rice paddy. In addition to the automatic-weapons and small-arms fire, the enemy began to drop mortar rounds into the LZ. Later we would learn that we had landed in the midst of an enemy infantry battalion that was assembling and preparing to join the Tet Offensive that would begin in a few weeks.

Despite my leg wound I crawled around the paddies administering to the wounded. During this time three mortar rounds landed near me and sprayed shrapnel into my back. A lot of other soldiers were also wounded by the mortars. These wounds were very painful because of the heat and the jagged edges of the shrapnel, but there really was not much you could do to treat them other than try to stop the bleeding. As I treated the wounded, I moved them to the many dikes that crossed the LZ to provide them as much cover as possible. Each platoon had a medic, but I was the only one who survived. And I survived a lot longer than a lot of the other guys. Consequently I ended up treating a lot of people regardless of what platoon they were in. In my mind there was no way I could not have gone to see about someone who hollered "Medic" or called "Doc." There was no way that I could justify not going or at least trying to go see about that person.

The fight continued into the afternoon, and I was hit twice more by machine-gun fire. I could no longer walk, but I could crawl, and I continued to move around the battlefield taking care of the wounded. I pulled myself through the water and across the mud by grasping rice stalks. It was kind of like swimming. Eventually I ran out of bandages and other supplies, but I continued to move the wounded to more-protected areas and to encourage those not seriously hurt to continue to fight. I felt that if I could get the guys up and fighting, we might all get out of there somehow. We were in danger of being destroyed. The only thing that prevented us from being overrun was the F-4 Phantoms dropping napalm and the Cobra gunships and Puff the Magic Dragon hosing down the enemy positions. Late in the day I was hit by another bullet—this time in the head. My mother always said I was hardheaded, and I guess she was right, because the bullet ricocheted, raising a huge lump and leaving me dazed for several minutes.

As darkness neared, the main body of the enemy battalion began to withdraw, but they left snipers behind to continue firing at us. For most of the night I tried to help wounded guys as they cried for their mothers, their daddies, somebody to help. Some cried, "I'm dying. Somebody help me." That is probably the worst thing I remember about the entire day. I did all I could. It wasn't until about 4:00 a.m. that we were able to evacuate most of our wounded. The final count of our casualties was thirty-four killed and fifty-nine wounded—almost the entire company.

I was on one of the last Dustoffs out and was treated at an evacuation hospital in country and then transferred to Japan for further treatment. It was while I was in Japan that I was told I had been recommended for the Medal of Honor. My first thought was that I had not really done anything above and beyond my duties. I had just been doing my job. Today I am particularly proud that I received the medal for saving lives, rather than destroying them. That's not to say anything against the combat soldiers who killed people. I do not mean to insult or belittle their accomplishment. In war someone has to do the killing. I don't begrudge anything like that.

After I recovered from my wounds and received the Medal, I was awaiting my discharge from the army when Gen. Earl Rudder, the President of Texas A&M University, called me to arrange a meeting. He offered me a scholarship. I entered A&M in August 1969, but I left before graduating. I've always regretted that because I'm an Aggie at heart and always will be.

Tom Darling (1954, B Athletics and Squadron 11) 824th Bomb Squadron, 1966

Newly promoted, I started my life as an Air Force major at Turner AFB, Georgia, in the summer of 1964. I was assigned to the 824th Bomb Squadron as a B-52 aircraft commander. Turner AFB was a typical SAC installation, with single squadrons of B-52s and KC-135s. Combined with various maintenance and support squadrons, the units formed the 484th Bomb Wing, a unit with a storied World War II history. The base was located in a rich farming area of southwestern Georgia near the town of Albany. Plains, Jimmy Carter's hometown, was thirty miles to the north. Albany residents welcomed military people and were glad to have the base in their area.

Turner's B-52 aircraft were some of the oldest in the SAC inventory. They were "D" models—two versions older than the "F" models I had flown at Carswell Air Force Base from 1958 to 1963. It was a bit of a comedown to be assigned to a unit with older aircraft and to begin my duty with a recently formed crew. It took some time and crew-member changes to gain the proficiency that I and the Air Force were looking for, but within a few months we were selected as the lead aircraft for several important training missions.

By 1964, things had gotten sticky in Southeast Asia. The Gulf of Tonkin incident prompted President Lyndon Johnson to initiate military action against North Vietnam, signaling the expansion of a war that would drag on for eight long years. B-52F crews, who already had been sent to Guam, were directed to deliver conventional bombs on targets in South Vietnam. The very first strike mission was a disaster. Two aircraft and crews were lost when they collided over the Pacific on their way to Vietnam. Mission results were less successful than expected. But this didn't deter the President, the Department of Defense, or the Strategic Air Command staff. Different procedures and tactics were quickly developed for SAC forces, and the B-52 took on a new, tactical role, becoming a major player throughout the conflict.

Early in the war, Defense and Air Force leaders developed a plan to modify all B-52 D, E, and F models to enhance their ability to carry and deliver gravity weapons. The modification allowed B-52Ds to carry a much larger load both internally and on pylons mounted on each wing. The units who flew these models were destined to be the backbone of SAC's Vietnam striking force. B-52 G and H model units were not included in the initial modification plan but remained at their home bases, dedicated to nuclear alert and strategic deterrence. Because Turner AFB was a "D" model unit, we knew our time to join the war would come soon.

In late 1965 Turner crews began intensive training for delivery of conventional munitions. Our silver airplanes were painted a camouflage scheme and modified to carry and deliver 80,000 pounds of gravity bombs per sortie. Soon we learned that our wing would deploy to Guam in March of 1966 to "conduct extended operations in Southeast Asia." Our orders were for 179 days, which made it temporary duty rather than a permanent change of station. The master plan was to have two SAC wings on Guam for six-month periods to perform bombing missions against targets in Southeast Asia. No one expected the war to last more than a year or two. Based on the might of US forces assembled in Southeast Asia, military leaders and media experts predicted a short war. There was no thought of units having to go back for a second or third tour. And there was no plan for the mobilization or significant use of reserve forces.

The wing began its deployment in early March. My crew launched on a flight that took more than seventeen hours and two in-flight refuelings to reach Guam. When we stepped off the plane, the temperature was 90 degrees and the humidity was just as high. The weather didn't vary much while I was there. It was always hot, muggy, and rainy.

The wing's KC-135s and associated flight crews deployed to Okinawa, their in-theater operating base. Arc Light was the operations code name for bombers; Young Tiger, for tankers.

The 28th Bomb Wing from Ellsworth AFB, South Dakota, which arrived the same week we did, was our companion unit for the next six months. We replaced units from Carswell and Mather AFBs, beginning a rotational shuffle that continued for the duration of the conflict. (Later in the war, more B-52s were added to the striking force and a second operating base was established, in Thailand.)

With a combined striking force of some thirty-five B-52s and fifty-five crews, our task in 1966 was to fly daily missions in support of the effort to prevent South Vietnam from falling to the Communists. Together the units formed a formidable strike force under the banner of the 4133rd Provisional Wing.

Our B-52 operating base on Guam was Andersen AFB, on the north end of the thirty-mile-long island. Andersen had a saddleback 12,000-

foot runway that ran northeast and southwest. At the north end of the runway was a 600-foot drop-off to the ocean surface. It presented an intimidating sight during daytime take-offs and landings. (At night it wasn't noticeable.) There was ample parking space for all the airplanes, including revetments for many. Crews were housed in a secure, fenced-in compound not far from the runway. Along the shore to the west of the base was Tarague Beach, a wonderful place for crews to relax and enjoy the water, white sand, and sun—when it wasn't raining. Rain and thundershowers were common, usually occurring several times a day. About ten miles to the southwest was Agana, the only city of any size on the island and the homeport for a number of US Pacific Fleet submarines. Because the rocky soil of the island wasn't conducive to growing crops, all foodstuffs were imported. The island natives, Chamorros, were a friendly, laid-back people who lived near the poverty level. Transportation was mostly old cars and motorbikes.

The next night, after a short sleep following our long flight to Guam, we were scheduled to fly a combat mission with instructors on board, to get us checked out on mission procedures and tactics. We were to be Red 3 in a cell of three aircraft in a stream of three cells (nine aircraft total). Spacing within the cell called for each succeeding aircraft to be one mile back and stacked up 500 feet. As Red 3, we were two miles behind Red 1 and 1,000 feet above him. Cells were separated by a specified amount of time, usually fifteen minutes or as prescribed for the mission. Depending on mission requirements, the number of cells in a stream could vary from one to ten, or more. We had practiced cell and stream tactics back in the States, so it wasn't a new thing for us. However, dropping a full load of bombs on an enemy target would be a first. We were keyed up and ready to go.

Our cell was scheduled for a 2:00 a.m. takeoff. That time, established by the wing planning staff, was based on the desired time for us to arrive over target. A pre-mission meal, served at about 9:00 p.m., was followed by mission briefings, which included target assignments, intelligence, weather, the chaplain's prayer, and a final pep talk by the wing commander. Charts, maps, and radar predictions were passed to each crew. In specialized briefings conducted for each crew position—pilot, navigator, ECM officer, gunner—every detail of the mission was studied and discussed.

At a predetermined time we were transported to our assigned aircraft, where we conducted an aircraft and systems pre-flight. We then stood by until the time to start engines, which was thirty minutes before the scheduled takeoff. Our takeoff began exactly on the scheduled minute.

Everything was accomplished in radio silence to ensure we didn't leak critical information. Our intelligence briefer had told us about a Russian fishing trawler anchored just beyond the territorial waters of Guam, watching and reporting every takeoff from the base. That was something that existed throughout the war that we couldn't change.

After a long takeoff roll we broke ground just before running out of runway. Our aircraft sank slightly below runway level as we entered the drop-off zone beyond the end of the runway. But after the gear and flaps were retracted, we quickly picked up speed and altitude. In the climb we reversed direction and headed toward a point between the Philippines and Okinawa where we would rendezvous with a cell of tankers. Early in our climb we picked up our cell leader, both visually and by radar beacon, and assumed our position, two miles back, stacked up 1,000 feet. Once cell formation was established and checklists had been run, we could relax a bit as we headed toward a tanker rendezvous about three hours away.

At about 150 miles from the rendezvous point, we picked up the radar beacon of a three-ship formation of KC-135s that were to be our tankers. Refueling, too, was essentially a radio-silence operation. As we approached the tankers, Red 2 and Red 3 assumed a right echelon position from our leader, Red 1. Red 2, and Red 3 were to maintain position off Red 1 as he maneuvered the cell into position for closure and contact. The tankers were also in echelon position, so my job as aircraft commander was to close and make contact with tanker 3, the one farthest to the right.

The night was black and the airplane heavy from a maximum-weight launch. In the darkness I spotted tanker 3 and eased up behind him until I felt steady and ready to move to the contact position. With adrenalin flowing as I inched the aircraft forward, I heard the boom make contact in the refueling receptacle (overhead and behind the cockpit of our B-52). On the interphone, my co-pilot called "Contact," followed by "We are taking on fuel." My job was to hang on for the next twenty-three to twenty-five minutes as we took fuel from the tanker. But as the aircraft got heavier, the task became increasingly difficult. Fortunately I made it without breaking contact—a "one-gulper." As veteran pilots, our goal was always to get the gas in one gulp, but turbulence, turns, and other factors sometimes triggered a disconnect. Remaining in the small refueling "pocket" took skill and practice. One-gulpers weren't easy to come by!

After refueling was complete, the three tankers broke away and headed back to their home base on Okinawa. Our Red cell of bombers made a turn that put us on course to South Vietnam. Target time was still three hours away. Other cells of B-52s were strung out behind us, making their way toward the refueling area.

Refueling was always stressful, but once it was completed we had time to catch our breath and have a cup of coffee. However a more stressful time lay ahead. That would be the time over target when bombs were released.

About one hour from South Vietnam, while still over the South China Sea, we completed our bombing-system checks to make sure everything was working properly. The gunner had already checked his .50-caliber guns, and the ECM operator had checked his jamming transmitters and the chaff dispensers. All crewmembers donned flak vests and rechecked to make sure their water-survival gear was attached. The aircraft was at 33,000 feet, our bombing altitude. All lights, inside and outside the aircraft, were turned off.

We could see Saigon and other cities near the coast as we approached landfall. Our target area was a dense jungle near the Cambodian border where we would drop bombs on enemy fortifications and troops to assist allied forces on the ground. The idea was to put a trail of bombs in a specified target box. The radar navigator was to place his crosshairs on a designated point and let the bombing computers trigger release at the desired time. My job as aircraft commander was to keep the needle of the BDI centered until release, ensuring that the aircraft was on the desired track. A flashing yellow "bomb release" light in the cockpit and at the radar navigator's position signaled that bombs were being released. After all bombs were out, we waited fifteen seconds and then made a hard turn away from the target. Looking below, we could see multiple orange flashes as the bombs contacted the ground and lit up the sky. At our altitude it was impossible to assess damage. That was left to the staff to determine after examining our radar film on return to base and reviewing reports from ground observers.

Although we were constantly on the lookout for enemy fighters, ground fire, and missiles, we didn't see any on this mission. At our altitude we were supposed to be above the effective range of enemy antiaircraft guns. That gave us comfort, but we didn't take it for granted that we couldn't be hit from ground fire. Mobile SAMs were always a worry.

The return to Guam was six hours of mostly straight and level flying at 45,000 feet. Flying at such a high altitude extended our range and usually gave us the ability to make it home without another in-flight refueling. However, the fuel reserve was always a matter of interest and closely monitored. At the midpoint of our return flight we passed directly over the Philippines. We could see hundreds of islands below.

On this and almost every other mission we had to circumnavigate storm clouds that built up along our route. The Pacific Ocean is a favorable environment for cloud development, especially during daylight hours. The weather always made it a challenge to maintain our position in the cell, a task requiring constant attention and work.

We made our descent in cell formation early in the afternoon, arriving over Orote Point (a tip of land jutting from Guam) and following with a GCA. The saddleback runway made every landing at Andersen interesting. After parking the aircraft we went to debriefings and turned in all our logs and radar film. Debriefing experts asked us questions about every phase of flight. We also wrote up all our maintenance problems so the maintenance crews could fix them and get the aircraft back into the lineup for the next day's mission. From our film, intelligence experts could evaluate the success of our mission. Finally, after a twenty-hour day, tired and exhausted, we had drinks and snacks under the palm trees just outside the debriefing room before heading for quarters and some needed sack time.

That first mission was an interesting and demanding flight that introduced my crew to what we would be doing over the next six months. Just knowing we would be scheduled to fly every third day (or night) made us tired. We knew our strength and endurance would be thoroughly tested. It meant getting rest when we could and keeping ourselves fit, ready, and mentally alert.

My first mission presented some things I hadn't anticipated. The initial surprise came at the end of the pre-mission briefing, when the wing chaplain made comments and led a prayer. He prayed that we would be brave, professional, and strong and have a safe return. He also prayed for our enemy. I was impressed by the tone and sincerity of his prayer. One could have heard a pin drop. I had said my own silent prayer, but hearing from the chaplain was good. It enabled each of us to focus on the frailty of man, the harshness of war, and the need for divine help.

A second discovery was that dropping tons of bombs on real people and places was a much more sobering experience than I had expected. I hadn't thought much about people being killed until we were approaching the target area. Knowing that within a few minutes, tons of explosives would rain down on the surface below us made me wonder about who would be hit and why were we doing this. My prayer from that day forward became, "God, grant us a safe mission and may our effort hasten the day of peace for the people we are bombing."

Another surprise was the impersonal nature of the war where the face of the enemy couldn't be seen from our bombing altitude of 33,000 feet. Our target area was obscured by thick jungle, and we never knew how many people were hurt or killed by our exploding bombs. Our job was to put the bombs in the target box. Someone else would do the damage assessment, leaving us with little or no feedback. It struck me as odd that six hours into the mission we were dropping bombs in a war zone and six hours later were back in the friendly confines of Andersen AFB, where there was a comfortable bed and plenty of good food and where the island people hardly knew a war was in progress.

Although my heart rate increased every time I saw the bomb-release light blink, I never doubted our purpose or what we were trying to achieve—a free South Vietnam left to its own self-determination. I was doing a job I had been trained to do, and I felt genuine pride in serving our country in a time of national need. In a sense I chose to be there by virtue of my decision to make the Air Force a career. I was doing what my country asked me to do.

After a night and a day of rest, we were back on the flying schedule. The second mission was similar to the first—a night launch, a stream of fifteen aircraft (five cells), and a target box in the jungles of South Vietnam. Everything went as scheduled.

One early problem we encountered on Guam was a lack of personal transportation. The officers' club, where we ate most of our meals, was a mile or so away. To get to the club, the beach, or anywhere off base, we needed wheels. The answer was to buy a clunker. Like most other crews, we found a "Guam bomb" that met our needs. A ten-year-old Plymouth, it was rusted and dented but seemed to run okay. Together we could afford the $250 price.

The squadron parking lot was filled with "Guam bombs." It was an interesting collection. One innovative crew bought a 1954 Olds 88 that they painted a camouflage color scheme similar to that on the B-52s. After each mission they painted a little white bomb on each door. It was interesting to watch the accumulation of white bombs as their mission count increased.

Two of my crewmembers went together and bought a used Suzuki 80cc motorbike that they made available to the rest of us when they didn't need it. A motorbike was a dangerous vehicle on the coral-based, rain-slick streets and roads of Guam, prompting constant reminders from the wing safety office. That didn't deter many crewmembers. Motorbikes were all over the place. Later my copilot became a victim of a motorbike incident, breaking his arm in a fall that required he be placed on non-flying duty for about a month. His loss meant I would have a substitute copilot on every mission we flew. I rode the motorbike on several occasions but always with caution.

Our clunker allowed us to get off base once in a while and see some of Guam's scenery and culture. One day we drove to the south end of the island to see what Ferdinand Magellan saw in 1521 when he landed and claimed official ownership for Spain. We drove by Tumon Bay, Agana (the capital city), Agana Harbor, Orote Point, and several small villages. On a different day, a Sunday afternoon, we drove to a small village to watch the cockfights, a popular weekend sport for Guamanians. We weren't impressed and left after watching only two or three matches.

On still another day we decided to visit Talofofo Falls, one of the advertised tourist attractions on the island. We drove to a spot below the midpoint of the island, and then we trekked uphill for an hour, walking through heavy brush and vines, over stones, and past wallowing water buffalo, until finally we discovered the falls. They were beautiful and looked especially refreshing after our arduous hot climb. Already soaked from intermittent rain, we dove into the water and then stood under the falls in our underwear for at least an hour.

About three weeks into our tour, word came that we would be flying the biggest mission (until that time) of the war. The plan called for thirty B-52s to strike the Mu Gia Pass, near the Laos–North Vietnam border. It was a deep, narrow pass on the vital Ho Chi Minh Trail. Our goal was to interdict the movement of supplies through the pass. The concept was to put tons of bombs on the steep sides of the pass, causing massive slides that would fill in the narrow trail, making it unusable to the enemy.

The mission came on Easter weekend, but we didn't know it was Easter except by the date on the map. The Andersen ramp was loaded with aircraft as a typhoon near Okinawa had caused an evacuation of all its tankers to Guam. Fortunately, the ramp could handle that many planes, and more.

That night I participated in what I think was one of the great aviation feats of the war. Sixty aircraft—thirty bombers and thirty tankers—took off exactly on schedule at one-minute intervals without a single delay or abort. Every aircraft completed the mission. To have big, complex airplanes perform so flawlessly in darkness and radio silence was a huge tribute to the maintenance and ground-support personnel who made it all possible.

In terms of difficulty, importance, and threat potential, everyone saw the mission as a major step up. We knew it would not be a milk run. Our route would take us into an area where enemy fighter attacks, ground fire, and SAMs were likely. Crewmembers knew they faced a risky task; fear showed on their faces and in their conversation. A few privately questioned why the lumbering B-52s were being sent on such a dangerous mission. But they took comfort in knowing that friendly aircraft would be involved in SAM suppression and on combat patrol to deal with enemy fighters. It was an excellent plan that worked just as it was drawn up.

We were operating in radio silence, but there was occasional frantic chatter on the emergency channel of our UHF radio. One F-4 operating in support of our mission gave a "Mayday" report that he had been hit by a SAM and was trying to make friendly territory. That got my attention, big time. I will not forget the sound of his voice as he faced an uncertain future. Other radio talk from support aircraft reported missile firings and antiaircraft fire. We could see the rounds coming from below, but none could reach us at 33,000 feet. My ECM officer, in conjunction with other B-52s in our vicinity, used his "jammers" and chaff to help confuse the enemy ground sites. It was an intense thirty minutes as we proceeded to the target and dropped our bombs. I couldn't relax until we left the coast of Vietnam and saw the South China Sea below us. The ride home was smooth and uneventful. We thought we had done a good job.

On the ground there were many stories of what crews saw and what actions they took. One crew claimed they had to seek a higher altitude to avoid ground fire. One B-52 fired at an enemy fighter. Others reported observing heavy AAA and detecting ground radars that were trying to track and fire on our attacking force.

The informal word following our mission was that it was a big success. The Mu Gia Pass had been closed. Unfortunately it didn't stay closed very long. Using thousands of workers with shovels and wheelbarrows, the North Vietnamese reopened the pass within a few weeks. We couldn't believe it. Other missions were flown against Mu Gia Pass but nothing like the mission flown on that Easter weekend.

Except for one other "up-north" mission, the strikes my crew made were scattered around South Vietnam and with an occasional target on the Cambodian border. We hit targets from Da Nang near the DMZ to Chu Lai, Pleiku, Nha Trang, the delta area below Saigon, and other places that became well known battle sites during the war. Occasionally our load included antipersonnel (fragmentation) weapons. These were carried in canisters that broke apart when released, allowing small bomblets to be spread over a wide area.

Some of our staff went to Vietnam to observe, from a safe distance, the actual release of weapons by B-52s. The stories they brought back were of unbelievable concussion, firepower, and devastation. Army commanders spoke glowingly of the effectiveness of B-52s and welcomed their use in support of ground forces. Other stories came from captured North Vietnamese soldiers about their fear of being hit by bombs from a high-flying B-52.

By midsummer my crew, like many other crews, had qualified for a break in the action. We were rewarded with a four-day R&R trip to Japan. Our transportation was a KC-135 tanker that had a scheduled mission to Yokota AB. The plane was loaded with all kinds of travelers. My crew was delighted to get away from Guam, even for a short period. Japan was about a three-hour trip, and I remember passing over the small island of Iwo Jima—one sight I will not forget. Just looking down on the island gave me goose bumps because I could remember as a kid the grim story of 20,000 casualties during the fiercest fighting of World War II.

In Japan we made it to various stores and tailor shops around Yokota, buying electronic equipment at cheap Japanese prices and ordering custom-made clothes from Japanese tailors who claimed they could outfit us in a new suit or sport coat in four days. They also guaranteed a perfect fit. The bargains were plentiful, and we did our part to help the Japanese economy, as our other buddies did when they were there. The only restriction on buying was that we couldn't get anything through customs that had been made in Red China. Chinese goods were strictly taboo. The electronic equipment we purchased was fine, but the clothes never seemed to fit, and we had no way to get them altered.

Riding the Japanese trains into Tokyo was a new experience in transportation. We couldn't believe how efficient the trains were and how people literally packed themselves into the cars. None of us had ever been to Japan or any other Asian city. The people, their dress, their customs, and their food looked very strange. But we made out fine and enjoyed the sights.

After four days it was time to head back to Guam to resume our business of flying combat missions. By this time we had started marking off the days until time to go home. Someone came up with a beautiful mermaid that had been divided into 179 little blocks to be painted in, allowing us to count down the days until there was only a wake-up before going home. Most crews had the mermaid posted on the wall of their quarters, showing exactly how many days they had left on the island.

On Guam the rainy season had begun. Seldom did we see the sun. During our missions, weather became an increasing problem. Twice we came close to evacuating all the airplanes from the island because typhoons were moving in our direction. Luckily it never came to that.

I remember returning from one mission when heavy weather buffeted the Guam area. Before we started our descent at 200 miles out, we were advised of strong winds and heavy rain at Andersen. Tankers were launched, and we took on fuel in case we had to divert to Okinawa. Later we were cleared to descend and make our approach. By the time we leveled out at 2,000 feet, we were being rocked by forty-mile winds and rain so heavy we couldn't see anything ahead. We set the crab of our landing gear at the maximum of 20 degrees because the prevailing wind was almost 90 degrees off our nose. I knew it was going to be a sporty course that would require my best effort to get the plane down safely. It was so rough I couldn't hold the heading within 10 degrees of what I needed. The airspeed was bouncing around and varying by fifteen knots from what I wanted to maintain. When we turned final approach, following the instructions of the GCA controller, the aircraft was so crabbed into the wind that I was looking out the side window to try to find the runway.

I fought the aircraft as hard as I could. Without a doubt this was the most difficult landing I had ever attempted. I thought, "Lord, help me through this," and He did. I knew that saving the airplane and the lives of the crewmembers depended on me. We broke out of the clouds at 400 feet and somehow I got the airplane on the ground in one piece. Everyone on the crew rejoiced in our safe landing, knowing we had experienced a close call. Some other airplanes in our formation made multiple approaches before getting down; others had to divert to an alternate base. Perhaps that is what I should have done, knowing it was my call whether to attempt a landing or divert. But my goal was to get the plane and crew on the ground at Andersen so both could launch again on scheduled missions. It was either luck or the grace of God that got us through. I think it was the latter.

There were two other missions when our flight safety was seriously threatened. One was on return from a mission on which things had gone fairly well. The only problem was that the thick clouds encountered during the latter part of the mission didn't permit us to see our cellmates. We were the third aircraft in a cell of three and had to rely exclusively on radar to maintain our separation from the other aircraft. We had to do this often, and it required close attention to maintain the desired distance between our aircraft and the one just one mile ahead.

On this particular mission, I had an eager young officer filling in for my regular copilot. The substitute had requested that I let him make the descent to traffic-pattern altitude. I had authority to grant it, and I did. He seemed like a sharp pilot who was on top of everything. During the early phase of descent he let the airspeed get too high and his descent rate too steep. Suddenly the radar navigator couldn't spot the aircraft ahead. In clouds and without information on the other aircraft, we had a very dangerous situation. Realizing the grave danger, I took control and began slowing the aircraft and its rate of descent. At about eight thousand feet, we broke out of the clouds, and I was shocked to see that we were not more than fifty feet directly above the aircraft that was supposed to be a mile ahead. A mere wiggle of the wings, and we would have hit each other. It was that close. I jerked the throttles back to try to gain separation. Again by the grace of God, we avoided a catastrophe. I relearned some lessons that day about discipline, safety, and being in charge. I pledged never to let that situation happen again.

The other mission when we got the daylights scared out of us happened near the end of our tour. It occurred just after bombs had been released and we were about halfway through our 180-degree left turn away from the target. Suddenly, in the black of night, we realized we were on a collision course with a B-52 approaching rapidly from our right. I pulled up hard, allowing us to miss the other aircraft. In flying language it was a "near miss" (worst case). Again we had escaped a potential disaster.

Later analysis showed that the other aircraft had misread the flight plan. On this particular mission, due to our proximity to the Cambodian border, we were scheduled to make an immediate 180-degree turn after releasing weapons rather than waiting fifteen or thirty seconds, as we had done on previous missions. We in effect turned inside the aircraft in front of us, putting him on a collision course with us. It was a terrifying sight to see another aircraft so close and a great relief to know we had avoided a collision. This close encounter kept us in an uneasy mood all the way home and constantly thinking about what might have been. Only time allows one to get beyond such situations.

As we moved into September, we had filled in most of the blocks on our mermaid chart. We anxiously waited for the day we could board an airplane and head home. Over the months we were deployed, we had been busy purchasing gifts to take back to our families and friends. Our purchases included such things as jewelry, electronic equipment, clothing, stereo equipment, dinnerware, and crafts. There were bargains everywhere, especially in Japan and at the gift shop on Guam, which featured goods from many Western Pacific countries. I don't think I missed a week visiting the Guam gift shop and Base Exchange, always looking for new items. My specific buys included a stereo amplifier and a tape deck (a hot item at the time). I recorded many tapes at the base hobby shop during my time off, so I was loaded with music when I came home. I had everything from Mantovani to Johnny Cash. I also had such things as a large Japanese hibachi pot, jewelry, cloisonné, monkey pod, tablecloths, decorative pieces, and various articles of clothing. Knowing we would be coming home on a military plane, we weren't restricted by space or weight factors. Our only concern was clearing customs.

During the second week of September, we flew our forty-fourth, and final, mission. I was proud of what the crew had accomplished. On several occasions we were picked to fly as the cell or stream leader. Every mission we flew was launched on time and flown as briefed. Bombs were delivered on target, as scheduled, every time. I'm not aware of another crew who could claim such accomplishments. To fly that many missions without a late takeoff or abort was unlikely. We had accumulated more than five hundred combat hours and the respect of the wing's command and staff elements. From the Air Force we received multiple Air Medals for our performance. As crewmembers we felt both satisfied and rewarded.

For the trip home we boarded a KC-135 that took us to Hickam AFB, Hawaii, and then on to Turner AFB, Georgia. On landing in Hawaii we were welcomed by hula girls who put beautiful leis around our necks. It was my first time in Hawaii, so after clearing customs, I soaked in what I could in the limited time available. Clearing customs was time consuming but not as bad as I had expected. On the next day we loaded up for the final leg home. It was a smooth flight with much anticipation about seeing families, friends, and home again. We arrived in late afternoon and were met by a crowd, including our families, who made us feel like conquerors and heroes. But we knew we were neither. We were merely guys who had done our job and were glad to be safely home.

Mac Phillips (1969, D-1) 1st Cavalry Division, 1970

As a member of the Class of 1969, I took an extra semester to complete my degree—not unusual for Aggies of all generations. I immediately reported to Fort Benning for the Officer Basic Course. Originally I had planned to apply for Airborne and Ranger training, but there was talk that the war was winding down, so I submitted papers for transfer to Vietnam as soon as possible. This decision was not out of a desire for excitement or simple bravado. Instead I identified with something I read that said, just as World War I and World War II were the defining moments of those generations, Vietnam was the defining moment of my generation—and I wanted to be a part of it.

I arrived in Southeast Asia late in the fall of 1970 and received my first "trial by fire" the first night I was in country. After arriving at Tan Son Nhut Air Base, we were bussed to the replacement center in Long Binh. There we completed necessary paperwork and were assigned quarters while we waited for our unit assignments. I joined seven other lieutenants in a sandbagged bunker with four narrow single bunks on each side.

Shortly after dark my bunker mates began playing poker. As I sat on my cot waiting for a space in the game, we heard explosions several kilometers in the distance followed by sirens going off everywhere. Being a good Texas Aggie and having been trained well by my Spider D upperclassmen (including the editor of this book) on how to get under our bunks rapidly and amuse ourselves for what seemed like hours, I was first in the bunker to roll under my bed.

Apparently the infantry creed "Follow me" had been well learned by my fellow officers. Five or six lieutenants "followed me" under my bunk—foot to head, crosswise, and on top of each other, until all four legs of my bunk were lifted off the floor and wobbled side to side.

About ten minutes later the all-clear signal was sounded and we began to untangle and crawl from under the bunk. Other than one bloody nose from being hit the face by a boot, there were no casualties. The injured lieutenant wondered out loud if he would get a Purple Heart while another, who has got under a different bunk and had it to himself, claimed he should receive a commendation for following the principle of "not bunching up when the shooting starts."

The card game soon resumed, and I was left wondering if I should contact the folks who write training manuals and inform them that the maximum number of lieutenants who fit safely under the standard US Army bunk bed is five. Unfortunately this was not the only combat experience, humorous or otherwise, I would experience over the next eleven months.

Ben Goodwyn (1962, D-1) 7th Marine Regiment, 1965

In early September 1965, intelligence sources located remnants of the 1st VC Regiment, which had been mauled in the recent Operation Starlite. This crippled regiment had evaded our forces and moved eight miles south of the battle area from the Van Tuong villages to Cape Batangan. Cape Batangan contained a village complex that later would become infamous: My Lai. That incident, however, was far in the future.

The Cape lay fifteen to twenty miles south of the Chu Lai Enclave. Once off the coast, the land became undulating hills and valleys crisscrossed by ravines, hedgerows, dikes, and plenty of cover—ideal for the quick, sharp encounters that favored smaller, faster guerrilla units. For years the Cape had been a haven for the Viet Cong. The insurgents were well established in the area, with an infrastructure whose tentacles reached deep into village society.

Once the enemy was located, General Walt, the 3rd Marine Division commander, did not delay. He called on his old comrade-in-arms, Col. Oscar Peatross, boss of the 7th Marine Regiment. Peatross formulated his plan, assembled his staff and his two battalion commanders, and issued the order for Operation Piranha. The S-2 indicated there could be as many as 1,500 enemy in the immediate Batangan Peninsula. Should they choose to resist, our casualties could be significant.

The plan called for the 1st Battalion, in which I commanded C Company (Suicide Charlie), to embark in the evening and for two companies to follow the next morning, coming abreast across the beach in Amtraks. We would then come online and initiate a search-and-destroy mission across the peninsula, driving the remnants of the NVA and any Viet Cong into the blocking positions of the 3rd Battalion—which would have been heli-lifted into position at first light. Support would be provided by naval gunfire from destroyers off shore and from A4-E Marine attack aircraft from Chu Lai.

At the assigned time Charlie Company assembled along with Bravo Company on the Chu Lai beach. Small boats landed nearby and lowered their ramps for us to board. Through the surf we waded and at thirty to a boat, some two hundred of Uncle Sam's finest headed to an LST anchored a mile offshore. As the water slowly changed from green to a darker blue, I wondered whether I would survive, how the men would perform under fire, and the most nagging question, "How many of that NVA regiment would stand and fight?"

The roar of my landing craft slowed as the bow nosed in toward the LST. After the throaty diesels had been gunned twice—mostly for show—we found ourselves alongside the ship and reaching for the heavy nets. With a great deal of effort the nets were wrestled into the boat and the first four men began climb up the side of the LST. At 170 pounds and with another 50 in equipment and ammo, negotiating twenty feet of swinging nets up to the weather decks was no cakewalk. My thigh and arm muscles began to strain and slowly tire against the steady pull of gravity, the surge of the sea, and the undulations of the ship. The exertions required frequent rests, camouflaged as reviewing from whence one came, how far one had to go, and whether one was crowding his confederates' path.

Once aboard I continued to wonder about the potential welcoming committee on the beach. Tension built. Few could sleep. Most of us talked well into the night. Michael Mok and Paul Schutzer of *Life* magazine were on board to cover the landing. Mike, the writer, had served his time in the Corps in the infantry during the Korean War. Paul, the photographer, had followed most armed conflicts all over the world for decades. Paul didn't know it, but he had only two years to live. His life reached a fiery conclusion as an Egyptian antitank rocket slammed into the Israeli halftrack he was aboard in the 1967 Arab-Israeli War. But his tragic end was far in the future that night. The hours dragged on until sleep became a necessity. As we drifted off to anxious dreams, the ship began to lose headway and slowly came to a point just off the Cape Batangan headlands.

Four thirty came damn early. Seemed as if only moments ago I'd been talking to Mike and Paul. With consciousness, the tension returns. On with the jungle utility trousers (light Dacron blend), then the utility shirt. No skivvies. Because skivvies hold moisture, they eventually cause "crotch rot." And even in the tropics damp underwear is cold and miserable at night. Next come the jungle boots, my cover, and the ever-present cartridge belt with that dependable government-issue Colt .45 automatic. I went down a stairwell to the galley, where I was met by a hot, oily, diesel smell emanating from somewhere deep in the bowels of the ship. All ships are the same—that same sickly sweet smell and the ever-present humming of the engines.

Steak and eggs for breakfast. Ever since Marines started landing on beaches, the Navy has served steak and eggs. Real steak and real eggs—not those green powdered abortions served at the company mess. Hot coffee—good hot coffee. I've often wondered why such fare at such a critical juncture. The heavy meal, along with diesel fumes and choppy seas in the landing, often results in nausea and vomiting. It also caused a real problem if you are gut shot. If you are hit in the intestines, excrement boils out of the perforation and contaminates the whole body cavity, resulting in an extremely painful recovery or death.

I don't recall much about the breakfast other than the steak and eggs. After eating we returned to our quarters, where we got our pack, helmet, and ever-cumbersome "Mae West" life preserver. I do remember the call for general quarters: the incessant "bong, bong, bong" and the command, "Marines, man your boats."

The morning air was cool, but the night was still upon us—as black as "nine foot up a bull's ass." Damn it was dark. I had to hold on to the Marine's pack in front of me just to maintain contact. We slowly began to move toward the glow of the red nightlights on the well deck. We would descend into this psychological inferno and then find and enter our assigned amphibious tractors. Two parallel lines of heavy-laden Marines, one on each side of the weather deck, were heading into "Harm's Way." Tension was increasing, and just before we descended into the din, a priest materialized out of the darkness, illuminated by the red glow from the decks below. In his stark white smock, with all those bloody ribbons around his neck, he stood blessing or cursing us in some old, forgotten tongue. Was this a warning from an ancient apparition summoned like Samuel before Saul's last battle? The hair stood up on my neck as fear traveled down my back and arms. Even today the vivid, shocking impression stands distinct in my memory.

The Padre passed as we descended into the hellish glow to the throaty roar of the Amtraks that sounded like angry creatures roused from a peaceful hibernation. The high, piercing whine of the starters was followed by guttural explosions as the huge engines caught. Their roar and the diesel fumes filled the area. Sweat began to bead under my steel pot.

Somehow the twenty of us found our Amtrak and struggled down into the troop compartment. Once we were settled, the steel doors of the hatch slid shut, sealing us into our metal cocoon. The heat quickly became oppressive. The humidity rose, and our breathing became strained. There was no space to move with all our gear. Just before the press of humanity became totally claustrophobic, the huge doors of the

LST yawned opened, and the tracks began their jerking movements as we headed toward the portal and the sea. One by one the tracks were spawned—down the ramp and into the ocean, bobbing and swimming like huge green turtles. The Amtraks formed pods, circling until all had emerged. On signal the leaders of each pod peeled off and were followed by the rest until twenty-five or thirty tracks were traveling in line parallel to the beach a half-mile away. Then, with a wave forward, all the tracks executed a 90-degree turn and, with engines at max, headed toward the beach. If the tempo of the engines didn't clue us to our direction, the shells roaring overhead from the 5-inch destroyer guns did. Like generations of Marines who had preceded us, we were heading in!

Each high-trajectory howitzer shell sounded as though someone had catapulted a heavy, slow, lumbering boxcar. Not a flat trajectory gun! That bitch scalds the air in a screaming moan. Eeeeyowww! Bam!! An eerie sound one never forgets. After the naval-gunfire bombardment reached its conclusion, the jets began their runs at possible targets on the beach. First the 250- and 500-pound general-purpose bombs, and then, as we drew closer, the 20-mm cannon and the rockets. Closer and closer they came to their targets, and closer and closer we came to ours.

Blood pounded in my temples. Every sense at a high pitch. A quarter-mile off the beach the machine gunner in the Amtrak opened up. Hot spent shell casings began careening inside the vehicle. The sweet smell of cordite reached my nostrils, and my adrenaline reached undreamed levels as my heart pounded, pounded, pounded.

The beach loomed through the track's apertures as the command passed to "lock and load!" The sound of rounds sliding into chambers, bolts rotating and lugs engaging, and safeties clicking followed. A second order followed. "Fix bayonets!" Cold black blades were withdrawn and clicked into place at the same time the clawing treads of the tracks grabbed sand. A surge, a return to the high whine, a firmer catch, the whine, a catch, a whine, and then, with finality, a surge of speed. Along four hundred yards of white, sandy beach emerged scores of green-black Amtraks, their machine guns spewing.

At the high-water mark, Marines pressed forward as the door cracked and then slowly, so slowly, opened. Seconds seem like hours as I focused wholly on the opening hatch—a door that likely would attract the attention of every NVA machine gunner on the Cape. At halfway open, the troops lunged. A Marine stumbled, the rest went over him. The tracks emptied as the squads formed platoons and the platoons formed their companies.

Following our training and experience we moved across the beach to a small hill to get organized and await orders. Meager enemy fire was drowned by the mass of Marine automatic weapons. Other than an occasional sniper, resistance quickly melted. Once again, United States Marines had taken the beach.

Operation Piranha concluded on September 10, 1965, with a body count of 178 VC and NVA and another 360 suspected enemy captured. Many of the local VC left the area before the operation and later returned to exert their influence on the peninsula.

Larry Sommers (1968, C-1) 4th Infantry Division, 1970

I had been an infantry platoon leader for six months when my RTO asked one of his constant questions. The RTO, who was from Louisiana, was always talking, asking about things, or wondering what if. This day he asked, "Hey L-T, if you had three doors to choose from, and behind the first door was death, the second a naked woman, and the third a ticket home, would you take a chance to pick a door?"

I told him I would choose a door because one out of three odds of being killed wasn't any worse than those of an infantry lieutenant's chances of surviving combat. Before he had an opportunity to ask which door I'd pick, we received orders to move to an NVA mortar-platoon site that had just shelled the battalion's firebase.

We moved out immediately and hadn't gone more than a couple hundred meters when we received intense fire from our front. I moved up immediately to get a better look when the familiar crack of AK-47 fire caused me to hit the dirt. As I was returning fire, wisps of dirt and leaves sprang all around me. Soon the contact ended and our only casualty was our point man, who had been shot in the hand and likely would lose some fingers. The enemy left one dead and numerous blood trails indicating several more were wounded. As we dusted off our wounded soldier, my RTO said, "L-T, you almost got shot. I saw rounds hit all around you, and look at your M-16, two bullets hit your trigger guard and magazine and as you were on your belly that meant the rounds were deflected down under your chest."

I replied, "Yeah, I just opened the first door and won." Shortly the battalion radioed we were to continue the mission as our contact was suspected to be with the NVA mortar platoon trying to flee the area.

An hour later, as we cautiously followed fresh signs the enemy was leaving behind, we came upon recently discarded packs and equipment. We must have been getting close as the enemy was lightening his load to be able to move quickly. We should have thought of him circling around to our flank to ambush our center; which is exactly what he did. This time in addition to AK-47 cracks, they fired two RPGs at my platoon CP. The first hit five feet away from my RTO but didn't detonate. He scrabbled behind a rock formation when a second RPG struck the tree he had just left—and did explode. Other than ringing in his ears neither he nor anyone else in the platoon got a scratch. The NVA quickly broke contact and continued to evade. Before continuing the pursuit I told my RTO, "This time you picked a door and won."

After another movement of about a kilometer, we finally arrived at the NVA mortar firing point to find six mortar rounds stacked against a tree. The NVA were nowhere in sight, but later they were engaged and scattered by the rest of our company moving to our location to reinforce us. We secured the location and prepared a demolition pit to blow the ordnance. However, no one wanted to touch the mortar rounds in fear that they were booby-trapped. I didn't think so, so I picked up two and carried them to the demo area. My first squad moved the rest. My RTO was shocked and said, "L-T, why did you pick up those rounds?"

I replied, "I already opened door number one today, so I was thinking door three."

Bill Park (1964, G-3) 55th Military Intelligence Detachment, 1966

In April of 1966 I was on temporary assignment with the 3rd Brigade of the 25th Infantry Division in the Central Highlands of II Corps near the Cambodian border. There were a lot of Aggies in the area. One day I was flying in an observation plane over the Ia Drang Valley, where five months earlier three battalions of the 1st Calvary Division engaged in the first major battle of the war with North Vietnamese Regular Forces. It was where Lt. Pat Payne (E-1, '64), from Waco, earned the Silver Star when he and his recon platoon prevented the North Vietnamese from overrunning their battalion headquarters.

On a flight a few days later our observation plane received ground fire that caused an oil leak in the motor. When oil covered the windshield, the pilot started trying to make it back to the dirt strip at the Brigade CP. I remember that all aircraft in the area were trying to track us and find out where we were in case we went down in the bush. Fortunately we made it back to the strip—but we were losing oil pressure fast.

Shortly after that flight I ran into Lt. Terry Scott (B-3, '64), from Coleman, who was a platoon leader with the 3rd Brigade of the 25th ID operating in the same area near the border. He looked as though he had been in the field a long time, and he said his troops looked even worse. They had spent many weeks operating out in the bush in the area of Chu Pong Mountain, near the border. Terry Scott ended up being a career Army officer and retired as a lieutenant general.

I was on duty at the 3rd Brigade HQ CP tent one day during this same period when Gen. William Westmoreland—Allied Forces Commander for South Vietnam—landed unexpectedly wanting a briefing on current operations. As a 1st Lieutenant I was the only intelligence officer around at the time. I presented our intel briefing to him, and although I was extremely nervous I think he was satisfied. He was very upset that the brigade had sustained casualties from friendly artillery fire. I heard later that several officers were relieved or reassigned for reasons related to the incident.

When I was at the II Corps Headquarters airstrip at Pleiku in late April, I ran into Lt. Lee Sanders (D-1, '64), a platoon leader with the 1st Cav. He was looking pretty good that day, but in 1969 he returned to Vietnam for a second tour and was wounded on Hamburger Hill, which left him on lifetime disability.

In April 1966, Aggies had several musters in Vietnam. I was fortunate to get a day off from the field and went to Muster with one of my bosses—Colonel McCord (G-2 for Army II Corps Area). He was from an A&M Class in the 40s I think and had seen a lot of action during his army career. His Assistant G-2 was Lieutenant Colonel Stiles (also an Aggie), from the Taylor, Texas, area.

Many other Aggies from the class of '64 participated in the Vietnam War, and several never returned. Our class hit it just right when the war was escalating. Many served during the first couple of years of the conflict, in 1965 and 1966.

Hale Burr (1965, Squadron 7 and Corps Staff)
13th Tactical Fighter Squadron, 1969–70

At 0330 the longest April Fool's Day 1970 in my life began routinely in my two-man room. The alarm clock rang to wake me for an 0430 flight briefing in our squadron building. A major, two captains, and I were all on our last combat mission with the 13th Tactical Fighter Squadron at Udorn Royal Thai Air Force Base, Thailand. After the flight we were scheduled to depart for the USA. I was on my second combat tour in Southeast Asia and during hundreds of missions had experienced more than my fair share of exposure to odds against returning. We were further concerned by the fact that one of our squadron's F-4s had been shot down while attacking a SAM site in North Vietnam the day before. Both of the crew had ejected from the plane over Laos and, luckily, were quickly picked up by USAF Jolly Green Giant SAR helicopters.

Our four F-4 Phantoms, call sign "Falcon 51," launched at 0630. Our takeoff was followed by an aerial refueling on "Lemon" track with a USAF KC-135 tanker flying out of U-Tapao Royal Thai Navy Airfield, in southern Thailand. We cycled through the refueling in 1, 3, 2, 4 order and continued to our target in an area called the "Fish's Mouth" or Barthelemy Pass between NVN and Laos. Because the passes through the mountains on that border had numerous logistics facilities that transported war materiel to their troops in Laos, Cambodia, and South Vietnam, they were heavily defended with AAA guns and SAM sites. Of course the passes were frequent bombing targets. The terrain is incredibly rugged with high mountains called karsts and dense triple-canopied jungles. Of the many American pilots downed near these passes during the war, very few returned. Search and rescue was difficult not only because of the terrain but also because of the large numbers of North Vietnamese and Pathet Lao soldiers in the area.

When we were about forty miles from our target, we made radio contact with our Tiger F-4E fast FAC from Korat Airbase. As he directed the strike, one of the F-105s attacking the target area was hit by AAA fire and came up on Guard emergency radio frequency frantically announcing for everyone to hear that he might be bailing out over Laos. Our pucker factor increased dramatically because we then knew it was a "hot" target area. While approaching the target, we saw all the 37-, 57-, and 85-mm active AAA gun sites shooting from both sides of the border.

The Tiger Fast FAC marked the target with a white phosphorus rocket, and our four F-4s commenced our circular attack on the white smoke from various angles to complicate the enemy gunners' tracking. Because I was number 4 in the flight and rolled in last on the target, I descended through a nearly solid cloud of black, white, and dark grey flak bursts that the AAA sites had fired at the preceding three F-4s. As I descended to drop altitude, I could see various colors of tracers coming up at my aircraft and passing by my canopy. It was like watching a World War II movie of B-17s flying over Germany! (A tracer round is usually only every fifth bullet, so I knew there was lots of incoming out there.) We dropped our loads of Mk-82 500-pound bombs and CBU-24s in one pass on the target and rapidly got away from the area. The Tiger FAC announced our BDA: two large secondary explosions (possibly ammo storage) detonated, two AAA gun sites destroyed, numerous enemy KBA (killed by air), and several fires.

Our four-ship flight quickly rejoined within ten miles of the target and headed back into Laos for the return trip to our Thailand airbase. It was an uneventful return except that before we set down at Udorn we flew a tight four-ship diamond formation in a very low pass over the runway. I was "Falcon 54," in the slot position and hoping the leader wouldn't drag me off on the ground. I always felt "bullet proof" as a young fighter pilot, but that day I wanted to make sure I got back to the "land of the big BX" safely. We made a tactical pitch up to the landing pattern and got the jets safely back on the runway.

As we taxied back in, all the guys in our squadron were waiting in the aircraft parking area to welcome us. When we climbed from our Phantoms, they hosed us down with water cannons on fire trucks. After toasting everyone with lots of cheap champagne and beer, we celebrated our successful tour completion by shaking the hands of squadron friends and other 432nd Wing well-wishers on the ramp. Then we changed to dry uniforms, grabbed our bags, and boarded the base C-47 "Gooney Bird" for the flight south. For our trip, the squadron had thoughtfully sent a garbage can filled with ice and beer—which we proceeded to drink all the way to Bangkok.

That afternoon we four "happy warriors" got on the "Freedom Bird," a military charter B707, that would take us from Bangkok to our homes in America. A slight delay was caused at the Bangkok airport when the ticket agents didn't want to let our flight leader on the flight because he was so intoxicated. But when we convinced him that the three of us would prevent any problems, he let us all aboard.

Because we crossed the International Date Line west of Hawaii, our long trans-Pacific Ocean flight to Travis AFB, California, arrived on what was still April 1. We all said our goodbyes and best wishes to each other and went our separate ways. I caught a flight from San Francisco back home to Texas, where I was met with hugs and kisses from my wife, Barbara, and my two-year-old daughter, Lara. The longest April Fool's Day was over. No jokes or pranks had been played. Nor had any bad luck happened. What a memory!

Michael Lee Lanning (1968, D-1) 199th Light Infantry Brigade, 1969

I remained overnight in College Station after commissioning and graduation on May 25, 1968. The next morning I drove from Highway 6 up to the Administration Building and made a U-turn so that I was headed east and could see Texas A&M in my rearview mirror. I was on my way to my future.

Over the next eleven months I attended the Infantry Officer Basic Course, Airborne training, and the Ranger Course at Fort Benning, Georgia—and spent several months with the 82nd Airborne Division at Fort Bragg, North Carolina. All the while I was afraid the war in Southeast Asia was going to be over before I could get there. I did not want to miss what I considered to be the most important and exciting event of our generation. To expedite matters I submitted paperwork volunteering for immediate transfer to Vietnam. This was one request that didn't suffer the Army's usual bureaucratic slowness.

I am pretty sure I was among the first of the Class of 1968 to arrive in the war zone when our flight landed in Vietnam. With the addition of a day when we crossed the International Date Line, I was unaware that it was April 21—Aggie Muster Day—until I had to sign and date some forms at the 90th Replacement Battalion in Long Binh.

We were kept busy all day in processing, briefings, and receiving uniforms. Near the end of the afternoon I spotted an officer with an Aggie ring. I introduced myself to Lieutenant Colonel Baker of the Veterinarian Corps. We held a minimuster as we talked about Aggieland and had a moment of silence for dead comrades. It didn't compare with the muster of twenty-five Aggies on Corregidor shortly before the island fell to the Japanese in 1942, but it would have to do.

Afterward we shook hands and went our separate ways. Deep inside I hoped my first Aggie Muster since graduation would not be my last.

Mike Richardson (1965, A-1 and 1st Brigade Staff)
First Marine Air Wing, 1969

I was with Animal A-1 my first two years and on 1st Brigade Staff my junior year. For my senior year I told A&M to stuff their Army contract, and I became a civilian student. I graduated in May of 1965, and that summer I was surprised to flunk my draft physical when they found I had a hernia. I was classified 1Y and was told I would not be drafted and had no obligation to serve. Perhaps I had no obligation to the draft, but I still felt an obligation to my Aggie buddies who were now in training and soon would be going to Vietnam. There was no way I would let them go without me. It took about six months to have the surgery necessary to fix my hernia and another six months to heal sufficiently to enlist. I joined the Marine Corps in the summer of 1966 and started OCS in Quantico, Virginia, in January of 1967. After commissioning and flight school I reported to Vietnam, where I joined VMCJ-1 with the First Marine Air Wing. The airplane I flew, the EA-6A, was involved in Electronic Reconnaissance. We flew both passive and active missions. A passive mission involved collecting electronic intelligence; an active mission generally involved jamming SAM missile sites in support of air strikes in North Vietnam. After the loss of a number of my friends in combat, I concluded that this aircraft and this mission were not for me. I really wanted to be at the tip of the spear, more directly killing the bad guys. In order to see more action I volunteered to be a ground FAC. I was scheduled to attend the FAC school in the Philippines, but before that could happen I lucked out and found a slot with H&MS 11 as an airborne FAC flying TA-4s in Laos as part of that secret war. It was there that I found what I was looking for. I could kill all the bad guys I could find.

Gerald Madeley (1964, Band) PACAF Procurement Center Thailand, 13th Air Force, 1971–73

On August 18, 1971, I completed my Master of Science degree program at the Air Force Institute of Technology and anxiously awaited orders for the next assignment—which I fully expected to be Vietnam. When the orders arrived, I learned that I was to be assigned as the Purchasing Officer at Nakhon Phanom AB, Thailand. The early September reporting date necessitated a real scramble to get everything done, including my M-16 marksmanship training. This proved rather challenging because all the military weapons training facilities in the Dayton, Ohio, area were closed for renovation.

I finally located an active range at Dyess AFB in Abilene, Texas. This worked out well because I had planned to stop in Stephenville to visit friends and family for a few days before leaving for the Far East. I quickly made a reservation for the next M-16 qualification session, to be held the last week of August. In spite of a three-inch rainfall at the Sweetwater range the night before my training, as well as the presence of rattlesnakes, I qualified on the M-16 rifle and successfully completed the course.

Following a trip to Dallas to catch my flight to San Francisco, I reached Travis AFB, where I boarded the thirty-hour flight to Bangkok via Honolulu, Anderson AFB, Clark AB, Hong Kong, and Tan Son Nhut AB. At Don Mueang Airport, in Bangkok, I caught a flight to Nakhon Phanom AFB. Upon my arrival at the Bangkok airport, Lt. Col. Burt Bailey advised me that my orders had been changed, that I had been reassigned to the newly organized Thailand Procurement Center (TPC), in Bangkok. This was great news; however, I had no idea what my new responsibilities might be. (I had noticed Colonel Bailey's Aggie Ring, Class of '51. He proved to be a great boss and the first of four Aggie bosses I would have during my working career.)

Because I was the last of six captains to arrive at the TPC, the regular captain positions in the office had been assigned. After checking their duties, I discovered that no one was interested in the contracts that the Center awarded to US businesses. This looked like a good opportunity, so I discussed the situation with the Services Branch Chief and Colonel Bailey. They were receptive to my suggestion that the Center create a "Special Contracts Branch" with me as chief (and the only person assigned).

At first my duties as Branch Chief included administering a multimillion-dollar contract for the operation of power plants, water systems, and sewer facilities at six Thailand air bases and several other sites used by the US Air Force. Before long I also took over contracts for the operation and maintenance of software and hardware at a secret site called Task Force Alpha (TFA) at Nakhon Phanom AFB.

My contract responsibilities continued to grow as the O&M contractor was assigned significantly more tasks over the next few months. Also, the TFA contracts were up for renegotiation, and I soon found myself on TDY to the various bases and sites most of the time. By now my branch included two senior NCOs. The O&M contract was very interesting—primarily because of its size and its impact on base missions. However, I found the TFA contracts more challenging.

Task Force Alpha was originally a part of a program called "Igloo White," which was to be an interdiction and verification barrier some ten miles deep and running across Vietnam and Laos from the Gulf of Tonkin to the Mekong River. It was to be seeded with road-denial mines and sensors that targeted trucks moving along the Ho Chi Minh Trail. After the US Air Force and Navy Campaign called "Rolling Thunder" began in 1965, Secretary of Defense McNamara became convinced that such a barrier was needed.

Eventually the barrier was canceled, but the Igloo White portion was implemented, and the trail was sewn with some 20,000 seismic and acoustic sensors. The infiltration surveillance center, a fenced-in area and a windowless building called Task Force Alpha opened in July 1967. Use of the Igloo White sensors was a key element of all seven Commando Hunt campaigns.

I spent many hours at TFA observing the contractors' operations and watching the activities on a large display board. New sensors had to be dropped by aircraft every few weeks because the batteries ran down and parts of the trail changed. Several types of sensor were used. Some just stuck in the ground. Others resembled plants or were designed to hang in trees. It was fascinating watching the sensors being dropped and then observing the movement of trucks along the trail. The contract guys often told stories about how the placement of the sensors sometimes allowed them to listen to conversations in the immediate area. Although the technology probably was sufficient, I never observed such activity.

TFA and its surveillance program remained classified for many years. Recently, however, I have read articles in military publications regarding TFA and its sensors. And in 2006 I saw a scale model of Task Force Alpha in the 8th Air Force Museum at Barksdale AFB, Louisiana.

Carol Micki Hunt, widow of Joe Bush (1966, A-1) Army Element, Joint US Military Advisory Group Thailand, MAAG Laos, 1968–69

February 10, 1969, began as an uneventful day. After Joe left for his tour of duty in Southeast Asia on April 21, 1968, my life had involved missing and corresponding with him, looking forward to his return, and caring for our infant daughter, Robin. Robin and I lived in Temple, Texas, so that we could be near my and Joe's parents while he was overseas.

Robin was born on Easter Sunday April 14, 1968—five years from the day Joe and I met and three years from the day we became engaged—affording us only a week together before Joe had to leave what he called "his little family." In addition to doting on Robin, I devoted endless hours to writing letters and sending "care packages" and audiotapes of our voices to Joe. I also greatly anticipated receiving letters, poems, and tapes from him. Joe and I were still very hopeful that after ten long months of being apart, we would be rewarded with R&R.

The knock came at midmorning. The door had a thick, amber-glass insert that made recognition of individuals on the outside difficult. I saw two figures, one in a suit and the other in what appeared to be dress blues. I immediately knew what it meant.

Opening the door, I saw Joe's Dad and a soldier. My greatest fears were confirmed. Joe was gone.

After learning some of the details of his death from the soldier, I felt a need to locate Joe's writings and poetry that had been in a large envelope since he left for his tour. I couldn't believe that I had not read these during his absence. I had always been obsessed with reading his poetry since he first wrote a poem for me in 1963. I had read them often in the previous years because they were of such comfort. He wrote only two poems from the war zone. I kept them at hand so that I could read them every day.

I was amazed that the first poem in the envelope was one I had never seen. It depicted a part of Joe that he had kept private. He obviously wrote it while Robin and I were in the hospital after her birth. After reading it, I knew why he never showed it to me. He knew it would have caused me great distress and worry. I suffer greatly when I think about Joe wondering why I hadn't mentioned this poem in my letters to him. He knew I loved his written words and how often I had read them in previous years. Did he wonder why I hadn't asked him about it? If I had read it, I would have told him selfishly to "get his butt back home." He would have minimized the danger and ordered me not to worry. More important, though, he would not, and could not, leave Muang Soui. That's the kind of guy Joe Bush Jr. was. He really thought that what he was doing was that important. I wish I felt that his sacrifice was worth it.

UNTITLED—APRIL 1968

There is something I know, and, well,
It's a story I have to tell.
It's not a story I wish all to hear.
It's the story of something I know, and fear.

Have you thought of how you'd die
And if anyone at all would cry?
Myself I didn't have to think of it.
It came to me. I know of it.

The morn will dawn that fatal day.
I'll not be home but far away
In the warm jungle growth, live and green,
When they tear through me, angry, mean.

I won't be quiet—but with dying gasp
Curse all around with that fatal rasp.
I'll go down fighting—fighting like hell.
This is something I know, and know it well.

Oh to be an artist, to paint that scene
With blood of red and jungle green
With me in the middle a frown on my face
As if to say from hence, which place?

But I haven't said what I wanted to
About that day when life is through.
But can I? Or will it be
It's down too deep inside of me?

Joe was born January 28, 1944, in Tyler, Texas to Joseph Kerr Bush Sr. and Marjorie Saums Bush. Joe's dad, Joe Sr., attended Texas A&M for two years before joining the US Army during World War II. Joe was two years old when Papa returned to his family. Joe, along with his parents and siblings George, Janie, John, Jim, and Janet, moved to Temple when Joe was fourteen. Papa worked six days a week as a furniture salesman. He was devoted to his children, spending every Sunday with them. Joe's mom worked in their home and was a highly respected seamstress and drapery designer. She employed four women, including her mother, Mamam Saums.

I was born to Lillie and Jerry Mikulas Sr. January 5, 1946, and named Carol Vickie Mikulas. My parents, grandfather, and five siblings lived on a farm ten miles east of Temple, between Seaton and Zabcikville. Our farm was self-sustaining. We raised nearly everything we ate—beef, pork, and chickens along with produce from a three-acre garden and orchard. The only store-bought items were sugar, flour, and spices. Both sets of my great-grandparents came from Czechoslovakia via Galveston Island. Our area in Central Texas is one of the largest Czech communities in the United States.

While Joe was at Temple High School I attended Rogers High. He played football and was active in student government. I played volleyball and basketball, ran track, and was president of our Student Council. He worked odd jobs, including a paper route, and I worked in the fields and garden on our farm.

Joe began writing poetry at an early age and his poems are revealing.

UNTITLED—1962

Here I am eighteen and alive
At an age I expected not to arrive.
Several months now and I'll be on my own,
But I'll have my memories. I won't be alone.
The old friendships I've had
Both good and bad.
Guys I've known—Mike, Calvin, Tim—
Hell raisers they were, all of them.
The old gang, the girls we knew-
Nancy, Rubette, Bobbi—the crew.
The Canteen, the Wagon, the places we'd go.
Dates to Frank's or the picture show.
Drunks at the tree, or Sefcik Hall.
Good times they were, one and all.
Think of all the fads we knew.

Some we remember; some we outgrew.
My silly poetry, little thoughts, many rhymes.
Belton and Troy and Zabcikville.
We'd explore a cave or climb a hill.
My old red Ford or Mike's Chevrolet.
Life was carefree, and youthfully gay.
Johnny, Juanita, T.A., Will and James,
Scotty and Brewster—countless names.
Of course they will fade, their memories dim,
But each will have a memory, sacred to him,
Of the wonderful carefree high school days
As we walk through life our separate ways.

TARNISHED CUPS—4-26-62

It's strange, very strange, or it seems to me,
How three tarnished cups hold eternity.
Two plain, one fancy, but all are old.
Tarnished they are, but not what they hold.

I'm sentimental; I cherish them much,
Even the soot that comes with a touch.
One is ornate, another is plain,
One has a letter; the other's a name.

One is my father's, his and mine.
They seem a part of a chain or line.
They record a small part of history.
They record the births of my father, his father and me.

To me it is so very, very odd,
This plan of life, made by God,
That changes and ages the best of men
But never touches these cups of tin.

What is it they seem to say?
In their dust gathering day to day.
"Earth is for rocks and things of tin,
While somewhere above is the place for men."

Joe graduated from Temple High in 1962 and later that year enrolled in Texas A&M. He was the ultimate Aggie. He was a member of the outfit "Animal" A-1 in the Corps of Cadets. When he was home on the weekends he often attended St. Mary's Catholic Church in Temple, and I went to Seaton Brethren Church in Seaton.

Just down the road, off Highway 53 from the Seaton Brethren Church, is the Tom Sefcik Dance Hall, also known as Tom's. It is one of the oldest dance facilities in Texas. Almost every Saturday night and often on Sunday night a band was playing at Sefcik Hall. And there are other dance halls within two miles of Tom's, including Flag Hall and Star Hall. Many young people from Temple and the surrounding area frequented the halls. On the night of Easter Sunday, April 14, 1963, Joe (age nineteen) and I (seventeen) were both at Tom Sefcik Hall. Joe intended to ask my younger sister, Trudy, to dance, but someone asked her first. So he asked me. (Trudy and I had always been mistaken as twins.) I remember that I was wearing a dress I had made. It was a pink, purple, and white print. Joe referred to my dress in a letter written a year later.

After that night, Joe and I began dating. He was a "fish" at A&M, and I was a junior in high school. He had no car and had to depend on Aggie buddies to give him a ride home. Or he would hitchhike from College Station so we could meet at Sefcik or Flag Hall. Sometimes Joe was able to use the family car. Soon we were writing each other four or five letters a week. In this correspondence Joe expressed his love for A&M and its many traditions.

In these early days Joe called me by my given game, Carol. His first letter came as a surprise.

4–30–1963

Dear Carol,

Hi! How are things at Rogers High School? All the Ags are studying hard as usual—me too. Hope this letter doesn't surprise you too much. Tim told me your address.

[Tim Miller was one of Joe's best friends. Later I would ask that he accompany Joe's body home from Laos.] I'm sort of crazy—aren't I?

Will there be a dance this weekend? I sure wish I could come, but I won't be able to come home 'til next week.

If you have a spare minute some time I'd love to hear from you. Tell

Diana "Hi" for me, okay? [Diana Engbrock, a dear friend, would later be in our wedding.]

That crazy Aggie,

Joe

5–15–63

Dear Carol,

In your letter you asked why Scotty Shallcross doesn't wear his hair short like Tim and me. He isn't a fish like us. Only freshmen in the Corps have to have short hair. He has a bad knee so can't be in the Corps.

Carol, Thanks so much for writing. You write the nicest letters—really. If you are at the dance Saturday, I promise I'll be trying to dance with you every dance. (If you want!)

Be seeing you soon.

Love,

Joe

Joe spent the summer of 1963 working in Temple, and I worked on our farm. Joe loved that I was "full blooded" Czech. He gave me the nickname Mickie, taken from my middle name, Vickie, and my maiden name, Mikulas. (I recently dropped the e to become simply Micki.) On weekends we would go to a dance, a picnic, or a movie or go exploring at the lake. Joe introduced me to pizza. I remember this clearly. I had never had pizza and didn't know how to eat it. I was too embarrassed to tell him that, so I said I wasn't hungry.

Joe wrote this poem after he returned to A&M in September of 1963.

MICK—1963

There is no time for lonesome,
Yet he visits me every day
When I chance to pause and think
How soon I'll be far away.

Far from the softest, sweetest eyes,
Far from the gentlest, kindest touch,
Far from the suave and misty form,
Of the one I love so much.

When it's still at night I'll be lonesome,
And by day I'll think of you
And those happy summer days,
Of a love and how it grew.

When summer turns to winter,
And the air begins to chill,
I'll remember the warmth when you kissed me,
And the thought will warm me still.

I wonder if I'd be lonesome.
If only for sure I knew
That when summer comes again
I'll still be close to you.

We continued to correspond. He wrote about yell practice, Silver Taps, and other A&M traditions.

9–15–63

Dear "Mic",

Here I am at Aggieland. If I could afford to, I would call you every night.

Gosh Mickie, I have a million things to do. It is 8 o'clock and I still have to iron a uniform, polish my brass, polish my shoes, and haze forty freshmen!

I didn't have any trouble hitchhiking back. Some Aggies picked me up. I sure wish that I could have stopped at your house on my way out. . . .

Love ya,
Joe

9–17–63

Dear Mickie,

I sure am broke! I had to buy about fifty dollars worth of new books. My haircut business is booming, though.

We had our first yell practice last night. I got cold chills when they played the War Hymn. I can't wait 'til the first home game!

We're having Silver Taps tonight. Impressive as the ceremony is, I hate to see them. This is the first one that I know the Aggie who died. I waited on his table last year. He was a good man.

Mickie, I miss you very much. I can't wait 'till Saturday. Write soon.

Love,

Joe

On a Saturday in 1963, Joe broke a date with me. He told me that he had made a date with a previous girlfriend. I was devastated, but Diana encouraged me to go to the dance at Flag Hall with her. Shortly after I got there Joe appeared saying that he was very sorry and that he had made a huge mistake. He said that he told the girl he loved me and had to break the date with her. I was very hurt, but I did not try to hurt him. This was the only time Joe ever hurt me.

10–15–1963

Dear Mickie,

If I ever wrote a letter in which I didn't know what to write, this is that letter. I know you can't understand why I made that date—and I guess I didn't explain it very well Sunday—but, Love, really, I wish I had not.

Mic, I guess you won't believe me if I say that I love you, but I love you anyway. . . . Please forgive me for hurting you. Hurt me back, Mic, if you want. I deserve it. Nothing can ever stop me loving you, though.

Yours,

Joe

P.S. I've loved other women,
Not one but a few.
You're not my first love,
But my last love is you.
If I cause you tears,
Please send me away,
For I want you smiling.
I love you that way.
I love you, my darling.
May happiness be thine,
And if you still want me,
May your love be mine.

A short time later I was hospitalized because of a severe case of food poisoning. Routine tests showed a kidney infection that resulted in a three-week hospital stay. Joe hitchhiked to see me at least three times while I was in the hospital.

10–22–1963

Dear Mic,

The Kingston Trio played here on campus last night, but it cost a dollar and a half so I didn't go.

Love, I wish they would hurry and let you out of the hospital. Just not knowing how you are worries me sick. I'm going to the Commandant's Office to see if I can go to Temple this afternoon. [Joe did come to Temple, and he brought me a picture of him in a plaid shirt.]

Love,

Joe

10–28–63

Dear Mic,

If I could afford to miss school I would pretend there was something wrong with me, and then I'd get them to put me in 329 (The room next to mine in the hospital.)! Then you probably never would get well.

Your very own Aggie,

Joe

11–3–63

Dear Mic,

Honey, I wrote a poem this morning. You may not think it's very good, but I kind of like it. Anyway here it is:

GREY SKIES—11–3–1963

The years we have to live are few,
And the time we have so small
That often we have not time to do
The things we would most of all.

For who has time in this busy world
To stop, to pause, and to wonder
At stars and suns and clouds so swirled
Or at flowers and bees or thunder?

One moment I paused, one early morning,
To notice the cold and crispy air,
The fluffy clouds, the earth adorning.
Thus a thought came to me then.

And who,
'Neath those same grey skies above,
Has time enough
To be with his love?
Your Aggie,
Joe

11–14–63

Dear Mic,

Did you hear about us swiping Bevo (the University of Texas longhorn steer mascot)? Crazy!

Your very own Aggie,
Joe

11–20–63

Honey,

The worst thing about the whole situation around here is that the crazy profs at this place never let up. I have a quiz tomorrow and Friday. You can't imagine what a college major quiz is like. Ugh!

I was very happy to hear that you can play basketball now.

Bonfire is started. They put up the center pole today. Gig 'em Ags. Ya know sumthin', Carol Vickie—we're gonna beat 'em!

Love,
Joe

12–4–63

Hi Mic,

How is my girl? Just thought I'd better check. Gosh, you sure have been sending me some sweet letters this week, as always!

Honey do you realize that we get seventeen whole days out for Christmas. Isn't that terrific! It means I'm going to have seventeen dates with you. Why don't you just ask your mother if I may sleep on the sofa. That sure would save me a lot of driving back and forth!

It is official as of today. I am a vice committee chairman for S.C.O.N.A. That is pretty good considering that I'm the only sophomore in such a position.

Your very own Aggie,
Joe

12–15–63

Dear Mic,

I just got back from church, and my spirits are high. The sermon was on prayer, and it really meant something to me.

We have, of all things, a delegation of Colombian Agricultural students staying in the dorm with us. There are fourteen of them and only one speaks English! My Spanish comes in very handy. They are all pretty nice fellows.

Guess what else is new—I got my promotion order yesterday. Now I can wear my rank (stripes). Sure makes a uniform look better to have some rank on your shoulder!

Your ole man,

Lonesome Joe

1–4–64

My Darling Mickie,

. . . Love, you can't know how much your love and letters mean to me—especially now when I'm beside myself worrying about finals.

Mic, I'm going to come home with a friend that you don't know. I have promised him for months that I would take him to Flag Hall some Saturday, so that is what he wants to do. His name is Ted Smith, and he is a great guy. Would you get a date for him? Maybe B. J.? [Betty Jean Zabcik, a very good friend and classmate who lived in Zabcikville.] We could go to the show and then to the dance—whatever would make you happy. . . .

Your very own,

Joe

2–27–64

Dearest Mic,

All of us sophomores decided that since we are campused we might as well enjoy it. We are going to buy four or five cases of beer and go to the Brazos Saturday afternoon. Wa!

Your lonesome Ag,

Joe

2–28–64

Dear Mic,

Here is all the "hot poop" on Military Weekend. I'm glad you decided to come Friday. The Combat Ball is informal. Your maroon dress with loafers would be fine. I will go home after my last class so I'll probably get home at 5:30 and pick you up at 6. You will stay with Linda and Richard Rubac. (I couldn't afford to stay in a hotel.)

Your love,

Joe

3–2–64

Dear Mic,

Mic, if you have a few minutes, please write a letter to Box 6666. It's Tommy Hargrove's box, and he is a friend of mine who never gets a letter. Just tell him that you heard that he was a great Aggie and you're my girl. He's a swell guy, and it would tickle him to death. If you could, please try to get a bunch of girls to write him? He's kinda nice looking too. [I did write Tom, and we exchanged a few letters after that, and we became friends. In 1994 Tom was kidnapped in Columbia. After his release nearly a year later, he went to a hospital in Ft. Worth for tests. He called me the day he was to leave the hospital and asked if I would pick him up. He wanted to go to Chili's for a burger. I took three of the letters he had written to me back in 1964 and 1965. His sons, Gettie and Miles, met us and enjoyed reading the letters written by their father years earlier.]

As long as you want me,

Joe

3–4–64

Dear Mic,

Wish you could have been here last night, Honey. This place went wild. Of course you know we won the Southwest Conference (in basketball). The minute the game was over everyone on the whole campus poured out into the Quadrangle screaming and running up and down and throwing firecrackers. It sounded like a war, and I'm not exaggerating a bit. Then the band marched down the Quad, and that sort of stuff went on for an hour or two. At 2:30 am the whole school turned out to welcome the team back.

Your very own,

Joe

3–19–64

Dear Mic,

Well, it's all over but the shouting. People are voting like crazy, and I hope they are voting "Bush." We won't get the results until tomorrow, so don't get anxious. Honey, I am so nervous it is pitiful. Gerald helped ease my anxiety some. He said that it is already decided, so worrying wouldn't help. [Joe is referring to his campaign for the position of Yell Leader.]

Loving you,

Joe

3–20–64

Dear Mic,

Honey, I wish I could have called about the election, but I didn't want to call collect, and I don't have any money, so I just told Mother to call you. Dockery won outright. Simmonds and I are in the runoff for the other position. The runoff will be the day after we get back from Easter. You can help me make posters over the holidays if you want to!

I love you Mic,

Joe

4–7–64

Dear Mic,

[Joe won the election for yell leader.] Frank Cox, next year's Head Yell Leader told me that we have our first meeting soon, so I'm looking forward to that. He's a terrific guy. Guess you'll get to meet him next year.

Yours always,

Joe

4–13–64

My Darling Mic,

Well, when you get this letter it will be Tuesday, the 14th. One year, Honey, and a wonderful one at that. Does it seem possible to you that we have been going together that long?

Yours as long as you will have me,

Joe

Joe wrote this poem about our meeting one year earlier.

UNTITLED—1964

A sunburned young lady
In a soft summer dress
Who I asked to dance
And who there and then said, "Yes".

And that was our meeting,
Only one year away,
But so simple a greeting
Made it one special day.

That soft, sweet young girl
Who I talked to that night
Set my mind thinking funny,
Set my heart beating light.

I've met girls since then,
And one year has gone by,
But I haven't forgotten,
When you caught my eye.

It doesn't seem strange
That I should love you so now,
I knew you'd be mine one year ago.
How you'd be mine, though I didn't know how.

4–21–64

Dearest Mickie,

I just got back from Muster. It is one of the most impressive ceremonies we have around here. Every 21st of April we get together and have a ceremony for all the Aggies that have passed away during the year. Someone answers "present" to roll call for their friends that passed away. What other school cares as much about its friends? That's why I'm an Aggie, Mic. There's not a school anywhere to compare with this one. Guess when we're seniors we can go to everything down here together.

Your own,

Joe

4–22–64

Dear Mickie,

Mic, Mother's Day is coming up soon, and I want you to be sure to come. Mother and Daddy will be with us, and you can bring Diana. I will get her a date.

Mike Jackson says "Hi." He is one of my Aggie buddies. . . .

All my love,

Joe

4–30–64

Dearest Mic,

Tonight I didn't get to mail your letter on time because of a water fight in the Quadrangle. Can you imagine four thousand Aggies fighting it out with wastebaskets full of water? It was terrific.

My body, my soul, my mind, and my love

belong to you, Darling,

Your Joe

5–10–64

Dear Mic,

. . . Final Review will be the 23rd, so plan to come. Watch out, girl. After the first march around I'm gonna plant one on you like nobody has seen before!

Your Aggie,

Joe

5–11–64

Dear Mic,

We have a Yell Leader practice this afternoon. Exciting isn't it? I'll bet I make a spastic Yell Leader. If I'm too funny I just won't bring you to any of the games! Only kidding, Mic. Really I'm looking forward to a big year next year. It should be a happy one for both of us.

Your own little Aggie,

Joe

5–12–64

Dear Carol,

How's that for a greeting? I love that name—maybe 'cause it's yours.

Honey, I'm so glad that I can come home this weekend, even if it's only for Friday night. Ugh! I hate to think about signing in the rest of the weekend, though. That isn't much fun, going to the guardroom every hour on the hour and signing your name on the line. [I don't remember why Joe was disciplined.]

I love you Mic,

Joe

5–18–64

Darling Mickie,

Honey, this morning I went to church as always, and I wanted so much for you to be there beside me. I said a prayer for us, Love.

I'm going to try to save enough for some kind of a car this summer and get an afternoon job next year. That would sure help us out, too.

Your own,

Joe

I had always intended to go to college directly after graduating from high school. However, I realized that I would have to postpone college if we were to marry. We both got jobs that summer, but we also had much more time together than ever before. The plan was to marry the summer of 1965 and for me to get a job on campus or in Bryan.

We bought a 1950 Ford for $100. It was difficult to start and stop. I remember having to put an object in the "butterfly valve" to start it. The brakes were always bad, so we had to be extra careful. We "wet" sanded the entire body for about a month and had it painted maroon. Joe's mom knew a man who installed custom seat covers and headliners, so ours were maroon and white of course. Joe's mom gave the guy a good deal on draperies, and we had the coolest car in Aggieland. Our friends would later say that it was a good thing that Joe and Micki Bush lived on a hill on College View as we had to "jump start" the "Bomb" every morning.

9–28–64

My Darling Mickie,

I'm so happy I really don't know what to say to you, Love. I am going to the student placement office and see about getting you a job and also to put in an application for an apartment. (Joe began to want to move up our wedding to December. I was resistant only due to our financial situation.)

Your own,

Joe

10–12–64

Darling Mickie,

. . . Honey, Saturday we are going to go talk to some of my married friends. I think that will help an awful lot to settle your mind and help you stop worrying so much.

Your own,

Joe

10–18–64

Dear Mic,

. . . Darling, I couldn't tell Mother or any of my friends either. I was just afraid someone would laugh and say they knew I wasn't serious all along. I guess I kind of talked you into it anyway. [Joe was referring to our decision to wait until the summer to marry.]

Your own,

Joe

10–20–64

Dear Mickie,

. . . All the boys in the M.S.C. [Memorial Student Center] had to smell your letter. (Joe had Tom Hargrove, Harry Tollar, and Charles Mella write me a paragraph in his letter.)

Your own,

Joe

10–29–64

Dearest Mic,

Honey, I had a big time last night. The fish tied me up in a mattress bag, wet me down, and threw me in the middle of the Quadrangle! Lummus had them do it 'cause I did it to him earlier!

Your own,

Joe

11–3–64

My Darling,

Angel, because of some stuff the junior class did, the junior yell leaders won't be allowed to lead yells in Dallas. The juniors are boiling mad about it.

I'll always love you,

Joe

I recall Joe being concerned that the joke he was considering telling at Midnight Yell was not appropriate. The joke went something like this: A stunning young girl was walking down a street on a windy day. After the wind blew up her skirt, some workmen nearby whistled and yelled out at her. Appalled by their behavior, she said, "It's obvious you aren't gentlemen." One of the men retorted, "It's obvious you aren't either."

11–11–64

Darling Mic,

. . . Well, you got your picture in the Battalion, but I'm kind of wrapped around you and it's hard to tell that it's you. [Aggies kiss their dates after every football score.] I'm saving one for you and sending one to your mother. Monday night after yell practice the fish mobbed the yell leaders and gave us a bath in the Fish Pond. Gig 'em!

Your own,

Joe

11–20–64

My Darling,

Honey, I guess what is really bothering me is just what I'm going to do about next semester. I really feel like I'm up against a wall. [Joe was concerned about how he would pay for tuition in the spring and whether or not to take a commission in the army after graduation. If he did, that meant he would get paid $40 a month—a lot of money back then.]

Your own,

Joe

12–2–64

Dear Mic,

I didn't get a letter from you today, but Tommy Hargrove did. Guess I could always go read Tommy's letter again.

Love,

Joe

Joe wrote this poem around Valentine's Day in 1965.

UNTITLED—1965

Love, If you looked into my heart,
The quietest, deepest, innermost part,

You would find but one thing there—
The only name for which I care.

If you read the name you would see,
Then you might discover what's dear to me.
The name? It's yours, and I think you'd know
That because it's there, I love you so.

2–25–65

Hi Darling,

Baby, I just got the cush [Aggie language for dessert or treats]. I love those how-ever-you-spell thems! [Joe is referring to kolaches.] You'd better get your mother to show you how to make them or I won't marry you.

Love,

Joe

3–8–65

Darling Mic,

. . . Are we going to celebrate on April 14? That is when I met you at Tom's!

Your own,

Joe

3–16–65

My Darling,

Honey, I'm going to enter you for Junior Class Sweetheart. Harris Pappas and Tom Hargrove are on the selection committee. [I won.]

Your own,

Joe

3–18–65

Darling Mickie,

Love, the election is today so it will be decided by the time you get this letter. [Joe was elected as Head Yell Leader for his senior year.]

Your own,

Joe

4-10-65

My Darling,

Well, the boys just got back from the river. I locked my door just in time to keep from getting thrown in the shower. The piss heads (sophomores) are feeling their oats. I'll have to give 'em a rough time tomorrow. There is no place like Aggieland. [Joe came home on the 13th, and we were engaged on April 14th.]

Your own,
Joe

4-20-65

Darling Mickie,

Did you get the 'Bomb' ticking again? I wish I could have found why it wouldn't start. We sure need to have it last us for a while longer.

Your own,
Joseph

4-27-65

Darling Mickie,

I found some boots finally! He wants $52 for the boots, spurs, hooks and three pairs of pants.

Your own,
Joe

The summer of 1965 was very busy for both Joe and me. I worked as a bookkeeper in Temple and moved to an apartment to be closer to my job. Joe worked at Wendeland's Grain in Temple. He was in charge of their pig farm and even brought home a 'runt' for the whole family to raise. As usual, we tried to save as much money as possible.

We married August 28, 1965, at the Seaton Brethren Church. We both wanted to have a dance, but that was not allowed by my church. (My dad always found it strange that both Joe and I loved to go to the dances on Saturday night, yet would always go to church on Sunday. I told him that I just loved to dance, didn't drink, smoke, or go sit in a car with a guy.)

After a short honeymoon we moved into our home on College View near North Gate. Our rent was $42.50 for a non-air-conditioned, furnished, two-bedroom apartment, all bills paid. In order to graduate as an accounting major in May 1966, Joe had to carry a huge load both semesters of his senior year. He was Head Yell Leader, which added to his responsibilities, and he worked every hour he wasn't in class. He was transferred to Company H-2, a married students' outfit, in the Corps. I worked at Lily Ice Cream Factory as a bookkeeper. Joe told everyone that I milked the cows.

Our financial situation was always an issue, but we were blissfully happy. Joe's mom helped us find some furniture, and by Christmas of that year we even bought a used TV. We often got by on only $5 for food in one week. We thought we were in heaven if we had ranch steak for dinner.

Joe had always succeeded at everything he attempted. He was a Distinguished Military Student, graduated with a degree in Accounting in 1966, was commissioned as an artillery officer in the US Army, and completed his basic officer training at Fort Sill, Oklahoma. He went on to graduate from Airborne and Ranger schools in the cold winter of 1967.

Joe then joined the 82nd Airborne Division at Fort Bragg, North Carolina, and we lived on base in officer housing. Both of our bedrooms had twin beds. Joe said that sleeping on a twin would be 'cozy' for us and did not want to ask the housing department for a full-size bed. We became pregnant during this time. We also made many good friends and enjoyed our free time, which was filled with many activities, including biking, tennis, and playing bridge with other officers and their wives.

Joe's orders for Southeast Asia had us first going to the Defense Language Institute at Fort Myers, Virginia, in January of 1968. We lived in Arlington and spent the weekends visiting museums and touring the D.C. area while Joe became fluent in the Lao language. Robin was born on Easter Sunday, April 14, five years from the day we met. One week later, on Aggie Muster Day, April 21, 1968, Joe left for Southeast Asia.

Joe initially served as an adviser to the Royal Thai Army from April to July of 1968. Again, we began corresponding via many letters. The only changes were that he now used the military way of writing dates and that he was much farther away than College Station.

1 May 1968

My Darling Wife,

Well here I am in Thailand. I am on loan to the Royal Thai Artillery school for two months. I live with two NCOs in a house that looks like a fort. The walls are 12 feet thick! There are also three house boys who can't seem to understand a word of anything. Lao isn't much like Thai.

Your man,

Joe

3 May 1968

Dearest Mic,

The town where I'm working is the ancient capital of Siam and has many ruins. The place is infested with monkeys! When traffic is slow one monkey will jump off of a fence onto a passing fruit truck. He then throws fruit to the other monkeys on the fence, grabs one for himself and jumps back as the truck nears the end of the fence. . . .

Your own,

Joe

12 May 1968

Dearest Mic,

Well here I am in Bangkok again. The battery commander invited me to stay and go to a wedding party. The food was delicious and the liquor was free. Of maybe 300 people guess who was the only Pharang (American)? Me!

Love,

Joe

15 May 1968

Dear Mic and Robin,

By the way, don't forget I go back to Laos on 20 June. It is little wonder that I got sick. I have eaten fish-intestine soup, stewed duck feet, raw chicken.....I never ask what the food is—but they often tell you anyway.

Love,

Joe

25 May 1968

Dearest Mic and Robin,

Last night we had a party at the battery. The Thais hired two bands and eleven prostitutes. You should have seen all those horny troopers in line to dance with them. Their dancing is quite interesting—slow or fast there is no bodily contact. Also they start singing songs that everyone knows, and then they go back to dancing. When the Major and I were leaving we saw all eleven girls heading for the barracks with about as many troops. I couldn't figure out how they decided who got the girls 'cause there were about 300 troops. Don't worry, they tried to get to me first but I very politely told them I couldn't.

Your old man,

Joe

30 May 1968

Darling Wife and Robin,

I am back in Laos for this week.

I took a Thai train to Bangkok yesterday. It was really fun. For miles there were only what you expect in the Orient—farmers in conical hats, water buffalo, bamboo, teak houses, rice paddies, and some old temples.

Love,

Joe

7 June 1968

Darling Wife and Robin,

Well, get out your map and look up Muong Soui, Laos. It is north of Vientiane. That will be home for 10 months. My job is Assistant Army Military Attaché for the Muong Soui subsector. The place is quite scenic, set in a valley with high mountains all around.

It sounds like our Robin is getting to be quite a girl. Gosh, she is a cute little button. I'll bet she won't let me near her for a while (when I finally get home) and that will just break my heart. Seems almost strange that I could love a little girl so much when I've only known her a bit over a month! But then again, I guess she's only a part of something that has been around several years now—our love. You two are the most precious things in the world to old Joe.

Loving you,

Joe

10 June, 1968

Dear Mic,

You asked what kind of plane I flew in to get to Laos. I went by C-130, to Udorn, Thailand, a C-47 (DC-3) without any doors or seats to Vientiane, and to Muong Soui in a C-46 (which was the original "jump aircraft" for U.S. Paratroops). I flew around Muong Soui in an H-34 helicopter and an L-19 Birddog. Seems as if I've spent half my time aboard aircraft since I left the States.

Your own,

Joe

14 June 1968

Dear Mic,

You asked what kind of fruit they have here. They have fruit you have never even heard of—Ngok, Turian, Breadfruit, Muang, Mangosteen, all kinds of melons. The Ngok has whiskers and is red. Most are quite good. You'd go wild.

Your own,
Joe

16 June 1968

Dear Mic,

Tuesday is a big ceremony day. I will get to meet the Prime Minister of Thailand—Ain't I something? He will present me with a Buddah Medal good luck charm to protect from bullets.

Your own,
Joe

21 June 1968

Darling Wife and Baby Robin,

You asked how close Muong Soui is to Vietnam. Not close, but within sight of the Ho Chi Minh Trail. There is a war going on in Laos only it's difficult to tell who is fighting who. There is fighting in and around Muong Soui daily but usually only small scale action. Don't worry though, I have plenty of bodyguards. Can't really say much about it, Honey (because of classification of mission).

Your own,
Joe

Joe's job description was mostly classified. A note added to the website The Virtual Wall states that Joe was assigned to the US Army Element of the Joint US Military Advisory Group Thailand (JUSMAGTHAI), which was headquartered in Bangkok, Thailand. However, JUSMAG was not his daily work place.

International accords guaranteeing the neutrality of Laos had been ignored by the North Vietnamese since the day they were signed, and by the mid-1960s the North Vietnamese Army was estimated to have some 35,000 soldiers permanently in place within Laos. Some engaged in direct combat with the Laotian forces; others maintained the Ho Chi Minh Trail, which provided a supply line from North Vietnam through Laos and Cambodia into South Vietnam. This placed pressures on the Royal Laotian government as well as on the Allied forces in SVN.

In 1966 the US government established Project 404 (sometimes referred to as Palace Dog), by which military personnel could be in Laos but technically stationed in Thailand or elsewhere. Individuals in Project 404 and their operations in Laos were classified for most of 1964–73. Being "in the black" allowed service personnel to perform military duties as a civilian operating in Laos under the supervision of the military attaches to the US Ambassador to Laos. A number of separate military efforts were established under Project 404, including advising Laotian loyalist and Thai mercenary forces, establishing a network to control US air support to ground troops, manning technical facilities such as Lima 85, and helping train RLAF pilots.

In late 1967 the NVA pushed the Pathet Lao aside and began concerted attacks against the Royal Lao forces and the "black" US facilities in Laos. The monsoon weather slowed the NVA effort until the beginning of 1969.

25 June 1968

Dear Mic,

Darling, believe me I try my best not to skip a day in writing to you. If my mail means as much to you as yours does to me then I know how you feel when the mailbox is empty. Whether or not I get a letter determines if it's a good day or not!

The Lao government controls only about half of the country and they are having to fight for that. From mountain tops in my area I can actually see bad guy trucks in bad guy land.

Your man,

Joe

13 July 1968

Dear Mic,

Did I tell you that the Lao usually have their dependents right with them? It looks funny to see Papa standing by a machine gun with his kiddo right behind him. Their poverty is appalling by our terms but they generally get enough to eat and a little Lao-Lao to drink and it keeps 'em happy. Quite remarkable folks.

Your own,

Joe

1 August 1968

Darling Wife,

Well today I became the Official Commander of U.S. Forces in Muong Soui, Laos. That must be some kind of a first for the Bush clan. My generators are out and my radio ain't working. I sure feel lonesome.

Our house is coming along fine. The two sergeants plan to move in about September. Guess some recipes would help out a bunch.

Your own,

Joe

11 August 1968

Dear Mic,

I'm allowed three days off per month so I may go to Vientiane next weekend. George (Legg) plays tennis so much he can beat me now. The Muong Soui Lawn Tennis Association ain't what it should be. Have you been playing?

Your own,

Joe

28 August 1968

Dear Mic,

I am writing you on our wedding anniversary from a little mountain top known as Phouxia, which appropriately means "Lost Mountain." I am on the edge of the Plain of Jars.

Sweetheart, of course today what I most want to write about is the wonderful three years we have been married. Old Joe just lays there thinking of his wife and daughter; and also getting out of the army so that I will never have to leave you again. If only I knew what kind of work I would be happy doing.

Your own,

Joe

5 September 1968

Darling Wife,

Joe is just sitting here munching shoestring potatoes. I got the care package. Thank you so much sweetheart. Lemon drops and butterscotch candies are my favorite candies.

We've hired a cook-houseboy. Only one small problem—he can't cook! He's a 19 year old Meo tribesman from a nearby village. He speaks passing

English which is good 'cause the Meo language is similar to Chinese and a bit difficult. . . .

Your own,

Joe

10 September 1968

Darling Wife,

The chow last night was particularly bad so I ate Vienna Sausage and the peaches you sent. It's not the local food that is so bad; it's the cook—he's terrible!

Your own,

Joe

20 September 1968

Dear Mic,

I thought the opium weights were kind of interesting. Of course they are used on balance scales for weighing opium. Don't try them out though—you might get arrested! Did you know I am in the middle of one of the largest opium growing areas in the world? [Joe had always teased me about the large field of Poppy Seed on our farm, which we used for my mom's Poppy Seed Kolaches.]

Baby, without you I am a lonesome creature. You and little Robin are so dear to me even so far away—especially so far away. It is really comforting to think of you as I do.

Your own,

Joe

29 September 1968

Dear Mic,

Today I was a real Tom Sawyer. This is one of the funniest things I ever had happen to me. For the new house we are constructing a barbwire fence. Having nothing else to do, I went to dig holes and set fence posts. Well, the Lao are very curious types and anything you do will draw a crowd, especially if you are a Pharang (Caucasian) building a fence because they have never seen that before. What's more they have never seen a post hole digger either and they were simply amazed by it—so guess who let everyone have a turn at trying it out? You guessed it! I got one hundred yards of fence posts set in only 2 ½ hours. Ain't that a story!

Your own,

Joe

10 October 1968

Darling Wife,

We didn't accomplish much at our monthly meeting in Vientiane. We had a cocktail party followed by a formal dinner. That night there was an eclipse of the moon and every one with a gun in the entire country was shooting at it! They are superstitious and think that a frog is eating the moon so they shoot to scare it away—how about that!

Your own,

Joe

13 October 1968

Dear Mic,

Yesterday I took a little helicopter trip out to a quaint hilltop village about 30 miles from here—but in my area of responsibility and was impressed. All of the people were lined up to meet the chopper and gave us flowers and greeted us quite traditionally. What was unusual to me was that it was pouring down rain!

Sweetheart, a plane just landed so I'm going to run to the air field and mail this. I love you very much.

Your own,

Joe

16 October, 1968

Dear Mic,

Yesterday I went to visit a village that is so remote you would not believe it. What we went for was the opening of the village's first school, built by U.S.A.I.D. When we arrived everyone in the village was lined up in a line—500 people long. We had to greet each one starting with the chief down to the school kids. Then we went for the school opening ceremony or "Baci." The elders give a bunch of chants and everyone comes and ties strings around your wrists and makes wishes for you—like "I hope you get to stay in Laos and help us for 8 or 10 years" or "I hope you will have many beautiful wives." With each wish and string you must take a shot of Lao—Lao whiskey and the result of a big "Baci" is a big drunk. Then there was a supper, more whiskey, dancing and music. The band consisted of two guys banging beer cans and one banging a 5 gallon gas can and everyone singing. That continued until dawn, then they butchered a cow for breakfast. It was something out of another world.

Your own,

Joe

23 October 1968

My Darling Wife,

When do I love you most? Do you know? Is it in the morning when it is cool like it is now; or is it in the evening when it is warm; or at night when I ache for you? Sweetheart, it is all of these and it is now. Each moment of the day I am in love with you.

Your own,

Joe

11 November 1968

Dear Mic,

Well, it looks like the Aggies just couldn't get the ball rolling this year. We are just going to have to beat T.U. to make it a successful year. Two years in a row—wouldn't that be nice!

Your own,

Joe

22 November 1968

Darling Wife,

I know this letter is probably the first for some time now and I'm very sorry. I was quite indisposed for a few days. I was making a reconnaissance of a road east of Muong Soui and unable to write. I spent the night in a place where no one could speak a word of English and I had to rely entirely on my Lao—which incidentally is getting to be quite good. I spent most of the night getting quite drunk on something called Lao Hi. They dug up two clay jars, popped the seals and added water. Then they put two bamboo reeds in one jar, gave one to me—one to the village chief said, "Doom" which means drink up.

I love you,

Joe

25 November 1968

Dear Mic,

Well my job has increased somewhat in scope. I now work one additional area—a little place called Vang Vieng, Laos. I am really quite snowed under with work now but at least that helps to keep the loneliness away.

Still no word on R&R. I know how that must worry you Love but Joe just can't do anything about it but bitch to HQs.—which I have done loudly.

Your own,

Joe

25 November 1968

Darling Mic,

I just listened to your tape and though it is midnight already I must at least tell you how wonderful it was to get and listen to your tape. I miss you Baby—so much. To hear you talk I can tell how much Robin loves her mommy—that made me sad in a way, because she doesn't love me too. Isn't that sort of silly. Well, I will have plenty of time for her to discover she also has a daddy when I get home.

I really had to laugh about you wanting to send gifts to "all the Muong Soui kids" for Christmas. There are 1,200 school age kids here! There are actually 19 villages that form Muong Soui. Any of the things you mentioned will be fine, Love. These kids really don't have much and love it all.

Your mother sent some much appreciated pecans.

Your own,

Joe

27 November 1968

Dear Mic,

I suppose they are burning Bonfire tonight—and tomorrow you get to see the game. Gosh I wish I could.

Sweetheart, I got the Christmas package you sent today. . . . It is so amazing to me that these people are so friendly and generous. They shared everything you sent.

Activity is really picking up and the bad guys are beginning to move as is typical for the dry season. That makes my job a lot more demanding.

I love you,

Joe

30 November 1968

Dear Mic,

There is a French army training mission in Vientiane and I ran into a Lt. Blardat. This guy couldn't speak a word of English and I can't speak French, but we got along beautifully in Lao!

Your own,

Joe

13 December 1968

My Darling Mic,

Today has been another long day at Muong Soui but at least now it is ended and I am that much closer to being with you and Robin once again. You know I actually enjoy this tour as long as I am busy enough to keep my thoughts from wandering back to you—but that is never for very long. It is almost strange that the one who has always made me so happy can now make me sad—because I miss you so much Darling One. I have been giving some serious thought lately to what else I could be happy doing. You know how much the army means to me—but then I have only one love and that is for my little family. Mic, it has been so very difficult for me to be away from you.

Mic, old Joseph still loves you, as you must already know and though the days grow longer the time grows yet shorter until these lonely arms hold you tight one again.

Your own,
Joe

22 December 1968

Dear Mic,

Well Sweetheart, I played Santa with the toys you sent and had enough for the kids from one small village. They have never heard of Christmas of course. We had a real all day celebration.

Your own,
Joe

27 December 1968

Dear Mic,

Thanks for all the gifts, Mic. The nut bread was delicious and devoured. I sent the pumpkin bread to my friends in Sam Thong including Maj. McManners and some to the guys up north who are even more isolated than I am.

I love you both,
Joe

DAYS OF REMEMBERING—JANUARY, 1969

Written thinking of Moung Soui, Laos and you.

Artillery sounds in the distance
And resounds ‘round the mountain chain.
Soldiers walk back from the front lines,
While I think of you in the rain.

Was raining the eve of our parting
But not when we said goodbye.
I remember you held me so gently
And tried so hard not to cry.

But now our parting is over
And we're half a world away.
While I'm here watching the soldiers
What's my love doing today?

The soldiers are muddy and dirty
And some of their comrades have died;
But gladly I'd shoulder their burden,
If you could be by my side.

I long for my wife and my daughter
But I have naught but the rain
And the sound of the distant artillery
As it resounds 'round the mountain chain.

ROBIN—JANUARY, 1969

So tiny, so needful, soft, warm and dear,
Cuddled up safely with mother so dear.
Rosy pink cheeks and little, tiny feet,
Small and lovely and ever so sweet.
Wee one we love you, your mother and I
And we will care for you as your years go by.
So smile little one, and gurgle and coo—
For always and ever, we both will love you.

2 January 1969

My Darling Wife,

The action has been fast and furious but our side came out smelling like a rose and though the action continues, your husband is safe and working his little butt off (little?).

I welcomed the New Year in by staying awake all night flying in an observation aircraft and monitoring a big shooting match. Quite a night, I hope you got more sleep.

Don't worry because I am being very careful and am safe. If things look too dangerous I will be evacuated to Vientiane. My heart and all my love belong to you and Robin.

Your own,

Joe

4 January 1969

Dear Mic,

Believe me, Sweetheart. I am safe. I even have guards 24 hours per day and can call for an aircraft on a moment's notice. I did think of asking to go to Vientiane, but I would let down a bunch of people who I think I am really helping to do their part in fighting a way of life that they would never be happy under. That is worth something, Mic.

The time seems to be creeping again. Honey, if you only could be here with me. The people in Muong Soui would love you—and I would be a whole man again. . . .

Your own,

Joe

26 January 1969

Darling Wife,

I know you said you aren't ready for another chub yet Mic. Have you changed your mind about having a bunch? I sure hope not 'cause I want at least eight!

Your own,

Joe

28 January 1969

Dear Mic,

Sweetheart, although it is so difficult for you and me to be apart our time to be together again is rapidly approaching. To know that does not make the hours go any faster, but it does help to know that soon our arms, separated these 9 long months, will soon be joined once more. And, if there is a happy thought that goes with the heartache we have known in parting, it is the thought of our meeting once more. If Heaven ever meets Earth it must certainly be waiting for that moment when my eyes behold that lovely form which now only my mind can see. My Angel, my Love, my Wife, I shall always love you for the life you have given to me. Kiss Robin for me.

Your Husband,

Joe

5 February 1969

Dear Mic,

Baby, as you have probably guessed by now R&R looks doubtful. I think the R&R set up for us is a dirty shame: Twelve quotas a year for 72 people. Sweetheart, I know that worrying about it has caused you a lot of heartache, but Joe has done all he could to try to get us to Hawaii. I feel like the U.S. Army has let us down on this one.

Well Baby, it looks like I will have about six new ribbons on my uniform when I come home. All of that is classified but if all the paperwork gets complete I will have received a little recognition for a generally thankless job. Also it is a little consolation that I have been asked to extend by our office which I politely refused to do and ordered to extend by the local commander; an order that thank goodness he cannot enforce! Don't worry old Joseph will be home to his wife and daughter in April as planned even if he has to swim the Pacific.

Keep smiling Darling for Joe thinks of you and loves you every minute of the day.

Your own,

Joe

My dear husband and father of our daughter, Capt. Joseph Kerr Bush Jr., was killed in action on February 10, 1969. His funeral with full military honors was attended by the Texas A&M Singing Cadets, the Ross Volunteers, the Fish Drill Team, cadets from Company A-1, and many other Aggies.

Joe was posthumously awarded the Silver Star Medal, the Bronze Star Medal with V Device for Valor, the Distinguished Flying Cross, and the Purple Heart.

Some of Joe's letters were published in the book *Dear America: Letters Home from Vietnam*. In 1987 the book was made into a television documentary, in which the actor Tom Berenger read one of Joe's letters. And Tom Hargrove, '66, one of Joe's best friends at A&M, included some of Joe's story in his 1994 book *A Dragon Lives Forever*.

In Southeast Asia Joe worked closely with personnel from Air America. These were civilian defense contractors, primarily pilots, hired by the CIA to assist the US military in operations in Laos. Joe's story is described in the book, *The Ravens: The Men Who Flew in America's Secret War in Laos*.

Joe's death triggered a national debate about the US role and involvement in Laos. The Nixon Administration added to this controversy by calling Joe's death the result of a "hostile action" as opposed to a "combat death." To add fuel to the fire, his tombstone arrived with the place of death listed as Vietnam instead of Laos. Joe's parents and I requested that it be corrected to read Laos. This furthered speculation that the US government was hiding something. The result was a multitude of national newspapers and television stations asking to meet with Joe's parents and me. We maintained that the US government made no secret of his death, his mission, or his whereabouts. We did not want his death to be made into a political issue.

Our daughter grew up without ever knowing her father. Robin enrolled in A&M in the fall of 1986. She recalls,

> When I was a Fish at A&M in 1987, I attended a re-dedication ceremony of a war memorial on the Quad. Dr. Malon Southerland '65 was the Assistant Vice President for Student Services at the time and the keynote speaker at the ceremony. He began speaking about one of the men he knew personally who was honored on the memorial. I was shocked and nervous but I knew immediately he was speaking about my dad. I asked the cadet I was with to introduce me after the ceremony, and Dr. Southerland said, "The last time I saw you I was holding you at your father's funeral." I knew after meeting Dr. Southerland my freshman year that I was in the right place—a special place.
>
> Throughout my time at A&M, and still to this very day, I continue to meet older Ags who are brought to tears when they find out who my father was. They feel compelled to tell me stories, and I love to listen. I have heard many times, "Your dad was one of the finest men I have ever known." Of course, initially, I believed they were just being kind and felt the need to say something nice. However, upon hearing it time and time again, I decided there must be some truth to it. I am the proud daughter of an American hero.
>
> Former Head Yell Leader and Governor of Texas Rick Perry, '72, has often spoken of my dad in his Aggie Muster speeches over the years, both on and off campus. At the dedication of the Texas Capitol Vietnam Veterans Monument in Austin on March 29, 2014, Governor Perry concluded his remarks by shouting, "This is for you Joe Bush."

After Joe's death, I completed my associate's degree from Temple Junior College, and in 1973 I graduated magna cum laude from Baylor University with a Bachelor of Science degree in Speech and Language Pathology.

I married again in 1973, but divorced in 1989. I was blessed with another daughter, Corbin, in 1977. I was employed by the Arlington School District for twenty-nine years as a speech and language therapist, first-grade and fifth-grade teacher. During this time I obtained my Master of Science degree. After I retired, in 2002, Robin and I bought a Curves franchise. I operated the successful business in Arlington until 2007. Now I spend my time playing tennis, working out, reading, and visiting my granddaughters. Robin graduated from A&M in 1990. While there she received the Buck Weirus Award, was listed in Who's Who among Students in American Universities and Colleges, and was named the Dean's Endowed Scholar from the College of Business.

Robin, her husband, Mike, and their daughters, Mackenzie and Macy, remain Joe's greatest legacy. After graduating, Robin was employed by Exxon for nine years. In 1992 she married Mike Sproba, Class of 1990 and a member of the Corps of Cadets. At the time of this writing, they live near Lake Conroe and have a successful real-estate business, Synergy Real Estate. Robin has served on the local school board for four years, and she and Mike have donated much time to the Conroe Lions Club, including his term as president. They have been active in the Montgomery County A&M Club for sixteen years, both having served as president. Mackenzie (age sixteen) is ranked second in her class of 500. She has played on the Willis Varsity Volleyball Team since her freshman year and is a member of the National Honor Society. Macy (age thirteen) has never missed a day of school and is also a member of the National Honor Society. She loves animals and wants to be a vet. Both girls want to attend A&M and are avid, select volleyball players, excelling in all sports.

Robin, Mackenzie, and Macy have grown up hearing about what a wonderful person Joe was. Mackenzie and Macy call him "Daddy Joe," and they call me "Mammy." I feel so blessed to see Joe live on in the lives of my daughter and granddaughters.

From Joe's valor citations:

BRONZE STAR MEDAL

By direction of the President, under provisions of Executive Order 11046, 24 August 1962, a Bronze Star Medal with "V" device for heroic achievement in connection with military operations against hostile forces is awarded posthumously to:

Captain Joseph K. Bush, Jr., Field Artillery, United States Army, who distinguished himself by exceptional heroism during the period 31 December 1968 to

1 January 1969. Captain Bush, disregarding his own personal safety, unhesitatingly volunteered as the night aerial artillery observer when the scheduled observer became ill. While directing the initial artillery barrage, the enemy engaged Captain Bush's aircraft with intense anti-aircraft fire. Despite the heavy ground fire, Captain Bush remained aloft for two and one-half hours, directing artillery fire on enemy targets and anti-aircraft locations. As a result of his outstanding heroism, enemy artillery fire was reduced, targets of opportunity were destroyed, and enemy pressure generally relieved. Captain Bush's exceptional devotion to duty reflects great credit upon him and the United States Army.

SILVER STAR

By direction of the President, under the provisions of the Act of Congress approved 9 July 1918, a Silver Star for gallantry in action is awarded posthumously to:

Captain Joseph K. Bush, Jr., Field Artillery, United States Army, who distinguished himself by gallantry in action above and beyond the call of duty while serving as Assistant Army Attache in Muong Soui, Laos on 10 February 1969. On the morning of that date, the quarters occupied by Captain Bush and his operations sergeant were attacked by an enemy force of 20 North Vietnamese Commandos using grenades, small arms, machine guns, B40 rockets and satchel charges. Captain Bush, realizing that only he and his sergeant were adequately armed to offer protection to the other Americans in the compound and who were without protective cover, quickly decided to establish a defensive position within the compound from which he could suppress enemy fire. Covering each other with protective fire and throwing grenades into the North Vietnamese positions, both attempted to reach the pre-selected position and to draw enemy fire and attention. The sergeant was seriously wounded short of reaching the new position. Captain Bush, without hesitation, attempted single-handedly to attack the enemy raiders, firing as he advanced and killing two of the enemy. It was during this assault that Captain Bush was mortally wounded. The heroism displayed by Captain Bush in giving his life while drawing enemy fire away from his fallen comrade and the other Americans enabled the sergeant to escape. Captain Bush's conspicuous gallantry, exceptional heroism and intrepidity at the cost of his own life are in the highest traditions of the military service, and his gallant actions reflect great credit upon him and upon the United States Army.

General Order 69–58, Chief of Staff, US Army

Loren Parsons (1968, E-2) 64th Finance Section, 1970

I received orders transferring me from Post Finance, Fort Sam Houston, Texas, to the 4th Infantry Division, Republic of Vietnam, in late May 1969. I was twenty-three years old with less than a year on active duty.

In late July I flew to McCord AFB, Washington, and boarded a contract commercial flight, arriving in Cam Ranh Bay July 31, 1969. During in-processing, I was told my orders had been changed and I was now assigned to the 64th Finance Section, Da Nang, in I Corps. I reported there on August 2, and the finance officer, Colonel Gabriel, informed me that I was going to become a Class B Agent Officer in charge of the 64th Finance Section under his command at Quang Tri. A jeep arrived the next day, and we drove up Highway 1 about sixty-five miles north of Da Nang to Quang Tri—the northernmost province of South Vietnam.

In Quang Tri I saw Howard Hoegemeyer ,'68 (D-1), a few times as well as Brian Davis, '67, brother of Mark Davis ,'68 (F-2). In March 1970 I was transferred to the Class B Agent Office in Phu Bai, about ten miles south of Hue as the officer in charge of unit payrolls as well as inbound/outbound processing. This Class B Agent Office was a much larger organization, with a captain in charge of two lieutenants, a warrant officer, two E-8s, one E-7, four E-6s, and forty or fifty enlisted men. The job was not all that exciting, but it was necessary. The troops deserved to be paid and to have answers to their pay problems.

When I discovered that Chuck Whitacre, '68 (F-2), was at Phu Bai as a Chinook pilot with the 101st, I went over to his area to visit with him on a number of occasions. He learned that there was going to be a Muster in Da Nang and wanted to know if I was interested in going. I said sure, that I would even drive us down. He knew another Aggie at Phu Bai who also wanted to go. When I picked them up in my jeep, Chuck told the driver to pull over to a Chinook on the nearest landing pad. He got out of the jeep, talked to the pilot, then motioned us forward. One of the crew lowered the rear ramp and instructed our driver to pull in. The Chinook crew strapped the jeep down and flew us to Da Nang. We landed, lowered the ramp, removed the straps, and drove off. It was much easier and faster than driving.

The Muster was to be held at the 80th General Support Group Officers' Club, so we headed over there and got transient quarters. The next day we went to the Muster, where the speaker was Lt. Gen. Ormond R. Simpson (Class of '36), commander of the 1st Marine Division. Texas Aggie Class of 1968 members in attendance along with me were Dave Harrigan (E-2), Howard Hoegemeyer (D-1), Greg Duesing (Sqd.14), Mike Swindle (Sqd. 14), Jim Reagan (G-2), Chuck Whitacre (F-2), Dave Powell (G-2), and Bob Huff (Sqd. 1).

Tom Durdin (1955, Squadron 2) 12th Special Operations Squadron, 1967–68

In 1967 I arrived in Vietnam as a pilot in the 12th Special Operations Squadron, known as Ranch Hand, based at Binh Hoa Air Base. Our mission was to dispense Agent Orange to defoliate vegetated areas from which the enemy might ambush friendly forces. This defoliation took the element of surprise away from the enemy, saving many American and Allied lives. We were probably one of the most shot-at flying organizations in Vietnam, but I liked the assignment because I did not have the responsibility of dropping bombs on people.

During my tour I flew 140 combat missions in C-123s. We carried a 1,000-gallon tank in the cargo area and had spray booms on both wings and in the rear. A boom operator, sitting in the cargo compartment in a box that was lead plated for protection from ground fire, operated the pumps that dispensed the spray. The 1,000 gallons of Agent Orange covered the width of a football field six miles in length. We normally flew three or four aircraft formations, but occasionally flew up to twelve on a single sortie.

On my first mission our plane took three hits from ground fire. According to policy, I had to buy champagne for the entire squadron after my first hit, so that night everyone celebrated at the Officers' Club. Our squadron used most of the champagne the club could get because we took hits on most missions. Although everyone laughed because I'd received hits on my first mission, I thought, "This is going to be a really long year."

Being shot at so much and living to talk about it were probably the reasons we had great esprit de corps in our squadron. You had to learn to laugh off close calls, or your nerves wouldn't let you function effectively on a mission. We were so vulnerable to enemy ground fire that we never flew without fighter support. On one mission, when we knew the enemy was entrenched in the mountains, our F-4 fighters strafed and dropped bombs to deter them from shooting at us. The fighters dropped their ordnance so close that we flew through debris in the air—but we still received heavy ground fire.

Early in my assignment, my boss, Robert E. (Gene) Marshall upgraded me to be the Ranch Hand Standboard Navigator. A fellow Aggie (Class of 1960), Gene was preparing me to be his replacement when he rotated home in January of 1968.

On my worst mission we returned to base with twenty-eight holes in our aircraft. In my role as Standboard Navigator I was giving a new arrival a check ride to ensure he was ready to lead missions. The cockpit area of the plane was reinforced with heavy plate for protection from enemy fire; but I was sitting behind the cockpit and five bullets came through the plane within a foot of me. During spray runs the navigator sat between the two pilots on a lead box. When the bullets came through the deck I almost shoved the new navigator through the instrument panel trying to share his protected area. The crew kidded me about hugging the navigator, but it didn't bother me. I'd been trying to avoid what sounded like a West Texas hailstorm of bullets.

One of my most interesting missions was to locate a road in a heavily forested area. The road, which ran from Cambodia into South Vietnam, was used by the enemy to move troops and supplies. I worked with the Army, and initially we flew in a helicopter to identify and map the road. During the flight we landed at a "friendly location" to refuel. Within thirty seconds after we had lifted off, a mortar shell hit the edge of the refueling pad. We received no damage, so we continued the mission.

Using the data we collected, I flew as the navigator on the first defoliation mission against the road. It went extremely well as we marked the area for later flights and exposed much of the road to aerial observation. The missions required much maneuvering to follow the roadway. At one 90-degree turn in the road, we had to shut down the spray and make a 270-degree turn to get back on target. This was all planned, so it was mostly fun—except having to fly through our own spray. The Army was grateful and awarded me a Bronze Star for our support.

Despite all the fire we took, my squadron lost only one aircraft during my tour. The loss occurred on a mission in the Delta area on the southernmost coast of South Vietnam. The formation took ground fire, so after the spray run they remained at 150 feet until they reached a safe distance out over the water. During the climb to altitude for the return to Bien Hoa an aircraft tried to contact the plane in front that it was trailing smoke from an engine. They received no response, and a few seconds later the smoking aircraft peeled off and crashed into the sea. One of the pilots was a close friend and was the most Christian person I knew. I remember him telling me more than once that Jesus Christ was his Savior and that he was prepared to die whenever God was ready to take him. I have often wondered if God took my friend and spared me and others because he was better prepared.

We squadron officers lived in eight hooches—long narrow structures built of wood and screened—with eight men in each. Occasionally the enemy launched 122-mm rockets against our base. One night one of these rockets hit our southernmost hooch, setting it on fire. The wind spread the flames, burning four more hooches to the ground. When it looked like mine was next, I ran back in to save my family picture album. Fortunately firefighters saved my hooch, but the next morning we had guys walking around in underwear because they had lost everything in the fires.

During another night a rocket made a direct hit on one of the perimeter bunkers, killing fourteen Americans. One of the dead was due to rotate home the next day. That same night other rockets came in all around our area. One just missed my hooch, landing about fifty feet away. A piece of shrapnel hit the wall penetrating a two-by-four and a half-inch sheet of plywood before going through a metal clothes locker and exiting through the tin roof. Debris put holes in a shirt I had hanging on a hook. During the attack I didn't have time to get to a bunker. I just lay on the floor and did some serious praying.

The Viet Cong attacked Bien Hoa during Tet of 1968 but were repelled before reaching our area. It is a wonder some of us were not injured as everyone was running around with loaded M-16s.

A break from the combat zone came when I had the opportunity to join a flight crew ferrying a C-123 to Taipei, Taiwan, for an overhaul. Soon after takeoff we had to abort and land at Cam Ranh Bay for repairs. When we took off again the next day, I couldn't get the Loran navigation system to work properly. About an hour offshore from Vietnam I finally got the equipment working and got an accurate fix on our position. Unfortunately we had used too much fuel to reach our objective and had to return to Vietnam.

The next day we made the flight with no problems. We spent a couple of days seeing Taipei, and when the overhaul was complete, we flew to Clark AFB, in the Philippines, for fuel and crew rest. While there I called home, but it was difficult to talk to my wife because just hearing her voice really broke me up. I had to hang up and call back later in the day, when I could better control my emotions.

Back at Bien Hoa I was scheduled for R&R with my wife in Hawaii.

About two weeks before the break I went into a shop just off base where the owner had a handkerchief covering his mouth and nose. As soon as I saw him I had a premonition that I had been exposed to something highly contagious. Soon I was sick. The doctors thought I had dengue fever, but it turned out to be a serious case of flu. I looked and felt terrible with fever blisters all over my chin and lips, so I rescheduled R&R for later in the year. When I finally got to Hawaii, I purchased thirty-three pounds of dried pinto beans and two pineapples to take back to the squadron. On my return we all enjoyed a big Texas red-bean cookout.

There were other lighter moments during my tour. Once during a rocket attack I was first out of our hooch only to fall as I exited the door. The other seven guys stomped me into the ground as they ran out. Nothing was broken, but I was so sore and bruised that I could barely get around for the next week. Another time, when we were playing volleyball, I went up for a spike only to fall on my face. I began to wonder what I was going to tell my children if they asked, "Daddy, did you get wounded in Vietnam?"

It was, of course, very difficult to be away from my family for a year. My wife did a great job of being both Mother and Dad during my absence. She also took time to write me almost every day. When you are ten thousand miles from home and people are shooting real bullets at you, Mail Call is the best time of the day.

After they came home, some Ranch Hand crewmembers began to get various diseases including cancers that many felt were caused by Agent Orange. Finally, in the early 1980s, the Air Force commissioned a study that was conducted for twenty years. Most of our Ranch Hand personnel elected to be a part of the study, which also included people never, or only occasionally, exposed to Agent Orange. Comprehensive physical and mental examinations were administered in the first, third, fifth, tenth, fifteenth, and twentieth years. I personally felt this was an outstanding study, and it did find that some of the problems our people were having were caused by Agent Orange.

Lee Sanders (1964, D-1) 101st Airborne Division, 1969

I was wounded late in the morning of May 19, 1969, as I commanded Delta Company, 3rd Battalion, 187th Infantry Regiment, 101st Airborne Division in our assault up Ap Bia Mountain (Hamburger Hill) in the A Shau Valley of South Vietnam.

We opened our attack at 9:00 a.m. after a thirty-minute artillery bombardment. Our route began with a 200-meter advance up a 20-degree slope that was almost devoid of cover or concealment. Then we faced another 100 meters at a 45-degree slope to reach the top and overrun the NVA defenses. Not far into the attack I passed three dead Delta soldiers. One will forever remain in my heart and mind. He had been hit by a machine gun burst that threw him back into some tall bushes. There he hung, standing like he had been crucified.

As I continued up the hill, machine gun and AK-47 bullets broke the sound barrier around me, making a near-continuous ripping and cracking sound. Bullets struck all around us. In previous fights during my two tours in country I had experienced leaves and branches falling on me as the result of intense fire, but nothing compared to that morning on Hamburger Hill. There was no place to hide or take cover. Our only chance was to bow our backs and move forward.

Suddenly a 7.62-mm machine-gun bullet struck me high on my right arm, where it attaches to the shoulder, and exited six inches above my elbow. I not only felt the bullet; I heard it. It sounded like a wooden bat hitting a hardball. Blood gushed and at times spurted from the entry wound. In addition to breaking my arm, it had severed my brachial artery.

When the bullet hit, it pitched me sideways, face downward into the ground. I was astonished. In earlier fights I had experienced grenade and rocket-propelled-grenade shrapnel wounds and even had had the top of my steel helmet ripped to pieces—but nothing was like this. It shook my body and soul to my core. I immediately realized with no doubt that I had been seriously wounded and initially thought my arm had been completely blown off.

I had no feeling at all below the hole in my shoulder. When I looked down and saw it was still there, albeit in pieces, I was surprised. It felt like a foreign appendage; I didn't know that all the nerves had been killed beneath the break. A medic crawled over to me and said the wound was too high up the arm for him to apply a tourniquet to stop the bleeding.

As my blood continued to pool on the denuded jungle floor, I entered into my first of many negotiations with God. He could have my arm if he just let me live. About that time I lost my color vision. My world became black and white, like newspaper print. It looked as though my negotiations had failed. Death seemed close. Letting go, I said to God, "Here I come."

I felt no fear. It seemed I was stating a simple fact.

My RTO, lying near me, told me I was hit bad. I was well aware already, but his voice shook me out my conversation with God. I knew I had to stop the bleeding or I would die. With nothing else available or in mind, I stuck my left thumb into the entry wound and pressed upward as hard as I could. The pressure immediately stopped the spurting blood. Color came back in my eyesight, giving me a glimmer of hope that I might live. Only later did I learn that my thumb had pressed against the brachial artery, resulting in the formation of a blood clot that plugged the artery and saved my life.

My RTO dragged me twenty meters down the hill, to a large bomb crater. He pulled me into the crater, making sure I had the best cover possible from the hail of enemy bullets that continued to cover Hamburger Hill. Upon seeing there was nothing else he could do for me, he headed back up the hill into the fight. I probably owe my life to this brave man.

I have no idea how long I lay in the crater, but from the time line of the battle it must have been about three hours. I passed in and out of consciousness. When awake I thought about trying to rejoin my company, but that was an impossibility. I knew that one of my lieutenants had assumed command when I fell and was leading them up the hill. I also knew that more of my soldiers were falling dead or wounded.

The pain was nearly unbearable. I had never experienced such intense pain. It centered at the point where the bullet had shattered the bone. It felt like white-hot fire with spasms that radiated up my shoulder into my neck. I tried to adjust my body position, but the slightest movement sent shock waves of increasing pain across my body.

Finally Charlie Company came up the hill to reinforce what remained of Delta. One of their lead soldiers rushed forward with an ammo resupply. As he leaped into my crater, while he was in midair, a bullet hit him like a hammer in his leg. More Charlie soldiers came forward and laid down suppressive fire so that I and the newly wounded soldier could evacuate. I stood in the crater facing the continuing enemy machine-gun fire. Ignoring shouts to "get down," I made my last aggressive gesture in combat. I shot the finger at those who were trying to kill me.

I had passed the mental point of caring about anything—even my own life. All I could do was stumble down the hill. I made it about ten meters past the Charlie Company line before losing consciousness again and collapsing on the trail. When I awoke, a medic was giving me shot of morphine. When I opened my eyes, he said, "We thought you were dead." Then he went on his way to administer to other wounded.

Sometime later I was carried farther to the rear and placed on a Medivac chopper. As we lifted off to the hospital I experienced a sense of pure euphoria. I had survived. I was going to live.

Mike Burroughs (1967, Squadrons 13 and 15) 553rd Reconnaissance Wing, 1969

Ten days after graduating from A&M, I found myself on active duty at Goodfellow AFB, San Angelo, Texas, where I attended a twenty-two-week signals intelligence officer training course. When it was time to forecast for an assignment, I put down four overseas choices, but being the only Texan in the class, I ended up in a mobile unit right there at Goodfellow. Everyone else but one went overseas.

Immediately after completing training, I took a couple of weeks' leave. When I returned I found that more than half my unit had been deployed to Korea in response to the incident with the USS Pueblo. What a missed opportunity!

A couple of months later I got a call from personnel telling me I had a flying assignment in Southeast Asia. Although I had earlier volunteered for duty in SEA, I was surprised when I finally got my orders.

After some additional leave, in the summer of 1968 I ended up at Korat Royal Thai Air Force Base, Thailand, assigned to the 554th Reconnaissance Squadron of the 553rd Reconnaissance Wing as a CICO. During the following year, I was a crewmember aboard EC-121R aircraft flying electronic-reconnaissance missions over SVN, the Gulf of Tonkin, and Laos.

The mission of the 553rd RW was to monitor sensors implanted along supply routes in SVN, NVN, and Laos and to develop and report enemy targets in an effort to interdict the influx of men and materiel from the communist North into the South. The back-end crew on each mission consisted of one CICO, eight CIMs, and two RMTs. The front-end crew consisted of two pilots, two navigators, two flight engineers, one radio operator, and for certain missions, two electronic-warfare officers. Typically each mission was eight hours on station, but one or more planes were in the air 24/7.

Korat was a safe, reasonably comfortable base—so much so that several wives came over to visit their husbands. We flew at a high enough altitude that we were not in the range of ground fire while on our missions, but there are inherent dangers anytime one takes to the air.

My roommate was the copilot on Crew 39. His wife, Jean Ann, flew from the States to visit for a couple of weeks, so whenever he was not flying, they spent time together downtown. On April 25 I walked into the officers' club dining room for lunch and found my roommate's wife sitting by herself. When I asked about her husband, she told me he didn't feel well and had gone to see the flight surgeon. I said I hoped he felt better soon and thought little more of it.

Crew 39 was flying that afternoon with a takeoff time of about 1600 hours. As I walked from the club back to my room I saw the CICO for Crew 39 walking toward the crew-bus area wearing his flight suit and carrying his flight bag. I wished him a good flight and thought no more of it.

Later that afternoon, a severe rainstorm swept across the base. After a while the downpour stopped and I ventured back outside. I was walking down the sidewalk when a fellow squadron member stopped and asked, "Did you hear that we lost one?"

I didn't understand what he was asking, and when I told him so, he said that Batcat 21, the call sign for the aircraft that Crew 39 was flying, had crashed. I stood there, stunned and absolutely numb. Something in me wanted to say, "You're joking," but the look in his eyes said that he was serious, that this was no joke. I thought about my good friends on crew. Some I had flown with many times; all I had met at one time or another.

I rushed to the squadron operations center. Someone had already removed the picture of Crew 39 from the wall, and the names of the members had been erased from the scheduling board. This was to prevent speculation as to who was on board, pending verification of who actually was on the aircraft and notification of next-of-kin. Then I thought of my roommate's wife. How was she going to handle this? Back in my room, however, I saw that his flight bag was still there, which meant he was not flying, as he never flew without it. Yet I still wasn't sure. Why did he not fly that day? Then I remembered: earlier he was not feeling well.

Later I learned that there were eighteen men on board and no survivors. Apparently the thunderstorm was one of the most severe in about fifty years. In the meantime I had tried to contact my roommate's wife at her hotel, but to no avail.

After dark I went to the officers' club, where I joined a major who worked in scheduling and several others at a table. Ordinarily he was a joking, crusty kind of man, but now he was somber and distressed. I learned that the flight surgeon had grounded my roommate that morning because of food poisoning. That flight had two other pilots scheduled, and another flight scheduled later that afternoon had four. The scheduling officer had asked a fellow major and a close friend to move from the later flight to the earlier to replace my roommate. He agreed and was switched. The scheduling officer was blaming himself for his friend's death. Those of us who sat with him tried to assure him that he had no control over things and that it was not his fault. He probably realized that, but still it was extremely painful for him.

While I was sitting in my room the following day, my roommate and his wife walked in. I was never so glad to see anyone, and I told him so! I was so thankful he was safe, but that didn't change the fact that eighteen other men were dead. Included in the toll was the wing's flying safety officer as well as a lieutenant colonel who was the aircraft commander. It was supposed to be his last mission before he returned to the States and retired from the Air Force. His wife was already in San Francisco waiting for him.

The accident investigation determined that when the aircraft took off, the severe weather forced it down, that it never gained more than a few hundred feel in altitude. The aircraft, tail number 21493, had made a reasonably good belly landing, but it hit trees, broke up, and, with a full load of fuel, caught fire and exploded. Although I never saw the wreckage, I got some descriptions from investigating officers, and it was horrible. Those men never had a chance.

That day the reality of war confronted me and many other members of the wing. For us the war had seemed something rather distant; we felt well insulated from it. Now, however, eighteen men were dead—sons, husbands, brothers, fathers. The youngest was nineteen, the oldest, forty-six. I lost some friends that day, and except for a fluke of nature, I would have lost a roommate as well. On the other hand, had he not become ill and been placed on quarters, his replacement would have remained on the other flight, his life spared. In retrospect I suppose that many times in our lives, we all brush close to death without realizing it One little change in time, space, or sequence could cause us to cross the line that separates the living from the dead.

John Erskine (1960, Squadron 2) 5th Special Forces Group, 1966

I entered A&M as an Air Force cadet but later turned down a contract to be a pilot because I didn't like the five-year commitment that went with it. Instead I accepted a direct commission into the army as an environmental engineer—and was surprised to find out that the specialty was a part of the Medical Service Corps rather than of the Engineers.

In 1964 I was assigned to Special Action Force Asia in Okinawa. SAFAsia included the 1st Special Forces Group (Airborne), the 97th Civil Affairs Group, and several other Special Operations units. My first tour in Vietnam came as part of a Mobile Training Team (MTT) that covered Thailand, Cambodia, Laos, and Vietnam. We worked with the Thai Special Forces in providing training for Border Security and in developing relationships with the local population. We advised on building schools and hospitals, setting up water and sewage systems (where my A&M degree in Civil Engineering came in handy), and developing the agriculture potential in the area.

In January 1966 I returned to Vietnam for my second tour and was assigned to the 5th Special Forces Group in Nha Trang as the Medical Operations Officer. In March we received word that Detachment A-102 at Ashau had been warned of a possible attack by as many as four battalions of the NVA 325th Division. We moved quickly to reinforce the camp, and I was sent to Da Nang to handle the medical resupply for the detachment.

Ashau was a typical Special Forces Camp, triangle shaped with 200-foot-long walls so that all the corners had interlocking fire. Initially the camp consisted of 10 Special Forces NCOs and 219 CIDG troops. On March 7 we were reinforced with a Mike Force of 149 Nungs.

The NVA attacked the camp on March 9. The fight lasted all day, through the night, and into the next day. Poor weather prevented adequate air cover and resupply. At 5:00 P.M. on the tenth, when we were running low on ammo, the camp was ordered abandoned, with the men directed to exfiltrate to a nearby LZ for helicopter pickup. Of the seventeen Americans, five were KIA and twelve were wounded. Four bodies were wrapped in ponchos and cached in the camp. One of the severely wounded died during exfiltration. His body was wrapped in a poncho and cached outside the camp near the LZ.

After the camp was abandoned, a mission was launched to recover the bodies. As the senior Medical Operations officer, I was in charge of the operation. The plan was to interview the survivors to determine exactly where the bodies had been cached and then to depart by helicopter from Phu Bai airstrip, Hue, land at Ashau, recover the remains, and return to Hue.

As we approached Ashau, the helicopters began to take fire from the surrounding area. We landed, set up a perimeter defense, entered the camp, and began the search for the bodies. Because the camp had been totally demolished by air strikes after it was abandoned, searching was extremely difficult. We had good intelligence, though, and one by one we recovered all four bodies in the camp. But despite an exhaustive search along the route to the LZ, we did not recover the fifth body, now MIA.

Jeffery Murray (1973, Squadron 6 and H-2) 281st Aviation Company, 1968–69

I remember talking to a pilot who had been in country much longer than I about how it was conceivable to spend a year in country and never take a round. That sounded good to me.

In 1969, during my time as a "Bandit" in the 281st Assault Helicopter Battalion, I flew with lots of pilots. More than one liked to impress anyone within earshot with his abilities. Some were qualified IPs. But I enjoyed flying with one in particular, Ken. I never knew what he would do. He was blissfully silent whenever I flew, and he let me fly a lot. As a result I learned a lot.

One day Ken and I were off to a place called LZ Courage to pick up a liaison officer and give him a lift to Da Nang to catch a plane home. I flew the approach, the passengers loaded up, and off we went. At an altitude of maybe ten feet I heard this loud crack under my feet and some stuff flew around. I looked down, depressed the mic switch, and asked "What the heck was that? Did I hit something?"

Ken yells, "Heck no! We just took a round."

I looked closer, and, sure enough, there's a round hole in my chin bubble. Ken got on the radio and told the ground guys what had happened, and we headed to another firebase. He let me keep flying while he talked, telling me to maintain 900 feet of altitude. As we got closer to our destination we both noticed I was getting closer to the ground but we were still at 900 feet according to the altimeter. That's when we figured out the altimeter had a round in it. We dropped off one guy, zipped over to Da Nang to deliver the other, and picked up an artillery lieutenant.

Ken got an offshore navy destroyer to prepare to fire some rounds into the area near LZ Courage where we had taken the round. But before the navy guys lit the joint up, we made a run with our door guns. One door gunner was our platoon sergeant. I clearly remember him firing a line of bullets up a rice-paddy dike toward a kid who was running like heck. A few feet before hitting the kid, the sergeant adjusted his aim to make an arc around him, leaving him unscathed. I had a lot of respect for him after that. Ken thanked him. The arty guy, however, was none too pleased. He had been sitting in the back when we low-leveled over the place shooting everything up. No doubt he talked like Audie Murphy when we got back on the ground. He probably marched off and put himself in for the Silver Star.

We returned to Phu Hiep for some Hamm's beer. Just another day in Vietnam.

Frank Bonvillain, (1967, D-1 and B-1) 173rd Airborne Brigade, 1969

Graduating from college is no easy task. It is exponentially more difficult if you sell your textbooks on the weekends to buy beer and then stay drunk most of the week. Throw in not going to class and sleeping through the ones you did attend, and, well, all those things made it somewhat of a challenge. That is why sitting in a coffee shop with the assistant dean of the School of Veterinary Medicine was like a dream. I had to keep pinching myself just to make certain he didn't turn into a bottle of Lone Star.

But I'm getting ahead of myself.

I grew up in the salt grass of the Texas Gulf Coast. We ran cows. Every kid wants to be a cowboy at some point in his life, and I was no different. But I was a cowboy already, and I knew that cowboy life sucked unless you were reading about it in a book—or owned the King Ranch. What I really wanted to be was a soldier. Don't know why. There are no soldiers to speak of in my family lineage. My Daddy was a Cajun. Cajuns like to drink and party. They don't like to fight. My Mother was an Indian. But she was Cherokee, one of the "civilized" tribes. Most of them didn't like to fight either. Further, the ones who did weren't very good at it.

Regardless, I wanted to be a soldier. But my Daddy wanted me to go to college. This was the 1960s. You didn't say no to your father in the 1960s. So we compromised. I went to a military college—Texas A&M. Getting enrolled was tough in those days. If you couldn't play football, you had to graduate from high school. You had to have $200 to cover a full year's tuition (including room and board). And you had to be able to fog glass. So when it came time for college, my Daddy had the money and I could breathe. I was a shoo-in.

The military part of college was a snap. Ranch life had put me in decent physical condition. I knew my left foot from my right, so I was a marching fool. I could salute, and I could say "Sir" at the start and end of each sentence. I also had a great memory for people's names and useless trivia that seemed to be very important. Hell, I was destined to be a General Officer.

But the academic portion of college life didn't go quite so smoothly. Probably every kid raised in rural Texas planned on being a veterinarian. I was going to be a soldier, but I figured being a veterinarian "on the side" would be a pretty good fall-back career if I got wounded or something. Besides, I knew a horse from a cow and could castrate calves all day long. Pre-vet courses were mostly a piece of cake, and I was doing pretty well—until organic chemistry. I could never figure out what all those "Cs" stood for that the professor kept drawing on the blackboard. So I changed majors. Somehow I stayed in college a full two years before my luck ran out.

I was engaged to be married to the most beautiful girl in Texas. She was also going to college, but I thought that was just to pass the time until I could get closer to graduation and we could get married, when she would quit school, go to work, and start cooking, cleaning, sewing, and having babies. Life would be good.

Well, it didn't work out quite that way. Seems she actually wanted an education. I had zero interest in it and could not understand why anyone else would be interested—especially a girl. If the alternative to an education was to get to go to bed with me, why would she want to go to college? She got mad, I got madder, and eventually I was left under the bus in the dust. Then my grades really went into the ditch. And, more important, I was in real danger of losing my contract for an Army commission, which for me would have been a fate worse than death.

It was easy to get into the Army in those days. It was even easier than getting into college. In fact, all you had to do was stand still, and Uncle Sam would grab your ass, cut your hair, give you some new clothes, hand you a rifle, and you were in the Army faster than you could say "Vietnam." However, during a brief discussion with my Military Advisor, he told me that although I would make an adequate officer, I would make an extremely poor enlisted man. As I recall, he said something like: "Frank, if you are drafted, you will go into the infantry, go to Airborne School, and then go immediately to Vietnam. You will be dead in a week. If you stay in school, pull your grades up, and get back into the ROTC program, I will guarantee you a commission as an infantry officer and a recommendation for Airborne and Ranger schools. You will be in Vietnam ten months from graduation rather than ten weeks. As an officer, you may have six months in Vietnam before you do something stupid and get killed. Moreover, I give you a ten percent chance of actually living through the war. Stay in college, asshole."

So I remained in A&M. My academic advisor in the School of Agriculture was an elderly, fatherly looking guy with snow-white hair. Maybe a hundred years old. He was a wonderful man and a legend in the School of Agriculture. He seemed to be able to see potential in boys right off Texas farms and ranches, even though they might be uncultured and not have the academic background of other students. He was also able to tell if college was just not right for you at this particular time in your life and if you'd be better off spending Daddy's money doing something else. He was an amazing man. He saw something in me no one else saw—hell, that I didn't even see myself. He gave me another chance.

I had lost my girl and damn near lost my chance of being an officer in the army. School was still of no great importance, but without school, no army. So this was my wake-up call—maybe like a drunk who hits rock bottom, decides he doesn't like what he sees in the mirror, and joins AA.

At this point you might be wondering why, if I wanted to be in the army so bad, I didn't take my own advice—just "stand still" and get drafted. It's embarrassing to admit, but I had had a really bad car accident that broke an awful lot of bones, so my military-enlistment category was 4F. That meant I could not be drafted. It's doubtful I could even have enlisted for a combat specialty.

So I had no girl, and I was at an all-male military college. I had no money. Moreover, I was on both military probation and academic probation. Hell, there was nothing to do but study. As hard as it is to remain in college if you skip class, stay drunk, and honky-tonk all night, I discovered it is just as easy to do well if you actually open the book and listen to what the professor is saying. And cut back on the booze.

I had to go to summer school, had to spend a little more of Daddy's money and slow down on my drinking. In two years I had turned my life around. Not only did I get off academic and military probation, I became a Distinguished Military Student, and upon graduation I was a Distinguished Military Graduate, which meant I received my coveted Regular Army Commission in the infantry.

A week before graduation I was sitting across the table from the assistant dean of the School of Veterinary Medicine. Although I had transferred out of the pre-vet curriculum, I remained in the field of Animal Science (and had figured out what all those Cs stood for). The assistant dean taught several classes I attended, and I had traveled with him on weekend trips to various ranches in Texas. We had a lot of fun, but he was not my academic advisor. I had taken most (but not all) of the courses necessary to be accepted into the College of Veterinary Medicine. So I guess he looked at my grades and thought I was worth at least a cup of coffee.

His proposition was simple: Stay in school another semester, pick up the courses I needed to qualify for Vet School, delay going into the Army, and give up my Regular Army commission. Assuming I made good grades in the courses required, he would assure me a slot in the next veterinary medicine class, and if I still wanted to go into the Army after Vet School, I could be a meat inspector and/or take care of the military dependents' dogs and cats until I got out of uniform and went into private practice.

A chance of a lifetime—I had gone from a hair's breadth away from flunking out of college to a very good chance of being a Doctor of Veterinary Medicine. Thank God my Mom and Dad weren't there to hear this proposition. Or, better stated, thank God my Mom and Dad weren't there to hear my response.

Running through my mind was . . . becoming a veterinarian would mean five more years of college. It would mean giving up my infantry commission. Most important, because the Vietnam War was winding down and might soon be over. I would miss my chance. Even if I went, I would be a meat inspector. God, help me! A meat inspector! When I gave the assistant dean my answer and the reasoning behind it, I actually thought he was going to have the Big One right there in the restaurant. He looked at me like I had just grown two heads.

Army training was pretty much like I thought it would be. Second lieutenants were not supposed to know anything, so I fit right in. Airborne School was tough. Georgia is hot and humid in the summer; hot like Gobi Desert hot. We almost died. To cool you off, the Airborne School had mounted sprinkler heads on a series of bars about 12 feet long and five feet off the ground. At the one-hour breaks, men were required to strip to their T-shirt (unfortunately no women went through Airborne School in those days), get down into a pushup position, and put their upper body under the sprinkler to cool down. You also took salt tablets. It was determined much later that excess salt was not good for your system, but at the time it was thought that the salt tablets would make you sweat more and therefore be the best thing you could swallow. I would suck on them like candy.

The days were long, hot, and miserable. By the time you went to bed, every muscle in your body screamed for relief throughout the long, hot, painful night. Air conditioning had not yet been discovered at Fort Benning. No fans were allowed, and the door to your room had to stay closed and locked, or you would wake up the next morning with nothing left but the underwear you were sleeping in. If you were on an upper floor in the barracks, you walked down the stairs in the morning using both hands on the guardrail to steady yourself or you would fall on your face. Your legs worked on flat ground but going up or down stairs was impossible without support. Men lucky enough to have rooms on the bottom floor would laugh at the rest of us as we struggled down the steps every morning. I hate those people to this day!

Jumping out of an airplane is an unnatural act. By the time I finally retired from government service I had eighty-three jumps. And I was scared eighty-three times. But it's really not all that risky. Thousands of soldiers go through Airborne training every year, and there are seldom more than one or two deaths per year. There are broken bones and minor injuries at almost every big jump, but if you did as you were told, chances were that good nothing bad would happen to you. Many soldiers love to jump, and many civilians do it as a sport. I did it because it was part of my dream to be an Airborne Ranger. What could be better? Just like the song said: "Put silver wings on my son's chest. Make him one of America's best."

"Yes sir, Colonel, I believe I will have an extra tall glass of that Kool-Aid."

Airborne School was followed by Ranger School. Like Airborne, Ranger School also began at Fort Benning, but Ranger School was eight-plus weeks, and training was conducted at three locations; Camp William O. Darby, at Fort Benning; the Mountain Ranger Camp (now Camp Frank D. Merrill), in north Georgia; and the Florida Ranger Camp (now Camp Earl Rudder), at Eglin Air Force Base, on the long western arm of Florida, under Alabama. Florida may be "the Sunshine State," but I have never been as cold as I was in the Florida swamps that December.

Airborne School was rough, but Ranger School was hell on earth. Some Navy SEAL recently wrote a bestselling book titled *No Easy Day*. Bullshit. SEALs have one excruciating week. The remainder of their training is challenging, but if you are part fish, it's doable. Rangers have two plus months of hell. They break you, build you up, and then break you again. You go until you can go no further. No food, no sleep. And then, when you are way past the human breaking point, you lead a group of men just as tired up a hill or through a swamp another five kilometers to attack and secure some training objective. At night. In the snow. You did the impossible. And then you did it again.

The first time I ever saw snow was in Dahlonega the morning of November 11, 1968—my birthday. Dahlonega is a small town in northern

Georgia that sits at the foot of the Appalachian Mountains. The mountains are beautiful, and never having left central Texas, I had never seen mountains. These were impressive. This was the second phase of Ranger School, the Mountain Phase.

It was snowing, and we were getting ready for our first patrol. I turned to my Ranger Buddy, a little Irish Yankee from Boston named Mike. They paired him with me with because we were the same height and weight. But that is where the similarities ended. He was a West Pointer, so he could march, salute, and say "Sir" just like I could. But I found out he had turned down Harvard to attend West Point. A lot of that may have had to do with money. Mike was so tight he squeaked when he walked. Nevertheless, he had turned down Harvard, and I had almost flunked out of a Cow College!

Mike was the first Yankee I had ever known, but he was a pretty good guy. He spoke with this Godawful accent that made me want to choke him, and he kept telling me about people named "Clausewitz," "Sun Tzu," and "Machiavelli." I had no idea who these people were, but I knew damn well they were not from Texas. Of that I was certain.

I was excited about the snow. It was coming down pretty good in big, fat flakes, and there was already a lot sticking to the ground. "Hey, Mike. Snow. It's beautiful! Isn't it neat? We should make a snowman."

"At midnight tonight remind me you said that," Mike replied, "Then you can tell me again how 'beautiful' you think this fucking snow is." I guess Mike had walked in snow before.

Two days later it was still snowing. It was no longer beautiful. In fact, I never wanted to see snow again the rest of my life. It was like walking in mud. When you walked, you sweated, and when you stopped, the sweat froze to your body. Men learned to sleep leaning on their loaded M-14 rifle propped in their armpit (muzzle end, not the stock). The stock under your arm would have been more comfortable, but the muzzle would be in the mud. When fired, the rifle would explode. Of course, had the rifle gone off with the muzzle under your arm, you'd have lost an arm, but an arm was a small price to pay for a few moments of sleep.

Finally, we were allowed to stop for our first meal. A live chicken. You had to catch, kill, and gut the chicken, then figure out some way to cook and eat the damn thing. I was reminded of a short story by Jack London, "To Build a Fire," that I had read in junior high school. The story was about some guy lost in the Alaska wilderness. It was snowing. He tried to build a fire. He couldn't. He died. In retrospect I am certain there was more to London's story, but at that moment all I could think about was not being able to build a fire and, along with dozens of other Ranger students, freezing to death on some unknown hill in the Appalachian Mountains surrounded by dozens of equally dead chickens. They would find our bodies in the spring.

But my problems were mounting. Mike came over to me with his chicken.

"I need some help."

"What kind of help, Mike? I'm not certain how we're going to build a fire either."

"It's not that," Mike replied.

"Well, what's wrong, then?"

"I can't kill my chicken!"

"What the hell do you mean, you can't kill your chicken? You just wring the bird's neck, and it will die."

"I can't do that. I can't wring its neck. I can't stand the sight of blood."

"Excuse me? Did you just say you can't stand the sight of blood? You are an infantry officer, only months away from going to Vietnam with the sole purpose of killing as many of the enemy as you can, and you are standing there telling me you can't stand the sight of blood? Do you see anything at all incongruous about that statement? Mother of God! How the hell did the South lose the war fighting a bunch of Yankees who couldn't stand the sight of blood?"

But before Mike could answer, I looked around at the other Rangers. Almost everyone had caught his chicken but was just holding it. I then realized for the first time that most of these kids were from cities. I don't guess many had ever actually killed a chicken. Probably they had never killed anything unless they had gone hunting with their Dad and possibly killed a deer. But that would have been from 200 meters away. The opportunity was too good to pass up.

"Hey guys, look over here a minute," I yelled. "This is how you kill a chicken." With that, I grabbed my chicken, put its neck in my mouth, bit down and shook my head. Hard. Blood went everywhere and the chicken, minus its head, went flopping off in the snow. I spit the head onto the ground. Mike still tells this story. However he leaves out the part of him not liking the sight of blood. That's probably because now he is an honest-to-goodness medical doctor. (I have seen the diploma.) He is a pediatric endocrinologist. I have no idea what a "pediatric endocrinologist" is or what one does, but I doubt endocrine glands are very important (probably like tonsils). Whatever they are, I will guarantee you they don't bleed.

Two months later we had completed the Florida Phase of training. We were cold, wet, dirty, tired, malnourished, and near death. However, we had graduated. We were now Rangers. There is a myth that the Ranger Tab keeps you dry and stops you from being hungry. That is not true. The Ranger Tab neither keeps you dry nor stops you from being hungry. It just insures you don't care if you are wet and hungry. You can and will complete the mission, "Though [you] be the lone survivor."

I will never forget our graduation speech. The Ranger School Commander was on the podium blowing so much hot air it's a wonder he didn't float away. A portion of his talk centered on an incident during training when we had to cross the Yellow River. The Yellow River runs through the training area of Eglin Air Force Base and empties into the Gulf of Mexico. During the winter months it is colder than the Milk River in northern Montana. During the summer, at a tremendous cost to the taxpayer, using tugboats the Ranger Department brings in icebergs from the coast of Greenland and places the icebergs at the head of the Yellow River. Therefore the river stays ice cold twelve months of the year. One year a Ranger Student swore that he saw a penguin swimming in the Yellow River. But that was not confirmed.

Anyway, we had to cross the Yellow River as part of the training. It was night, we were naked, and the water was cold. Real cold. The only thing saving us from certain death was a rope tied across the river about four feet above the water that was pulled across and tied by a fellow Ranger who had swum to the other side. Each Ranger student would strip naked, tie his clothes in his rubberized poncho, tie the poncho to his wrist with a small cord, and jump into the water holding onto the rope. He pulled himself across the river by sliding his hands along the rope. Once on the other side, he put on the clothes wrapped in his poncho and then continued the mission. Because I want to be totally honest in this story, the river was about fifty meters wide at the crossing point. Some Rangers (who like to exaggerate) will tell you it was a mile across. Don't believe them.

For whatever reason, the colonel chose to cite this training as an example of our intestinal fortitude. A part of the speech went, "I'll bet when you were out there in the Yellow River, naked and freezing, you didn't think you were going to make it, did you?"

At that point, Mike turned to me and asked, "I wonder what the hell he expected us to do? Let go of the fucking rope?"

That was the real lesson of Ranger School and perhaps the real lesson of life, "Never let go of the rope. Never even think of letting go of the rope. Quitting is *not* an option. Once you start something there are only two courses of action remaining: finish or die in the attempt."

I was an infantryman, and I was now an Airborne Ranger. With two notable exceptions, marrying the girl I loved and getting a Combat Infantryman's Badge, I had accomplished everything I ever wanted in life. And I was barely twenty-one years old.

"Yes sir, Colonel. I believe I'll take *two* tall glasses of that Kool-Aid."

It was about a twenty-five-hour flight, with stops, from Travis Air Force Base, California, to Binh Hoa Air Base, Vietnam. It was a commercial airplane leased by the government. There was very little small talk on the plane. I don't think people knew what to say. For some it was their second or even third trip, but for most of us it was our first. For many of the men on that flight it was a one-way trip.

Some, like me, were volunteers. It was what we wanted to do or, if not exactly "wanted to do," were willing to do. Others were living a nightmare. These were the years of conscription in America. Many of these men had to choose between being on that airplane or in Canada or some other country that would take them. Some had wives, families, and jobs back home. Many had spent a fortune on a college education, which they thought was being wasted. They felt ill-used. They wanted nothing to do with the Army or the war.

The war was very unpopular in America and, in fact, was tearing the country apart. A lot of Americans did not think we belonged in Vietnam, and a lot of others, who initially supported America's involvement, had their fill of the bloodshed and came to realize that the war was unwinnable. Even many patriotic Americans wanted America the hell out of Vietnam. And this was a sentiment shared by a lot of people on the plane. They didn't feel America should be in Vietnam; *they* sure as hell didn't want to be in Vietnam. A tough position. I felt sorry for them. Me? Hell, I couldn't get there quick enough.

As our plane came in over the South China Sea, I could see the fishing boats below, the rice paddies and mountains of central Vietnam and Saigon, and the large, bustling capital city about thirty kilometers away. We flew over the large Long Binh Military Compound just outside the city. Bien Hoa was the airbase, and Long Binh was the Army Base, but it was one huge compound and as safe as Fort Benning. Of course, no one on the airplane knew that. I believe everyone thought they would get shot before they left the tarmac. I was no exception.

Soldiers moved out as fast as possible. I in-processed, got finances squared away, and, the day after I arrived, left with an assignment to the 173rd Airborne Brigade (Separate). The "Separate" meant that, unlike most brigades, the 173rd was not part of a division but was a separate command and worked independent of a division. For me it was the dream assignment. The 173rd had been in Vietnam longer than any other Army unit and had the reputation of being the brigade that was always "in the shit." I didn't know if that was true, but it made a great story, and there was no question the 173rd Airborne was an extremely tough unit and had participated in some of the most difficult and bloody fighting of the war.

I had been in country three days when I arrived at brigade headquarters on Landing Zone English and reported for further assignment. The standard job for junior infantry officers was as a rifle-platoon leader. If you survived six to eight months as a platoon leader, you were usually reassigned to a job on the battalion or brigade staff. The idea was to round out an officer's professional development leading troops in combat with time as a staff officer supporting combat troops. Of course the unstated fact was that it also helped keep you alive. The trick was surviving the first six to eight months.

When I reported to the Brigade S-1 for my assignment I was shocked. The 173rd (like all major commands) had a Ranger Company attached. Although the Ranger Company carried the 75th Infantry designation, there was no 75th Infantry Regimental Headquarters. Each company operated under the control of the brigade or division command to which they were assigned.

Officers in Ranger companies were graduates of Ranger School, but the soldiers did not have to attend the training. Only a very few NCOs were "tabbed" Rangers. However, all had combat experience and had attended an "in country" Patrolling/Reconnaissance Course was taught by the 173rd. It wasn't Ranger School, but it gave the soldiers basic irregular-warfare skills. Without overstating it, the Ranger Company had the most battle-hardened, professional infantrymen in the brigade. In fact, modesty was the only thing preventing them from telling you just how damn good they were!

This was my dream assignment. But it was very difficult to get a position with the Rangers. There was only one company for the entire Brigade, so there were lots of candidates for very few slots. You had to be a Ranger-qualified officer, but there were plenty of them around. Moreover, normally you were not considered for the Rangers until you been in a traditional infantry company for six months. Many Rangers, officers and soldiers, were on their second Vietnam tour. So it was very unusual for a green, unproven 2nd Lieutenant even to be interviewed for such an assignment.

However, the impossible happened. November Company, which had suffered a terrible hit the previous week, had lost several officers and soldiers either killed or wounded. They needed replacements. As luck would have it, the Brigade S-1 was a fellow Aggie, not a classmate, a few years my senior, but we knew each other. He was also a good friend of the Ranger company commander. He could not guarantee me the assignment, but he could get me an interview. That was all I really wanted and more than I expected. "Face time" with the company commander was worth its weight in gold. That way, in six or eight months (assuming I did well with my line platoon), when I applied for a slot with the Rangers, the commander would remember my name, and I would be a step up on my contemporaries.

The next morning Captain Crocker, the company commander, and I talked for about an hour, with him asking a few relevant questions about my background and experience and about my youth, family, and schooling. He was an impressive soldier and leader. I was even more impressed when he told me that I did not have to wait for the job. It was mine. I had captured the most prized slot in all of Vietnam. Life could not get much better.

Giving up drinking and carousing, having to study, turning down the opportunity to become a veterinarian, getting dumped by my old girlfriend, almost dying of frostbite in the Appalachian Mountains, nearly freezing to death in Florida's Yellow River; none of that mattered now. It was all worth it. I was about to become a platoon leader in November Company, 75th Infantry Regiment.

Early the next afternoon I walked to the company headquarters that sat on a small hill at the edge of the LZ English perimeter. The 2nd Battalion, 503rd Infantry was co-located with Brigade Headquarters as were the artillery battalion and various support outfits. But the Ranger Company was well separated from the other units.

As I carried my rucksack up the hill, I had no idea what to expect. I was not yet armed; realistically, I was in very little danger on a large Fire Base like LZ English. Of course, there were mortar attacks almost every night, but, armed or unarmed, there was nothing you could do about that, and there had never been an all-out attack on a major fire base since the Tet Offensive in January of 1968. This was my fourth day in Vietnam, and I had yet to hear a shot fired, much less see a VC. So I was not particularly concerned about not having a weapon. I knew that one of the first things I would do once I signed in to the company was draw a rifle.

The CO said my first few days would be spent acclimating to the weather; LZ English was in sight of the South China Sea, and the humidity was stifling. Being from the Texas Gulf Coast I was used to the dampness, but I still looked forward to a few days to get my legs under me before actually going on a mission. I had to learn the company SOP, radio call signs and procedures, team makeup, and a dozen other things. Most important, I needed an aerial reconnaissance of the Brigade Area of Operation.

The Ranger mission was to fly from the Fire Base well into enemy territory, find the enemy, and kill him. It was a little more sophisticated than that, but when you cut through all the fancy talk, that was what it amounted to. There were no "front lines" in Vietnam, but for the most part you knew where you were, and you knew where the other friendly units were, and therefore, you had a pretty good idea of the general direction to where the enemy was—or at least was supposed to be. The problem was that when a conventional platoon or company went on patrol, oftentimes the enemy could see the platoon coming and would just withdraw into the mountains. The Viet Cong either would not fight at all or fought on his own terms, which was never good.

Ranger Operations were different. Their tactics were just as unconventional as the enemies'. The company would fly small teams, usually six men, deep into "enemy" territory, where there were no other American units. The Viet Cong expected relatively large American units to come from the lowland into the mountains. Rangers fought them on their own terms.

The area was considered a no-man's land. If you saw something that was not supposed to be there, you were free to kill it. As I said: "Find and kill the enemy." But this was all I knew, and I knew it from my one-hour interview with the company commander the previous day. I didn't even know where I would sleep.

As I walked up the hill my mind was going in a dozen directions. The men in the company were used to seasoned platoon leaders, officers who had proven themselves in battle on numerous occasions. Me, I had been in Vietnam less than a week and didn't know shit. Maybe I shouldn't have accepted the job so quickly. Perhaps I should have gone to a regular infantry platoon first and then tried for the Rangers after six months—

or maybe not taken on the job until my second tour. Or maybe not taken it at all. Mother of God, what had I gotten myself into?

I soon found out.

A wooden sign with the black and gold Ranger Tab above a black scroll with red trim stood in front of the company headquarters. On the left side of the scroll was the letter "N," on the right "75." In the center, in white letters, was written "Airborne Ranger." Under the scroll was written "The Eyes and Ears of the Commanding General." I took a picture.

A black mongrel dog was the first to greet me. Behind the dog was possibly the scariest man I had ever seen. He looked Vietnamese—olive skinned, jet-black hair combed straight back in a ducktail, maybe 5 feet 5 inches tall, and with the coldest black eyes I had ever seen on a man. He shook my hand and said: "Hi, my name is Tad. Don't worry about Tango. He loves everyone; he's just happy to see you. Welcome to November Company, Lieutenant. You will find the Old Man and First Sergeant in the Operations Room straight ahead." Pleasant guy. Friendly, courteous. I don't know what scared me about him. I think it was his eyes; his eyes were dead.

I found out much later that Tad had been in Vietnam longer than anyone could remember, maybe since the war started. It wasn't certain where he was from nor his ethnicity. He was already a legend in the Rangers. Many years later a major US newspaper ran a story about Tad. It was called, "The Original Rambo." Supposedly he had more medals than you could buy in the Post Exchange.

I walked into the Orderly Room, gave the Company Clerk my papers, and signed a log book, making me officially a part of November Company. I then walked over to a wooden building surrounded by sandbags with a tin roof—the Operations Room. The small building had several people working at various desks. The CO and the First Sergeant were standing, looking intently at a map on the wall. They turned to greet me with large smiles. Both men shook my hand, introduced me to the Operations NCO, and began explaining the various maps showing the Brigade Area of Operation. There were red squares marked on the various maps with grease pencil. The OPS Sergeant said they represented where Ranger Teams were currently deployed.

He and I then walked outside, where he pointed down the hill to the aviation unit I had passed coming up. He said there were two aviation units co-located. "Lucky Star" provided transportation to the mission location, and "Casper" flew the gunships that provided covering fire.

Medevac helicopters were also part of the aviation support. The helipad was less than a five-minute jeep ride from Ranger Hill. We were just outside the door of the Operations Room when we heard loud screams coming from the radio inside.

"TIMBER, TIMBER, TIMBER" was being repeated over the radio, and the laid-back atmosphere of only a moment ago turned into quick, precise moves to telephones, maps, and radios. Everyone had a job, and everyone seemed to know what to do. A crowd of Rangers now stood outside. We pushed through the group and then were standing in the middle of a beehive of activity.

It was explained to me quickly that the signal "Timber" meant a Ranger Team was in serious trouble and needed immediate extraction. The exact type of trouble was unknown, as were the number killed and/or wounded and how many enemy they had encountered. Nothing. All that would come later. All the Ops Center knew at present was that a team was in serious trouble. The Brigade HQ was notified what was happening. Another call went to the helipad to notify "Lucky Star" and "Casper" to get birds ready to fly. Yet another call went to the Medevac helicopters to stand by.

The CO turned around with a folded map in his hand. Looking at me and the OPS NCO, he said, "You two go get those men. There are six Rangers. Two are wounded. Their last known location is plotted on this map. The choppers will be waiting when you get to the helipad. Lieutenant, you are the only officer I have available. The men are in your platoon. Bring them home."

We flew out the door. Tad was already behind the wheel of a jeep. We jumped in and sped down the hill. As we drove to the helipad, the OPS NCO asked how I wanted to handle the situation. I had no idea what he was even talking about; I had *no* idea what to do. If I had ever read a map from the air, I was damned if I could remember when. I think he could see all that in my eyes, so he spared me any embarrassment. "Lieutenant, being as you don't know the area yet, I recommend I fly in the C&C helicopter and direct you in on the target. The team will pop a smoke grenade when they're on the LZ and ready to be picked up. They'll throw the smoke grenade. You'll call them on the radio and tell them the color. If they confirm the color, you'll take the bird in and pick them up. That's all there is to it. I don't know if they still have their radio, so I recommend that if you see men in an open area with smoke on the ground, you go in and get them. But it'll be your call. I'll watch from above. If you get in trouble, I'll bring in gunships and come get you. There should be nothing to it." Nothing to it? Jesus, Mary, and Joseph!

When we arrived at the helipad, the choppers were already idling. The crew chief and pilot for each chopper met us. The OPS NCO made a quick introduction, laid the map on the hood of the jeep, and showed both pilots the team's last known location. He also gave them the team's call sign and radio frequency. He said, "They should be within 200 meters of this point. With luck they've already found an LZ and are waiting for us. There are six men, two shot up pretty bad. That's all we know right now. Once airborne we will lock onto their radio frequency and should have a much better idea of what we are going into by the time we get there. The lieutenant will be on the extraction bird, I'll be on the C&C. Let's go."

The crew chief handed me a communication helmet as I got on the chopper and showed me how to operate the toggle switch to talk on the intercom and to listen on the Ranger Frequency. The pilot spun up the RPMs on the engine, raised the chopper into a hover, tilted the nose down, and we headed down the runway a few meters before transitioning to lift and gaining altitude. Then we were fully airborne with LZ English quickly shrinking to our rear. As soon as we were at altitude, I flipped the switch to intercom. "Hey, guys, I don't want y'all to think for a minute I can't do this once we get on the ground, but I need to tell you that today is literally my first day on the job. I just arrived in country four days ago. I have never read a map from the air and even if I had, I have no idea where we are on this damn thing."

The pilot replied; "Not a problem, L-T. I know where we're going and will let you know when we get close. All you have to do is look for their smoke and let us know if you see it before we do."

Relieved that I didn't have to be overly worried about navigation, I flipped the toggle to listen to the C&C bird and any communication from the Team or the Company HQ. The radio was quiet.

Despite everything that was going on, I was amazed by the beauty of the country below. This was the first time I had seen Vietnam flying low and at a relatively slow speed. It was gorgeous. Bright-green rice paddies separated into large squares by berms and dikes were directly below us, and I could see the people knee deep in the paddies planting rice and walking along the dikes. Mountains quickly replaced rice paddies, and then we were flying over lush foliage, so thick in places you couldn't see the ground. I looked at my map. It was dotted with little black squares that indicated houses, but those houses were no longer there. I didn't have time to think about where they went.

The radio came alive, "Lucky Star, this is Silver 6. I have you in sight and am popping smoke at this time. Identify." I looked between the pilot and the copilot. In a few seconds, perhaps two kilometers directly to our front, I saw yellow smoke drifting towards the heavens. We were dead on target. God in heaven; I didn't even know my own call sign! I would use the chopper call sign, "Silver 6, this is Lucky Star. I see yellow smoke. We are coming to get you. What is your situation?"

"Confirm yellow smoke. Two hurt bad. Moving to LZ at this time. Will be there when you are. Not, repeat, not receiving enemy fire at this time. Do you copy? Over."

"Copy. We will be there in two shakes. Secure LZ as best you can. Out."

The pilot came on the intercom. "Lieutenant, the team popped smoke too early, they are not yet on the LZ, but I can see where they are headed. I can get in there with no sweat. Just get your boys on the bird as quick as you can, and we will get the hell out of there."

Looking out the front of the helicopter between the two pilots, I could also see the LZ. It was a fairly large field of grass surrounded by trees. Perhaps at one time it had been a garden that someone had cut out of the forest to raise vegetables for their village. Either way, from my training I could tell the LZ was large enough to land and take off successfully, even under enemy fire. I got ready to help the men onto the chopper.

The primary helicopter used in Vietnam was the UH-1 Iroquois. It was called a Huey—I guess because the "UH" sounds like "Hugh." There were different models of the UH-1. The one used to airlift troops in Vietnam between 1968 and 1970 was the UH-1D. However, the only discernible difference between various models was that the "D" model was larger with a bigger engine than earlier models, so it could carry more passengers. It was about sixty feet long.

A Huey carried a crew of four: pilot, copilot, door gunner, and crew chief. Once airborne, the crew chief acted as an additional door gunner. The "slick" (a Huey used to transport troops) had two M-60 machine guns, one mounted in the sliding-door opening on each side. A Ranger Team consisted of six men. The maximum load of a UH-1D was ten plus crew. The more men it carried, the more difficult it was to maneuver and the more space it needed to take off.

A helicopter can come in straight down and go out straight up, but that is seldom done unless in an emergency (or to impress girls from the States on a USO tour). It takes too much power. Going straight up or down also puts the aircraft in what is considered the "Dead Man's Zone" for an extended period of time. The Dead Man's Zone is that part of the flight envelope where there is not enough airspeed or altitude to perform a successful autorotation if the engine fails. Moreover, even with enough power, straight up and down makes the aircraft more vulnerable to ground fire. Come in hot (machine guns firing), and get out low and fast is the best way to avoid ground fire.

One of the jobs of a Ranger Team was to be on the lookout constantly for a "good" LZ just in case it was needed. The chopper needed at least forty meters to land at all, and the more room the better. A Ranger team of six would add approximately 1,500 pounds to the flight load, a significant weight if you're trying to get out of a tight LZ under enemy fire. The chopper was your ticket to safety, so finding the best possible LZ was in everyone's best interest. Yes, you could be extracted by a rope ladder dropped from the helicopter, but that was to be avoided if at all possible. It was very difficult to hold the helicopter steady while men climbed the rope, and the men on the rope were sitting ducks to ground fire. A Ranger did not want a rope extraction!

A helicopter can take a lot of rounds and still fly. Even a hit to the tail rotor or main rotor blade usually allows the pilot to fly far enough away to make a safe landing; same with a round in the transmission. A hit to a control lever, fuel line, or cable makes for a bad day, but those are small targets and hard to hit. But a bullet hitting the engine—and, obviously, a bullet hitting both pilots—will ruin everyone's day.

Like a bumble bee aerodynamically, a helicopter is not supposed to fly. So it would only make sense that the men flying them would be barking mad. They did stuff no sane person would even attempt. Regardless of how many bullets were flying on the ground, if you needed extracting they would come get you. They cared a hell of a lot more about the infantryman on the ground than they did about their own safety. The greatest guys in the world. However, as I said, crazy as a March Hare. You wouldn't want your sister to marry one.

Our chopper came in low and fast, and as it settled in the tall grass of the LZ, the nose came up, much like when pulling on the reins of a horse. True to their word, the men were already running to the chopper before we were fully on the ground. One was being carried/dragged by two others, and another was carrying an extra rucksack and rifle. The wounded

Ranger was bleeding badly from a leg wound, and it looked like his right hand was gone. (It wasn't; I just couldn't see it because of the blood). I stepped off the chopper to let the men board. Attempting to help would have slowed things down; his buddies carefully laid him on the floor of the chopper. I was about to signal the pilot to get out when I realized there were only five Rangers, not six.

I grabbed the last guy getting into the chopper by the sleeve, "I was told there were six men on this patrol. Where is the sixth?" The kid looked at me with wild, scared eyes as big as saucers. "I think he's dead; we left him on the trail. Couldn't carry him. Fire was too heavy." He tried to break my grip on his arm and get into the chopper, but I wouldn't let him go. "You left him? You fucking left him? Where the hell did you leave him?" I screamed.

One of the men helping with the wounded man pushed the other man into the chopper and yelled in my ear, "Sir, we had no choice. We could't carry them both. I think the other man is dead." Pointing to my rear, "He is on the trail just inside that treeline. We dragged him as far as we could, but we had to leave. There was nothing we could do."

Mother of God. Now what? I grabbed the door gunner and yelled in his ear that there was one man still in the wood line. I was going to get him. Tell the pilot to get the chopper airborne, and tell the C&C ship to come in and pick us up as soon as he sees my smoke. I thought to myself, "I have about as much business out here as a bulldog on a coon hunt. How could this be happening?"

I turned around and ran for the treeline where the Ranger had pointed. I had no idea what I would do or how I would do it. All I knew was I could not leave a man behind. There is now a written creed that says exactly those words, but in those days there was nothing in writing. Nevertheless, it was drilled into every Ranger: "No Ranger Left Behind." We didn't need it in writing.

The chopper rose in the air about three feet, dipped its nose and started forward, with the pilot hoping to gain enough airspeed to clear the trees to his front and to not take enemy rounds. I didn't wait to see if it cleared the trees. I was running fast to the treeline. So far my luck had held. We took no enemy fire coming in, on the ground, or going out. The entire operation had taken less than ten minutes.

When I reached the brush, I could hear the chopper in the background. It had cleared the trees and was quickly moving out of the area. I could see where the Rangers broke onto the LZ and quickly moved to where the brush was flattened from the men running and dragging the wounded man. The Team Leader was correct; the wounded Ranger was on the trail just a few meters inside the brush.

Suddenly, or so it seemed, it was deathly quiet. I could no longer hear the rotor blades from the Huey. There was no wind, no birds, no sound, no nothing. Only then did I realize that in all the haste to get on the helicopter, no one had issued me a weapon. I had no rifle! The "Timber" call had come in, and in everyone's excitement I jumped into the jeep and was so worried about what I was supposed to do, what I was going to do, and how I was going to do it that I never thought to ask for a weapon. God, what was I doing here? My own stupidity had put me in a situation that no soldier should ever be in. I was scared, really, really scared, maybe for the first time in my life.

I focused my attention on the wounded Ranger. I could see his rucksack where the men had dropped it as they were rushing to the LZ, and, praise God, I could also see his weapon. I raced to the rifle, insured there was a round in the chamber, grabbed the rucksack, and then went to the body. The kid was not moving. Initially, like the men on his team, I thought he was dead. However, as I eased him onto his back, he opened his eyes and tried to speak. I told him I was not going to leave him. We were getting out of there, and he had nothing to worry about.

It was still deathly quiet. Nothing was moving. I could almost hear the sweat pouring out of my body. I gently lifted the man and, after the second attempt, got him into a fireman's carry, with his right arm over my neck resting on my left shoulder and my right arm over his right leg. I grabbed his right hand with my right hand and tried to stand up. But I couldn't do it. He was too heavy, or, better stated, I was too weak. In addition to his actual weight, he also still had on his equipment, including ammo and grenades, items I could not leave behind for the VC to use on us at some later date. I grabbed his rucksack and placed it at my feet. Bracing myself against it, I was able to stand. I had no idea what was inside the rucksack. I prayed it was not full of ammo, but I had no choice but to leave it. I was not even certain I could carry the Ranger, but I knew I could not carry him and his rucksack. I started to walk, carrying his rifle in my left hand by the carrying handle. If I came under fire I would be dead before I could ever get the rifle to my shoulder, but at least I now had a weapon.

I wanted to run, but I could barely walk under the load. It wasn't like in training; there the guy you were carrying "helped" you. He wasn't supposed to, but he did just the same. This man couldn't help. He was truly dead weight. I took a few steps and stopped. I had to catch my breath. If I went down with him, I'd never get back up. I started walking again. The trail was stifling; it took my breath away. I felt as though I'd used up a week's worth of oxygen.

Knowing the other chopper would land as soon as I reached the LZ and popped smoke, I reached for a smoke grenade on the Ranger's web gear. But I lost my balance, and down I went. The Ranger moaned when he hit the ground, so I knew he was still alive. But I had lost my hold on him. I would have to put him on my back again. Pulling the smoke grenade off the Ranger's web gear, I put it on the ground and again tried to pick him up. I got him over my shoulder but couldn't stand. I had left his rucksack, so I had nothing to support me. I was not strong enough to do a clean lift with no support. Hell, I could barely stand up myself. I would pop the smoke grenade where I was, wait for the chopper, and get help when it landed.

I laid the Ranger gently on the ground and reached for the grenade. There was still no sound. I heard nothing. But suddenly I felt a hand on my back, "Hey, Lieutenant, let me help you." The OPS sergeant had come from nowhere. I looked behind him and there was the C&C bird sitting not more than thirty meters away. It had come in without my hearing it. Moreover, the NCO was able to walk right up to me, and I never even knew he was there. I was proving myself to be just one hell of a Ranger. Maybe I could get a job as the Quartermaster Officer, making certain everyone had clean socks. Shit.

I ran back, retrieved the rucksack, we put the wounded Ranger between us, and we moved to the chopper. The door gunner helped us lift the Ranger onto the chopper, I jumped in and the OPS sergeant followed. I sat on the floor just behind the pilot's seat. I put the Ranger's head in my lap. The sergeant got a bandage and wrapped it around a wound in the Ranger's leg. Another bandage went onto his stomach, where there was a hole but not much blood. The NCO told me to hold the compress tight against his chest, and I did as I was told.

The Ranger had opened his eyes again and was looking directly into mine. I told him he would be okay and that we would have him home in a few minutes. He said nothing, only looked at me. He lifted his right arm and placed his hand over mine (the one holding the bandage). I released pressure on the bandage and held his hand. Tight.

As we were coming in for the landing, I felt his hand grip even tighter. Then it just sort of froze onto my hand. His eyes looked at me and then rolled. His mouth opened a little and then his entire body went limp.

His shallow breathing stopped. The kid had died in my arms. When the helicopter landed, even before the blades stopped turning, medics with a stretcher were at the door. I helped them ease the Ranger onto the stretcher and, still holding his hand, ran with them into the aid tent on the edge of the helipad.

Inside the aid tent, the medics transferred the Ranger from the stretcher to a table. Someone, I think it was the company commander, gently took my hand and told me to wait outside, saying I had done all I could do and they would take care of him now.

It was dark when I walked out of the aid tent. It was probably dark when we landed. I don't remember. But I walked over to some sandbags and sat down. A medic walked up and asked how I was doing and if he could help. I looked at him funny and wondered why he would ask such a question but said I was fine and asked for a cigarette. He gave me a smoke but said I should get a doctor to look at me as soon as possible. Still not understanding what he was talking about I looked down at my uniform for the first time. It was soaked with blood—pants, shirt, everything. The medic thought I was bleeding to death. I told him I was fine, that I would change clothes when I got back up the hill. He gave me another cigarette and left me alone.

As I was finishing the second cigarette, someone else walked by, and I bummed another smoke. After finishing that one I got up and started walking back to the company. I had no idea where I was except that I was in the building complex near the helipad. I walked between some wooden buildings and finally came out on the main road leading up the hill. I saw brigade headquarters to my right, so I turned left and continued to walk. I passed the brigade chapel on my left. I stopped. No reason. Nothing to do with God. I was just tired and needed to sit down a minute. There was a bench in front of the chapel.

I walked to the bench and sat down. I could not understand what had just happened. That kid had died in my arms. I didn't want him to die. I didn't want to die. I no longer wanted anyone to die. I was not mad at these people. If they wanted to be Communists, what business was it of mine? I didn't want to hurt them; I didn't even know them. Hell, I didn't want to hurt anyone. I didn't understand why they wanted to hurt me. I didn't want to be a Ranger anymore. I didn't want to be a soldier anymore. I wanted my girlfriend to hold me. I wanted my daddy to hold me. I wanted to go home. I started to cry and I kept crying. I could not stop. I cried all night.

I never even knew the Ranger's name.

Thomas Zapata (1967, E-2) 525th Military Intelligence Group, 1969

I arrived in RVN on March 10, 1969, and was assigned to the 525th Military Intelligence Group, where I spent two months with its 3rd Battalion Headquarters in Bien Hoa. After that stint I was assigned to a small MI team attached to MACV Advisory Team 47 in An Loc, Binh Long Province, in what is known as the Fishhook. The province was bordered on the west and north by Cambodia. After a couple of months I took over command of the team.

The MI team operated independent of the advisors. Our mission was to work with the Hmong tribesmen looking for NVA and VC units operating in the area. Any intelligence we received was provided to the combat units. At that time those units were the 3rd Battalion, 1st Air Cav and the 11th Armored Cavalry Regiment.

Binh Long Province had some large rubber plantations bordering the thick jungle. It was quite a dichotomy: neat rows of trees and triple-canopy jungle. Some plantations still had the remains of grandiose homes belonging to French owners or caretakers. When I traveled to Loc Ninh, farther north and much closer to Cambodia, I dealt with Hmong tribesmen from Cambodia. There was a small detachment of US advisors, no more than ten soldiers, in Loc Ninh. The compound was secured by Regional Forces/Popular Forces. Next to that compound was a Special Forces Compound that was occupied infrequently.

The MACV Team in Loc Ninh employed a cook who previously had worked for a local French plantation. He was excellent in the kitchen, and it was a refreshing change from our normal menus.

I am one of the lucky ones who made it back from Vietnam unscathed. Some of our Aggie buddies were not so fortunate. In my opinion the leaders of our country failed us, and the suffering and waste of life is on their conscience. We don't seem to learn the lessons of history.

Mac Phillips (1969, D-1) 101st Airborne Division, 1971

In early March of 1971 my infantry battalion in the 1st Cavalry Division stood down for redeployment back to the States. I had been a rifle-platoon leader for five and a half months, but that wasn't enough time for me to go home. Instead I was transferred to the 101st Airborne Division, where I took over a platoon in A Company, 1st Battalion, 327th Infantry. We worked the area from Camp Eagle at Phu Bai westward along Route 1 to the Ashau Valley. On the east side were high mountains; on the west was Laos. In between were several FSBs, including Bastogne and Birmingham, that received the occasional rocket or mortar attack. We spent most of our time patrolling the jungle, setting up ambushes, and performing bomb-damage assessments. My company commander, Capt. Martin Niskanen, was a West Pointer, an excellent company commander, and a great guy to work for.

On April 19, 1971, we entered FSB Birmingham after several weeks of patrolling the bush to provide security and to get a short break from humping the jungle. The first night several of us were sitting around talking when I told the captain about the traditions of Aggie Muster and that there was to be one at Camp Eagle. The next day, after we had established guard posts and performed other FSB duties, Captain Niskanen approached and said, "Phillips, I need you to catch a ride to Camp Eagle tomorrow morning [April 21, Aggie Muster Day] and pick up the company mail. Make sure you make it back before dark." He made no mention of Muster. That was just the kind of leader he was.

The next morning I caught a ride to Camp Eagle, where I joined about a half-dozen Aggies in meeting for fellowship and to pay our respects to those who had died in the past year. There wasn't much drinking. All of us had duties to return to quickly. I barely made it out of Eagle before the curfew gates were closed to ground traffic. My ride was with a couple of ARVNs who said they would get me and my mailbag to Birmingham—about an hour away—before dark.

Everything went routinely until we reached the Perfume River bridge. The ARVNs decided to go off the main road to a nearby village to drink a few beers. I knew that wasn't going to happen. I had them let me, my mail bag, and my M-16 off on the bridge. I walked to the middle of the structure and backed up against a metal support beam to protect my backside. A lot of locals were on the bridge, but I was the only American in sight, and it was less than half an hour to full darkness. I decided to wait a while in hopes another vehicle would come down the road headed for the FSB. If one did not show up soon I decided I would calmly walk off the bridge into the nearby jungle and escape and evade until the next morning. Thoughts of being killed or even captured by the enemy during the night went through my mind.

I was scared—scared shitless as the troops used to say—to the point of wetting my pants. Just as I was about to move off the bridge and into the jungle, a jeep approached with two American NCOs who were in a hurry to get off the road and into the fire base. I jumped in the vehicle and soon was inside the wire of Birmingham. Captain Niskanen took the mailbag but said nothing other than, "You cut it kind of close didn't you?"

I don't think I've missed an Aggie Muster since. However, none compares to the one in Camp Eagle and the fear and borderline panic I felt trying to get back to FSB Birmingham before dark.

Larry Vetter (1964, A-1 and I-3) 3rd Marine Division, 1965–66 and 1968–69

I served in the United States Marine Corps from 1964 to 1970 and was in Vietnam for eighteen months, in 1965–66 and again from mid-1968 to mid-1969. On my first tour I was a 2nd and 1st Lieutenant with the USMC Engineers as a platoon leader and with the 3rd Reconnaissance Battalion as a platoon leader and patrol leader. When I returned for my second trip I was initially a brigade-engineer officer, and during the second half of the tour I commanded an infantry company.

I wrote two books about the conflict that were published by Ivy Books, a division of Random House. The first is historical fiction, *Blood on the Lotus*. Although it's a novel, it's basically a true story about my experiences and those of a Vietnamese woman who fought against us whom I encountered shortly before returning from my second tour. She initiated a change in my way of thinking about the war.

The second book, *Never without Heroes*, is a history of the 3rd Recon Battalion's four and a half years in country.

After Vietnam and the Marine Corps, I got my master's in city planning from A&M in 1971. Subsequently I served for twenty-five years as a city-planning director in three cities including Kerrville, Texas. My wife died in 2010, and two years later I returned to Vietnam, where I now work with the victims of Agent Orange, which we sprayed and dumped on this land and people (as well as our own troops). I have lived here since 2012 and love the experience. The land is beautiful, and the people love America, or at least are very interested in it and us. They also dislike, distrust, and almost hate China. Plus the dollar goes about five times as far here as in the States. You don't even know you work and live in a country ruled by one political party.

Our community of ex-pats is fun and interesting. Da Nang, where I live, is one of the most beautiful places you will find, with about forty miles of beachfront along the north and east. The non-resort restaurants there are pretty cheap, and nearby are two championship-caliber golf courses sponsored by Greg Norman and Colin Montgomery.

Steve Hightower (1968, D-3 and A-2) 101st Airborne Division, 1969

On July 21, 1969, after a very short year of marriage, I left my wife and boarded the bus from downtown San Francisco for Travis Air Force Base. While I was in the waiting room at Travis with hundreds of others en route to their year in Vietnam, I watched Neil Armstrong become the first man to walk on the moon. I remember thinking, "Wow, this is a special moment." And it was, in more ways than one.

After my in-country processing in Long Binh, I was assigned to the 3rd Brigade, 101st Airborne Division. I took a C-130 flight to Camp Eagle, near Phu Bai, and then a CH-47 up to Camp Evans, where I found myself, along with two other replacement officers, at the 3rd Battalion, 187th Infantry Battalion headquarters. My welcome to the battalion was memorable. We three lieutenants were standing in front of the Battalion S-1 getting our assignments and a brief orientation. As we began, one lieutenant, whose name I forgot immediately, said, "Excuse me sir, I have allergies and have to have shots every day. Will I be able to get them if I am in the field?"

The other lieutenant and I exchanged looks, which I can only describe today as, "What the ****!" The S-1, who looked pretty haggard, came around the desk, handed the lieutenant his paperwork, and pretty much threw him out of the building with the comment, "Go back to brigade, and don't ever let me see you again." I ran into that allergic lieutenant several months later when en route to R&R. He had become the division's R&R officer.

I was assigned as the 3rd Platoon Leader in B Company, 3/187. In mid-May 1969, B Company, along with the rest of the 3/187, had borne the brunt of the fighting in the assault on Hill 937 (Ap Bia Mountain) or, as it later became known, "Hamburger Hill," in the A Shau Valley. During the week-long battle, the battalion had suffered more than three hundred killed or wounded, including two of its four company commanders and eight of its twelve platoon leaders.

After Hamburger, the battalion had been declared "combat ineffective" because of the number of casualties and was sent to guard a bridge over the Perfume River outside Hue City. For the remainder of May and June the company received replacements and began an intensive training program. These new infantrymen included many "kids" fresh out of AIT.

It also included a number of replacements whose only "infantry" training had been in Basic. Then they had trained to become cooks, chaplain assistants, clerks, you name it. However, with the manpower shortages in our battalion, many had been reassigned to the infantry. I ended up with several of these new, unwilling, infantrymen in my platoon.

By the time I joined B Company in July, the company had been deemed "combat effective" and began performing operational missions, one of which was to make an assault back onto the crest of Hamburger Hill and establish a temporary fire base in support of other operations in the western A Shau Valley. I flew out to join B Company on Hamburger with my battalion commander, Lt. Col. Weldon Honeycutt (call sign "Black Jack"), who was piloting his own Loach. Because the company was receiving some light mortar at the time of my arrival, the helicopter copilot turned around and shouted, "We can't land, so when I point at you . . . jump." I did and was quickly met by my company commander. Capt. John "Butch" Chappelle, an experienced officer on his second tour of duty in Vietnam, had taken command of B Company when the previous company commander was wounded during the May battle for Hamburger. I quickly grew to respect Butch Chappelle.

During the next several days, as I met my NCOs and troops of the 3rd Platoon and began to settle in, we received intermittent, but increasingly heavy, mortar fire. I distinctly remember the undertone of conversations among the few remaining veterans of Hamburger: this was "bad shit," and we were going to get a ground attack soon. On the third or fourth night the enemy attacked. Captain Chappelle had one of the new Starlite scopes and was using it to scan out in front of our company's positions. Later he told me that when one of the sappers (who were crawling into their assault positions) turned his head slightly, he saw the sapper's cowlick through the scope. At that point, Chappelle quietly passed the order to "stand by for a sapper attack." On his command we began firing and preempted and spoiled the assault.

Like most leaders in combat, I was so busy during that first firefight that I don't remember many details other than trying first to ensure that I didn't "screw up" and get one of my soldiers wounded or killed and second to control and direct the fire of my platoon. At first light we checked the ground in front of our positions and found a number of NVA soldiers dead and numerous blood trails leading off the hill toward the Laotian border. The company had suffered no casualties. Much of the credit for this goes to Butch Chappelle.

The immediate and noticeable impact of the sapper attack on my platoon was that much of the talk changed, from pessimism to cautious optimism regarding the f'ing new guys' ability to soldier and fight. The pessimism persisted of course. "Just wait 'til we hit the *really* bad shit, and we'll see how you do." But we moved off Hamburger Hill a changed unit, still green and unproven but a bit better than we had been.

After moving off Hamburger Hill my platoon was cross-attached to an armored cavalry troop with M-113 ACAVs and M-48 tanks operating on the floor of the A Shau Valley. As I recall, this was the first deployment of armor into the A Shau and, for us "grunts" of the B/3/187, getting to ride instead of "humping" was a great deal . . . at first. Not long after we joined the Cav we learned that because armor was loud, it served as a magnet for any and all NVA units within earshot. We received increasing mortar fire in our NDPs and several ground attacks—all focused on knocking out the armor.

My company filled in the gaps between M-48s and ACAVs in the perimeter at night as the Cav troops had a tendency to stay on, and in, their vehicles. We quickly learned that, although the armor seemed like great support, it's hard to beat a hole in the ground for protection against direct rifle and RPG fire.

One night, at about 2:00 A.M., we received an NVA sapper attack. The opening shot was a direct RPG hit on the M-48 tank next to my foxhole. It definitely got my attention. The explosion also woke up and scared the hell out of my new RTO, who had been with us for only about a week. In my brief initial conversation with the young soldier, he told me he was a devout Christian and had been a chaplain's assistant and that he was one of those who had become a "reclassified infantryman" after the Battle of Hamburger Hill. I quickly got on the radio to for instructions from my CO and to get a handle on the status of my platoon during the attack. As I was talking on the radio, and otherwise distracted, I felt the handset being slowly and steadily pulled from my hand. As I turned to see what was going on, my new radio operator suddenly jumped to his feet proclaiming, "God will save us!"

I grabbed him, pulled him to the ground, and told him, "Keep your ass on the ground, and don't move unless I do." He stayed low. The rest of the night was one of intermittent probes against our positions with sappers and RPGs and some 60-mm and 82-mm mortar fire. The only US casualty was the M-48 tank that had suffered mechanical issues previously and was parked with its rear engine compartment facing the outside of the perimeter. The RPG had hit in the tank's engine compartment and it was now definitely "red-lined," or "dead."

The next morning, my platoon sergeant, a staff sergeant on his second tour in Vietnam, came up to me with both a smile and an extension cord for my radio handset, saying, "L-T, you may want to use this."

I did, and I also found a new, less-excitable, RTO.

Ed McDaniel (1965, D-1) Naval Intelligence Liaison Officer—Quang Ngai, 1969

As a part of my duties as a Naval intelligence officer, I was flying one day with an Army Aerial Observer in an 0–1 Bird Dog aircraft—a tandem-seat Cessna. It was late in the afternoon when we saw a young man walking along the beach, a rather unusual activity: all the young men in Vietnam were either in the South Vietnamese military or working for the VC unless they were physically disabled—and this man appeared to be in fine physical shape. Carrying no visible weapons, wearing only a shirt and shorts, he seemed to ignore us and kept walking along the beach as we flew by. Even more interesting was the fact that he was in a "free-fire zone."

I radioed the US Army advisory team co-located with the District Chief (a Vietnamese Army colonel), reported the sighting, and requested instructions. After five or ten minutes the District HQ radioed us with instructions that we were cleared to fire.

The 0–1 Bird Dog had no weapons, and the pilot usually had only a pistol, but I always carried an M-16—except on this trip. For some reason I had taken an M-79 grenade launcher, which definitely was not designed as an air-to-surface weapon. But we decided, "What the hell. Let's give it a try."

As we flew back over the guy, I leaned out of the window and popped off a round. The grenade launcher puts spin on the projectile (to arm it) but much less than a rifle or machine gun. We both figured the grenade would travel more or less straight toward the target. Neither the pilot nor I had considered the effects of physics. (The only course I had at A&M was "Physics for Agriculture Students.") The plane's forward motion coupled with the projectile's spin placed an exaggerated rotation on the grenade, the diameter of which grew exponentially. It landed and detonated on the beach well behind my aim point, causing no harm, just redistributing some sand. Based on our previous experiences, the pilot and I expected the Vietnamese to run for cover beyond the treeline, only thirty yards or so from the water line. The pilot yelled for me to reload as he put the plane in a steep downward dive. In short order, I was back in firing position at the ready.

But the Vietnamese did not run for the treeline. Instead he stood with arms straight out to the side, pivoting to keep facing us, as we spiraled down. When we drew abreast of him again, at three hundred feet or less altitude and a few hundred feet away, I could clearly see his facial features—even made eye contact. He never took his eyes off us, and he kept his arms stretched out—behavior totally inconsistent with our experience and expectations. I leaned out, took aim, stopped, sat back down, and told the pilot, "I don't think the guy is a VC. But if he is, he is damn smart, and this country needs some smart citizens." The pilot agreed completely, and we flew off into the sunset, returning to base.

I never had any moral qualms about pulling the trigger, but I also never fully accepted the free-fire-zone concept. The rural Vietnamese lived a hard life, much of which was a struggle for daily subsistence. They often entered free-fire zones out of ignorance to gather firewood or for other economic considerations. From that perspective, there simply were not enough indicators to convince me the guy was a VC. Maybe he was. Who knows? But it is still terribly funny to recall that M-79 projectile's downward spiral.

During my twelve months in Vietnam, I had the experience of being shot at by a wide variety of weapons in a diversity of contexts. But perhaps the most vulnerable I ever felt was during a "social event" with a group of our allies.

One evening while I was working with the MACV SOG team based at NAD Da Nang, the OINC (a Navy Seal) decided we needed to conduct a visit to the RVN Seals Club, where activities were in full swing. It reminded me of a Dodge City bar with a group of just-arrived trail herders. This being my first visit, I was quickly introduced to several of the Vietnamese Seals. It is probably worth noting that many of these men were originally from the north and had relocated to the south in 1954 when the country was divided. Thus they were much more motivated than the typical ARVN recruit. Moreover, this group had run clandestine missions into North Vietnam until a US policy change terminated the program.

Aware of their feats and reputation, I had considerable respect (even awe) for this group of men. So I was rather astonished when, after our introduction, one Vietnamese Seal sat in my lap and planted a very wet French kiss in my ear.

When relating this story, I'm always asked, "What did you do?"

To which I reply, "I sat very, very still."

Larry Sommers (1968, C-1) Infantry Officer Basic Course, 1969

Upon graduating from A&M in June of 1968 I was gung-ho and proud of my commission as a 2nd Lieutenant in the Infantry. All nine graduating seniors from Saber C (Compay C-1) looked forward to serving and answering our country's call for Vietnam.

Shortly after commissioning I headed over to the Trigon to get my reporting date for active duty and instructions for initial entry into the Army. As the Army was in a major buildup to meet the growing demands of President Johnson's escalation of the war, I was told I would be scheduled for my IOBC within six months, and would receive my orders in November for a January IOBC class. I was disappointed at the delay but accepted this as a temporary pause in my goal of leading men in combat.

In November I anxiously started checking my mailbox for reporting instructions—only to be disappointed when no orders showed up. Just before Thanksgiving I called the Trigon to get a status update and was told my orders would come from the ROTC command at Fort Sam Houston. A&M would follow-up for me. Just sit tight, and I would be contacted soon. Being new to Army bureaucracy, I didn't know better than to just sit tight and wait.

When mid-December came, I knew I'd have to do something if I was going to get an IOBC class in January. After numerous calls I finally got the assignments clerk at Fort Sam Houston—only to discover they had no record of my graduation and commissioning. Several days had passed when I received a call back. They were glad I had called. My file had to be reconstructed, and had I not contacted them, in all likelihood I would never have received orders. Three days later orders arrived directing me to report to the June, 1969, IOBC class.

I often wonder about my fate had my records not been misplaced and had I entered active duty on my expected January 1969 date. Certainly my Vietnam War stories would have been different. Such is life.

James H. Willbanks (1969, D-2) Advisory Team 87, 18th ARVN Division Combat Assistance Team) 1972

While at A&M I was very much aware that we were in a war. Many Aggies in the classes ahead of me had gone to Vietnam after completing their officer training. I was in the Corps of Cadets, and everyone expected to go sooner or later. After graduating, in May 1969, I reported to Fort Benning, Georgia. Vietnam permeated every phase of the training at Benning. The introduction to every class was: "Listen up. You're going to Vietnam. You need to know this stuff, or you'll get killed or get your people killed."

All the instructors were Vietnam veterans, and most had multiple tours. They tried to prepare us for Vietnam, but I got orders for Germany. I departed for my new assignment late in 1969, eventually reporting to 2nd Battalion, 30th Infantry, 3rd Infantry Division, in Schweinfurt, Germany. I became a rifle-platoon leader in C Company.

At that time the US Army was in desperate trouble in Germany. I had only about half the personnel I was authorized to have, and a number of those assigned were actually in confinement at Mannheim for various criminal offenses. The Army in Europe was rife with drug abuse and race problems. And we lacked adequate operating funds. At one point, because we didn't have enough money to maintain our vehicles, we placed half of them in admin storage. The barracks were falling apart. The whole situation was pretty much a mess.

The situation was so bad that I volunteered to go to Vietnam to get out of Schweinfurt. I was also afraid that I was going to miss the war—a thought I revisited several times in the coming months. It took four tries, but finally my application went through and I received orders to Vietnam as an advisor. I departed Germany and signed in at Fort Bragg, where I attended the Military Assistance Training Advisor course at the JFK Special Warfare Center. The eleven-week course focused on how to be an advisor with the South Vietnamese Army. We also got a little bit of language training. That was built on when I went to the Defense Language Institute Southwest Branch, at Biggs Field, adjacent to Fort Bliss, Texas.

I departed for Vietnam early in December 1971. After landing at Tan Son Nhut, we were bussed to Camp Alpha, a holding area for those coming or going, while we waited for assignments. While I was there, an

NCOs told several of us that the war was over, that we wouldn't even get a Combat Infantryman's Badge. As it turned out, he was wrong on both counts. I soon found out that I was going to Bear Cat to work with the Royal Thai Army in Vietnam. They sent somebody in a jeep to pick me up.

After a month I was told that the Thais were preparing to return home and that I should go find a job. I ended up in an advisory slot with the 18th ARVN Division based at Xuan Loc in eastern Military Region III. I reported into the 48th Regiment, which was located at Long Giao (known as Blackhorse when it was occupied earlier by the 11th US Armored Cavalry Regiment). The regimental advisory team consisted of a lieutenant colonel, three captains, and three NCOs. When a battalion from our regiment went to the field, at least two of us accompanied the unit. I went out on my first operation soon after joining the unit. On the third operation I was wounded. We were conducting a search-and-clear mission in a rubber plantation about ten kilometers from our base when we ran into a regiment-sized ambush. Apparently we got too close to one of their base camps, causing them to react violently.

The ambush looked like one of the examples from a Fort Benning tactics class. We were caught in the kill zone of a large L-shaped ambush. I took cover behind a tree and began to return fire. An RPG-7 round hit the tree, and when it detonated, a fragment of the round struck me in the right leg. In all the confusion, the Vietnamese battalion commander and his staff withdrew, leaving me behind with a bunch of walking wounded. Unfortunately, when they pulled back, they took my radio with them. So for the next twelve hours we continued to fight, attempting to get out of the kill zone. Eventually we were able to break contact. We made our way through the rubber trees for several hours until we reached a road that bordered the plantation, and then we walked to an ARVN outpost, where I borrowed a radio and called my headquarters to provide a situation report. Because it was after dark and none of the wounded, myself included, was critical, we were directed to spend the night at the outpost to be picked up the next day.

After a short stint at the Long Khanh Province Hospital, I was dusted off to 93rd Evac facility in Long Binh. I was there for a week or so. Upon release I was on crutches and could not return to the field, so I reported to the 18th ARVN Division compound at Xuan Loc. While I waited for my leg to heal, I served as the headquarters commandant responsible for downsizing the American compound and turning over part of it to the ARVN.

On March 31 the North Vietnamese Army crossed the DMZ and launched what became known as the Easter Offensive. They attacked first at Quang Tri in Military Region I and followed with major attacks at Kontum in the Central Highlands and in Binh Long Province, just over the border from Snuol, Cambodia. These attacks were part of a massive, three-pronged conventional attack that involved fourteen North Vietnamese divisions and twenty-six separate regiments—more than 130,000 troops and some 1,200 tanks and armored personnel carriers.

In the southern front, the NVA targeted An Loc, the Binh Long provincial capital. The attacking enemy force included the 5th, 7th, and 9th Divisions, plus the 69th Artillery Command, more than 35,000 troops. The initial objective of the attack in Binh Long was Loc Ninh, a district town between the Cambodian border and An Loc. The town was occupied by a regiment and a couple of other units, including an armored cavalry troop, all from the 5th ARVN Division. On April 4 the 9th VC Division (actually an NVA division) surrounded and attacked the town with artillery, rockets, infantry, and tanks. After forty-eight hours the NVA overran the ARVN defenders and their American advisors.

Shortly after taking Loc Ninh, the NVA continued south to attack a two-battalion task force from the 52nd Regiment from our division, which occupied two small firebases between Loc Ninh and An Loc. Under heavy attack, the ARVN troops withdrew toward An Loc. In the course of this move, the three US advisors with the task force were wounded and evacuated. Thus the remainder of the task force that made it back to An Loc had no advisors. Back in Xuan Loc, our colonel asked if anyone wanted to volunteer to replace the evacuated advisors. The cavalry squadron advisor and I volunteered. (I had been off the crutches for a few days.)

We took off in a jeep and drove from Xuan Loc to Saigon and then up to Lai Khe, where we boarded a helicopter that flew us into An Loc. We arrived on April 12 to find a grim situation. Artillery rounds and rockets were falling steadily inside the city. The helicopter that brought us hovered only long enough for us to jump off into a freshly dug hole in the city soccer field. During a lull in the bombardment, we linked up with the task force from our division and began to prepare for the inevitable battle that was to come. With the fall of Loc Ninh, it was clear, the NVA planned to move on An Loc. Maj. Gen. James F. Hollingsworth (Texas A&M, Class of 1940), commander of Third Regional Assistance Command, radioed the advisors in An Loc: "Hold them, and I'll kill them with airpower!"

Just after midnight the NVA began shelling the town with rockets and heavy artillery. In the next fifteen hours, they fired more than seven thousand rounds into the city. At dawn they launched ground attacks from three directions. Our unit was in the north end of town astride Highway 13, which ran from Snuol, Cambodia, sixty-five miles south to Saigon. The attack in that part of the city began when a column of Soviet-made T-54 tanks and several PT-76s drove down the highway from the north directly into our position. Our task force had no antitank weapons, and we had to fall back.

The enemy armored column was finally halted when a soldier from the local territorial forces destroyed the lead tank with an M-72 light antitank weapon. By this time Cobra attack helicopters had arrived, and they took the remaining tanks under fire. Shortly thereafter, a flurry of USAF A-6s, A-7s, F-4s, and A-37s and Vietnamese Air Force A-1s and A-37s arrived, and we began working with a USAF FAC orbiting overhead to put in the airstrikes against the NVA attackers. The battle lasted all day and into the night. We advisors spent our time coordinating the airstrikes and directing the attack helicopters against available targets. At night we worked with the AC-130 Spectre gunships that provided support during the hours of darkness. During the day B-52s from Thailand and Guam pounded the enemy staging areas in the rubber plantations that surrounded the city.

The fighting was bitter, and on several occasions the ARVN defenders nearly broke as the NVA made repeated human-wave attacks. At one point the NVA tanks advanced to within two hundred meters of the 5th ARVN Division CP, firing into it and killing several staff officers. By this point in the battle, the ARVN held the southern half of the city, and the NVA held the northern half. The city was completely surrounded by the NVA and isolated from outside reinforcement by an NVA division that cut Highway 13 between An Loc and Lai Khe. The besieged South Vietnamese defenders, who numbered about three thousand soldiers initially, received a boost in morale when the 1st ARVN Airborne brigade and their US advisors arrived by helicopters east of An Loc and moved into the city to join our defense.

With the aid of US TAC air, attack helicopters, B-52s, and AC-130s, we helped the ARVN hold their positions by coordinating air strike after air strike. The first big push to take the city lasted about seventy-two hours. By April 16, US air support in all its forms had helped turn the tide. The NVA backed off to regroup.

The situation inside the city, however, remained desperate. The enemy continued to pound us with round-the-clock artillery. It was dangerous to leave the bunkers. We were running low on food and ammunition. Because the enemy had ringed the city with air-defense weapons, helicopters were unable to land, and C-130s, forced to take evasive action to avoid intense enemy ground fire, made many air drops outside friendly lines.

On April 19 the NVA launched their second concerted attempt to take the city, attacking with five regiments. Once again the ARVN, strengthened by the addition of the airborne brigade, "circled the wagons" and held on tenaciously while attack helicopters, fighter-bombers, and B-52s pounded the NVA from the air. The ARVN fought doggedly until the air support again turned back the attack.

The situation inside the city continued to deteriorate. Most of it was in ruins. The streets were rubble and were littered with bodies, military and civilian. The smell of death permeated the air. Under these conditions, diseases, including cholera, ran rampant through both military and civilian ranks. To avoid a full-fledged epidemic, bodies were buried in mass graves during lulls in the enemy artillery attacks. Many bodies had to be reburied after exploding shells churned up the original graves. Supplies, particularly of medical gear, were dangerously low. Shortages became so critical that two ARVN doctors boiled nylon from sandbags for use as sutures to stitch up the wounded.

The fighting raged for nearly two more months as the North Vietnamese continually shelled and made repeated attempts to take the city. The ARVN defenders and we advisors continued to use B-52s and TAC air to keep the enemy at bay. In early May, I was extracted from An Loc and replaced by another advisor from my team. After I departed, the North Vietnamese made their last big push to take the city. It was a close-fought battle, but once again air support made the difference. This proved to be the last big attempt to take the city. The artillery and local attacks continued, but the air support had taken such a heavy toll on the enemy that they could not mount another multi-regiment ground attack.

The situation inside the city improved somewhat. The Air Force had devised a method using high-altitude–low-opening parachutes to insure that more of the air-dropped supplies landed inside the city. There was also a lessening in the number of artillery rounds that fell daily.

Later that month I joined one of the fresh regiments from my division that had not been involved in the fight at An Loc. Helicopters from Task

Force Garry Owen from the 1st Cavalry Division inserted us along Highway 13 just south of the city. We made our way into the town to relieve the task force I had originally been with. Things had calmed down considerably, but the city was still technically under siege, taking sporadic artillery fire and coming under periodic local ground attacks.

On June 18, in a surprise visit, South Vietnamese president Nguyen Van Thieu flew into An Loc to congratulate the victorious ARVN defenders. They had taken everything the North Vietnamese could throw at them and held on to the city despite overwhelming odds. Before flying back to Saigon, Thieu declared the siege of An Loc broken. Nevertheless, the enemy continued to shell the city periodically and the road south was still blocked by an NVA division.

More fresh troops flew in, and over the next few weeks they began to expand the perimeter. On July 9, General Hollingsworth's deputy, Brig. Gen. John Tallman, flew into the city with three of his staff officers. Another advisor and I went out to meet the general's helicopter. As they landed, the enemy began to shell the landing zone. The other officer and I directed the general and his party into spider holes that had been dug in the area. When it appeared that the artillery fire had stopped, we all came out of the holes and began to run for the command bunker, but another round landed right in the middle of the group, killing the three staff officers and a South Vietnamese soldier instantly and mortally wounding the general. The other officer and I were both wounded. Other advisors called in a helicopter, which picked up the grievously wounded general, the other officer, and me. Both the other officer and I survived our wounds, but the general died on the operating table at 3rd Field Hospital.

After a month in the hospital in Saigon, I returned to my unit headquarters at Xuan Loc, but I never went back to An Loc. I served out the last few months of my tour and returned to the States in December of 1972.

(Willbanks is a prolific author on military subjects. His Battle of An Loc {Bloomington: Indiana University Press, 2015} more thoroughly details the above story.)

Hale Burr (1965, Squadron 7 and Corps Staff) 20th Tactical Support Squadron, 1967–68

In 1966 assignments after pilot training were based on numerical class standing. I selected the only guaranteed combat-tour aircraft available to my class—an F-4 Phantom tour in Vietnam (as opposed to F-4 bases in the States, Europe, or Japan). About ten months later I finished three survival schools (SERE in Washington State, Water Survival in Florida, and Jungle Survival in the Philippines), and my six-month F-4 training checkout in Florida.

I was then assigned to Cam Ranh Bay Air Base, South Vietnam. The Air Force policy for completion of a Vietnam combat tour was flying 100 missions over North Vietnam (usually completed in six to nine months) or one year in country, whichever came first. Because Cam Ranh Bay is on the coast in the middle of South Vietnam, nearly five hundred miles from primary NVN targets, most NVN combat sorties were flown by F-4 pilots stationed at bases nearer NVN, at Da Nang AB, or at Ubon and Udorn Air Bases in Thailand. Our F-4 wing flew mostly interdiction and Close Air Support sorties in SVN and Laos.

During my first combat tour, in 1967–68, the losses of US aircraft were very high. This was true not only of our fighter planes but also of our FAC aircraft. The US Army and Air Force had an agreement that to be a FAC with an American army unit, one had to be a current and qualified fighter pilot. After six months in the 557th Tactical Fighter Squadron at Cam Ranh Bay AB, I had flown only about 20 missions over NVN. I knew I'd never get to 100. So when a personnel request came down from 7th AF Headquarters in Saigon for replacement Forward Air Controllers, I immediately volunteered. In five days I was reassigned and checked out in the Cessna O-2A at Phan Rang AB before heading north to I Corps.

One of the most significant events of my life took place while I was at Phan Rang. Our first daughter was born in Nederland, Texas. The Red Cross notification arrived three days after her birth. I bought cigars and cognac for the instructor pilots and my fellow students. We enjoyed it while sitting on the Phan Rang Officers Club patio on a hillside overlooking the airbase.

After only five days of checkout I went from a supersonic Mach 2-capable F-4 Phantom jet fighter to a twin-boom Cessna O-2A Skymaster whose tandem-mounted engines pushed it along at an airspeed of about 140 miles per hour.

Besides aircraft performance, there was a significant difference in living conditions. At Cam Ranh Bay I lived in an air-conditioned hooch with the rest of the pilots in my squadron. We had hot showers, and local Vietnamese cleaned our rooms, shined our boots, and did our laundry. Our 557th Squadron had, in addition to the base Officers Club, its own bar and patio adjoining our quarters. Two Aggie buddies, Sgt. Buddy Bullock, Class of 1965, who was not commissioned out of A&M when we graduated and was subsequently drafted as an enlisted man in the Army, and 2nd Lt. Russ Stein, Class of 1966, were stationed at Army installations near the air base. Both frequently brought a box of steaks over to my squadron and were warmly greeted and plied with adult beverages while we fighter pilots grilled their offering on the patio. Also, after we flew for five or six weeks straight, we received five days of leave. Because Cam Ranh Bay was an aerial port, we could catch space-available flights to Japan, Hong Kong, the Philippines, Singapore, Bangkok, and other sites for some R&R.

So what was life like for a fighter pilot serving as a FAC with the Army? I was assigned to the 20th TASS at Da Nang but lived with the four thousand officers and soldiers of the 3rd Brigade, 82nd Airborne Division, for the next six months. In mid-February 1968, after the end of the Tet surprise attack, the 3rd Brigade had shipped out from Fort Bragg to Vietnam and was under the operational control of the 101st Airmobile Division. Our FAC contingent consisted of five officers: one Major ALO, who was in charge of three Captains and one 1st Lieutenant (me). Being a FAC was a dangerous job. During the Vietnam War the 20th TASS lost more than seventy pilots and 108 aircraft: 31 O-1 Bird Dogs, 55 Cessna O-2 Skymasters, and 22 OV10 Broncos.

I flew an O-2 out of Da Nang and Phu Bai AB just south of Hue city. I lived in Camp Rodriguez (named after the first 82nd Airborne soldier KIA in Vietnam). I was in a two-man tent surrounded by a four-foot wall of sandbags and slept on a cot. I shared the tent with an Army 1st Lieutenant until he was so badly wounded that he had to be Medevaced back to the States, leaving the tent to me. My shower was a community 55-gallon drum of cold water with a faucet. I never did get the ever-pervasive red dust off my skin until I rotated back to the USA. I did get hot meals for breakfast and supper but usually ate C-rations for lunch. And because there was limited ice or refrigeration, I learned to like warm beer and soft drinks.

Besides flying once a day, I had to pull regular shift duty in the brigade TOC with the S-3 Air element. We monitored the radios, planned future air-support missions, responded to immediate requests for CAS from our units under attack, and briefed the senior leadership of the Brigade on all this activity at the daily Stand Up Briefing. This independent Brigade was commanded by Brig. Gen. Alexander Bolling. He was a real gentleman and during the daily Stand Up frequently expressed his gratitude for what the Air Force was doing to help the unit. From April to September 1968 I participated in all the big battles, directing fighters, B-52s, and naval gunfire to targets around Hue and west to the A Shau Valley.

One of my most memorable missions was when I patrolled over a company of troops walking down a dirt road in the mountains west of Hue. They were going to one of the fire-support bases we had built to support operations in A Shau Valley. We flew these missions routinely, and usually they were boring because nothing happened. But this day the infantrymen were ambushed by the North Vietnamese and Viet Cong. We always maintained contact with the ground unit over the FM radio. When the shooting began, I was cruising about 1,000 feet over them. (The customary altitude was 1,500 feet, to stay above small-arms fire, but obviously the lower you get, the more you can see.) A panicked voice crackled over the radio when the troops starting taking fire from the jungle. I could see the soldiers finding cover in ditches along the road and returning fire. The RTO, probably a young enlisted man, yelled they were taking casualties. I tried to find out where the fire was coming from and at the same time on the UHF radio requested close-air-support fighters from the DASC for "troops in contact." Then a cooler voice spoke up on the FM. The company commander calmly told me where the enemy fire was coming from so that I could put the air strikes in accurately. I was really busy now talking on three radios (FM, VHF, and UHF) and figuring out the map coordinates I was flying. The DASC, located at Phu Bai Air Base, immediately diverted some airborne fighters to me. They arrived within five minutes. I marked the enemy positions with rockets and put in two flights of F-4s and F-100s. After the 500-pound bombs and napalm dropped, it got real quiet on the ground as the surviving enemy retreated from our air attack back into the jungle.

About a week later I was pulling a shift with the S-3 Air in the 82nd TOC when an Army captain entered and asked for "Gimpy 35" (my FAC call sign). I told him I was "Gimpy 35," and this captain in dirty, muddy fatigues, who smelled like a pig, came up and bear-hugged me. While holding on to me, he said, "You saved my ass and my company." He was accompanied by his 1st Sergeant. They had just gotten off the helicopter after being airlifted back from the base camp. They gave me a captured AK-47 and an SKS assault rifle.

And now for the rest of the story. After reading several articles in *Stars & Stripes* about GIs being arrested for shipping live grenades and automatic weapons back to the States from Vietnam, I decided not to put the two Russian rifles in my hold baggage. I had them mounted on a wooden plaque with an inscription and donated them to the 20th TASS in Da Nang for the squadron operations building wall. I did ship an Army issue Colt 1911 .45 caliber pistol that another Army guy gave me (another war story), and it arrived without being found by customs. I still have it, and my grandsons will inherit it. Sure wish I had that AK-47 and the SKS!

Another vivid and memorable mission was when I was doing visual reconnaissance above mountainous jungle on the eastern side of A Shau Valley. I was down around 500 feet above the ground "jinking" (moving in random motions side-to-side and up and down, making it more difficult for the enemy to hit you with ground fire than if you are flying in a straight line). Suddenly I spotted twelve to fifteen NVA troops, dressed in tan uniforms and pith helmets, jogging down a trail. I always flew with a CAR-15 (short barrel M-16 with a collapsible stock) that I grabbed and stuck out the left-side window. I started firing at the figures on the ground while pulling my O-2 in a tight turn to keep them in sight. That's when my airplane stalled and started falling out of the sky. To use an old Texas expression, that "scared the daylights out of me." I pushed the throttles to full power and lowered the nose of the O-2 to break the stall. My front windscreen was filled with nothing but jungle rushing up at me! As I gained airspeed and broke the stall, the trees started to get real big. I eased back on the flight controls and pulled out about a hundred feet above the jungle canopy. With my heart in my throat, I knew how close I came to dying in a fireball of my own making. I climbed to a higher altitude and continued the mission—and never fired my rifle out the window again.

Another night I was sleeping soundly about 2300 when I was awakened by lots of automatic rifle fire that was very close. I jumped off my cot, pulled on my flight suit and boots, grabbed my CAR-15, and ran about a hundred yards to the TOC. On the way, numerous illuminating flares filled the sky, creating a surreal visual effect over the base camp. I actually saw a couple of NVA sappers throwing satchel charges that exploded about two hundred yards away. I hunkered down in the TOC that was my duty station in case of attack. It was a beehive of activity as the commanders tried to gather information and figure out what was happening. There was lots of ground fire, but it soon ceased. An Army officer who worked with me in the TOC S-3 area, a Citadel graduate, earned a Silver Star for leading a group that counterattacked and killed the NVA sappers.

The next week I finally got some leave and left Vietnam to meet my wife for a week's R&R in Hawaii. I slept soundly in the Honolulu hotel (no night ground attacks) and gained weight eating at the fabulous restaurants before I had to go back to 'Nam. I sure missed my wife for the next three months and was determined to survive and get back to her in Texas.

Upon my return to Vietnam I was dispatched to Da Nang Airbase to pick up cases of beer and soft drinks for our FAC unit at Camp Rodriguez. While I was at the 20th TASS building, I met a fellow FAC who wanted a ride to the Hue Citadel airfield, where he was stationed with a small detachment of O-1s and O-2s. Hue was the old imperial capital of Vietnam, and the Citadel was a large walled fortress where the royal family lived. It was the scene of very heavy fighting in the Tet '68 battles. Our flight from Da Nang and our landing on the very short Citadel runway were uneventful. After taxiing up to their operations building and dropping off the captain, I proceeded to the end of the runway. But I failed to consider several important facts in preparing to take off. It was a very hot and humid day, and my load of beer and soda probably gave me an over gross weight and aft center-of-gravity condition for the O-2. With these atmospheric conditions, an experienced pilot would anticipate a much longer takeoff distance and a reduced climb rate after liftoff. Being a young lieutenant, I just didn't realize what a marginal and unsafe operation I was attempting on a short runway. After I pushed the throttles up to max power and released the brakes, I soon noticed the slower acceleration. When I finally got to takeoff airspeed and lifted off very near the end of the runway, I knew I was in deep trouble. The runway ended only a few hundred feet from the massive brick fort wall on the north side of the Citadel. As the aircraft approached the wall, my life slowed down, and I thought I was going to crash. I rapidly pulled the landing gear up and flew just a couple of feet over the top of the wall. What a relief to be alive! I never repeated that mistake in the rest of my thirty-year flying career.

Soon after I was safely back at base, we had a visit from an Air Force major from Nellis AFB, Nevada. An instructor in the FWS, he was on TDY in Vietnam to observe various air-combat operations so that students back in the States would have access to the latest information regarding how we were fighting the war. He wanted to observe an O-2 FAC mission and was assigned to fly with me. After a long discussion about what our mission in I Corps with the 82nd Airborne entailed, I gave him a detailed flight briefing on the scheduled air strikes and targets I had for that day. As luck would have it, right after we got airborne one of our companies out toward A Shau Valley became engaged with the NVA in a heavy firefight. I flew over to their location and talked to the company commander on the radio. During a routine patrol they had come under heavy fire from a bunker complex. I had him pop a colored smoke grenade (that I identified as green smoke) to confirm his location, and he told me the direction from the smoke to the enemy. I could see what I thought were bunkers on the side of a tree-covered hill. When my first flight of two F-100s came overhead I gave them all the target information and specified the enemy and friendly locations. They had me in sight, and I made a rolling left turn to mark the target with a white phosphorus smoke rocket. They dropped eight 500-pound bombs in two passes in the general area of the bunkers. The ground commander liked what they had done but was still receiving some fire from the bunkers. In the meantime, two F-4s carrying 750-pound bombs and napalm arrived overhead. After my in-flight target briefing to the F-4s, I started rolling in to fire another rocket on a marking pass. When I was in the nearly wings-level-nose-low attitude to fire the rocket, a small-arms round shattered my left cockpit window and sprayed glass all over the major and me. The bullet missed both of us but scared him so much that he went ballistic and started squealing like a little girl. I told him to calm down, that we were okay. I continued on my pass toward the bunkers and fired the rocket to the ground. Although it was very windy in the cockpit, I pulled up and radioed the F-4s to "Hit my smoke"—which they did with great accuracy. After the napalm dropped on the target, the Army captain on the ground was very happy because the enemy positions got real quiet. I'm sure the major was embarrassed; he didn't say a word all the way back to the base. There was no battle damage to my airplane except the broken window.

A favorite aunt of mine had given me a Saint Christopher medal that I put on my dog-tags chain around my neck. During two Vietnam War tours and 525 combat missions in the F-4 and O-2 I always wore that medal. I took numerous hits but never got a scratch. Thanks, Saint Christopher!

Finally, it was time to go home. Many of our fellow Americans, mostly living on the East and West Coasts, were against the Vietnam War and treated returning servicemen very badly. There are numerous stories of our warriors in uniform going to or coming home from Vietnam being harassed, cursed, and spit on. I did not actually experience that, but if I had, I would have punched out the perpetrators. One of my most vivid memories is returning from my first combat tour in Vietnam. Like so many others before and after, I had just come home from an extremely dangerous life experience that only combat veterans know. It was comforting to be with my wife, Barbara, and six-month-old baby daughter, Lara, in very familiar surroundings back in Texas. As we drove to see my parents and other relatives in my hometown, I saw a banner hanging from the I-10 overpass on Main Street (Highway 105) that stated, "Welcome Home Hale." I knew then that although I had left Vidor, Texas, to serve in the war, Vidor, Texas, had never left me.

René Saenz (1967, A-2) Headquarters, US Army Vietnam, 1969

My tour of Vietnam has been etched on my brain. Lady Luck was good to me. While in country I saw Tom Zapata and Don Vogel, who were Aggie classmates. Seeing friends from "the world" was wonderful.

I did not get a commission at A&M and ended up in Vietnam as a Spec 4 clerk typist at USARV Headquarters in Long Binh. Highway 1, the primary north-south road in South Vietnam, ran right outside our compound. I used to think of it as Highway 6 back in College Station as it ran both ways—but I never had any thought of going AWOL. Long Binh was a fairly secure area, but along with other clerks, cooks, mechanics, drivers, and additional support personnel I pulled perimeter guard and served as part of a reaction force in case of attack.

Usually things were quiet, but during Tet of 1969 we earned our pay when enemy rockets slammed into our positions. Most of us were fortunate not to return home in a body bag. It's said that the two things guaranteed in life are death and taxes. No one adds it, but "change" is just as sure. All of us had to change when we got home.

Mike Jackson (D-1, 1966) 1st Cavalry Division, 1967–68

After graduating from Texas A&M in 1966 I finished my ROTC summer camp and received my commission as a Reserve Officer in the Transportation Corps. Within two weeks I received notice of my selection for a Regular Army Commission in the Artillery Branch, but I turned it down because I was horrible with maps and math and might get someone killed while being a forward observer.

I reported for active duty at Fort Eustis, Virginia, in November 1966. My Tactical Officer was Capt. Pat Payne, A&M Class of 1964. An infantry officer with the 3rd Brigade of the 1st Air Cavalry Division in Vietnam, Pat had been in the relief battalion that went into the Ia Drang Valley to help relieve the 1st of the 7th Cav in the battle that became the book *We Were Soldiers Once and Young* and the film *We Were Soldiers.* He survived an intense ambush. Two years later he returned to Vietnam for a second tour as a Transportation Officer.

My initial assignment at Fort Eustis was as an instructor in the Transportation Officer Candidate School. After a couple of months I was reassigned to the 116th Terminal Transportation Company in Cam Ranh Bay, Republic of Vietnam. There I found my classmate Lt. Russell Stein, '66, working at the Replacement Battalion and Lt. Bob Palm, '65, assigned to a nearby quartermaster company.

I reported to my company commander at the port area. Port duty was very difficult—twelve hours on and twelve off. After several months I requested a transfer to a different part of Vietnam. I had decided to make a career of the Army and felt that my current duties would not prepare me for future transportation jobs.

I went back to the personnel company where Russell Stein was assigned, and he helped me with the intra-theater transfer request. My transportation company, battalion, and subarea commanders all denied the transfer, but it went forward to the Military Command Vietnam, and they approved it. I was assigned as a Movement Control Officer to 1st Brigade of the 1st Air Cavalry Division, located in An Khe.

At the Division Base Camp I ran into Billy Johnson, '65, who was assigned to the 1st of the 9th Cavalry regiment. My assignment was with the 1st FSE for the Division's 1st Brigade. A Medical Company, Artillery Headquarters Company, an Ordinance Company, and a Quartermaster Company made up the FSE, and I was the only Movement Control Officer assigned. I had a specialist who worked a "Sling Out" platform for deployed battalions and companies assigned to the 1st Brigade. He called in large CH-47 helicopters to perform these deliveries.

I also had a specialist who worked in an aerial terminal (a tent or a building) to handle troop movements to and from the Division Headquarters. He also called for planes to evacuate wounded and killed soldiers to a hospital or a mortuary unit. I also interfaced with any logistic effort that involved a part of the 1st Brigade. Normal operations included support by a C7-A Squadron from the Air Force. These aircraft held about thirty soldiers, a jeep with trailer, or a 105-mm artillery piece. On a daily basis the C7-As operated out of the three brigade base camps, several logistical areas, and the Division headquarters, at An Khe.

When large numbers of replacements arrived in country, we often secured C-130s, a much larger aircraft, for their transportation. The Division Movement Control Officer normally alerted me if we had C-130s coming into my location. Almost all these flights operated during daylight conditions, but the three times when the 1st Cavalry moved battalion-size or larger units, the flights came in at all hours. We also used C-123s; however, they were used primarily to handle the remains of soldiers killed in action. Every day I had to send a report of the passengers and supplies coming into and departing the airfield.

While at Bong Song, we were mortared four or five times a week. When we moved farther north, the mortar attacks continued and every few days were joined by 122-mm rockets. While I was assigned to Bong Song or LZ English, we experienced several memorable events. One evening around 1600 we received an urgent message from a firebase called LZ Two Bits that they were short of artillery ammunition. We had sufficient rounds to send, but because there was no CH-47 available to sling the ammo to them, we organized a ground convoy to deliver the ammo even though it was nearing the time for the roads to be closed for the evening.

As the Movement Control Officer in the Forward Support Element, I was the Convoy Commander. We arrived with no problems in about an hour and unloaded the ammo. I then called my commanding officer for further instructions. I was hoping to stay at the LZ and drive back in the morning after the engineers had cleared the road, but his orders were to drive back as soon as possible so we would be off the road before total darkness. We did make it back, but it was well past sundown.

While we were at LZ English, the ammo dump was hit by an enemy mortar round and blew up, keeping us pinned down in our bunkers for more than an hour. During this time I learned that one of my classmates, Larry Kennemer, '66, who had been in the band, was featured on the cover of *Newsweek* magazine when he was wounded and being carried off the battlefield at Dak To.

In December 1968 I became very ill and was evacuated to Quy Nhon, where they had a better hospital. I was there over Christmas but got back to LZ English in time to help move the entire division north. More than a thousand sorties were required to move troops and equipment organic to the Division. One of my specialists and I stayed at LZ English until late January, when all the units had been flown out by helicopter, C7-A, or C-130. The arrival airfield, at Phu Bai, was congested by a complete brigade of Cavalry moving in without any wheeled vehicles to relocate them to their areas of operation. We also had to coordinate flights bringing casualties from Khe Sanh combat base into Phu Bai. To help move the troops and equipment farther north to Quang Tri via Highway 1, we requested several truck battalions from USARV.

I went as a part of the Brigade advance party to the Quang Tri Airfield, home of a Marine helicopter unit and a Seabee Battalion on one side of the road and of the Division Forward Headquarters for the 3rd Marine Division on the other. The airfield provided lift capability for all armed forces in the Quang Tri area, so we interacted with Marine, Navy, Air Force, and non-divisional Army units.

The accommodations were not great. The night I arrived I dug a foxhole next to an Air Force Jeep and two airmen who had brought in the C-130s. It was monsoon season, and my foxhole quickly filled with water. My second night I found an Army Radio Relay unit that let me sleep on the matted steel floor of their bunker. The next day we were so busy with incoming flights that I again spent the night in a foxhole near the tarmac.

Meanwhile my headquarters moved to the other side of Quang Tri City, to LZ Jackrabbit, about five kilometers from the airfield. They advised me to stay put until the majority of the division had moved through the airfield. The Seabees began constructing a terminal for both the Army and the Air Force, but it wasn't completed by my fourth night. My specialist and I moved into a different foxhole, complete with sandbags, that was big enough for two cots. About 0100 hours, 122-mm rockets hit the new terminal. Regrettably there was an infantry battalion command staff in the building, and all were killed. Another rocket exploded where I had slept the night before. All we could hear was ringing in our ears as the sandbags surrounding our two-man foxhole leaked sand from shrapnel holes.

Part of the 1st of the 7th Cav had set up on a hard-top surface next to the terminal building, and several of their gasoline-powered mules loaded with ammo and white phosphorus began exploding. Medics ran all over to check on the dead and wounded as my specialist and I welcomed two cav troopers to our foxhole. We made room for them by throwing out the cots. The next morning my executive officer arrived to check on me. During the visit he picked a piece of shrapnel out of my flak jacket, which I had been using as a pillow.

After most of the troops and equipment had been moved off the airfield, I relocated to LZ Jackrabbit. On January 31 we were awakened by a two-hour mortar barrage. The weather was gray and foggy, so we couldn't get any Aerial Rocket Artillery helicopters launched. We soon learned that there was action all over Vietnam. The Tet Offensive had begun. LZ Jackrabbit was well defended. We had all the 1st Brigade Headquarters Units as well as a battalion of the 101st Airmobile Division and a part of a truck battalion. The NVA had planned their attack in the Quang Tri area before the 1st Cavalry moved north. They were not prepared to face such a formidable force. Once the fog lifted, the 1st Brigade infantry units were flown into positions that would block the NVA advance against the 1st ARVN Division Headquarters and the Quang Tri American and Australian compounds. The 1st Cavalry gunships basically destroyed an enemy regiment, and after a day of fighting our engineers dug mass graves for more than two thousand dead enemy soldiers. In LZ Jackrabbit we had several casualties but very few dead. Earlier the 8th Engineer Battalion had dug us a bunker, and we had installed an Air Force pallet as the roof along with several layers of sandbags.

We spent the first night of the Tet Offensive in the bunker. Along with the tension of the raging battle, I realized that I had lost my A&M Class ring. I borrowed a flashlight and looked around until I found it. My last official action during the Tet Offensive was to get to Cam Ranh Base to leave for my R&R in Australia. My commanding officer had arranged for another lieutenant to take my job at the airfield during my absence. Getting out of Quang Tri airfield was a chore, though. Some soldiers who were to leave country and others whose enlistments were over were awaiting transportation, and all the aircraft were supporting efforts to counter the offensive.

I finally found a 229th Helicopter Company chopper that had been shot up and was heading to Red Beach, a little north of Da Nang, for repairs. I remember seeing several holes, and the floor was sticky with blood. We flew at treetop level for about an hour. From Da Nang I caught several more hops until I finally reached Cam Ranh Bay. I arrived with no money and no civilian clothes to wear on R&R. Russell Stein took care of both, and on February 9 I flew to Australia. While there I called my mother in Texas. She was frantic because news about the Tet Offensive was all over the newspapers and television, and she'd had no word from me for weeks.

I spent half of my week-long R&R on a large sheep station near the center of Australia. I also enjoyed several days in the Kings Cross area of Sydney. Upon my return to Vietnam I caught a C-123 headed to An Khe. Once we took off, though, the left engine quit and we had to glide into Nha Trang. Eventually I got back to An Khe and then to Quang Tri, where I resumed pushing supplies to forward locations. The Seabee Battalion assisted by developing a beachhead that could be used to offload cargo directly from offshore. I led the first convoy off Sunder Beach with no problems. The second convoy was ambushed with mines on the road and small-arms fire from the surrounding jungle.

Although actually assigned to LZ Jackrabbit during this time, I stayed at the airfield in a makeshift bunker next to the terminal and ate with the Seabee Battalion. In late March we began planning Operation Pegasus to relieve the pressure on Khe Sanh. Along with my duties on the airfield I also acted as a courier, carrying information about the operation between Camp Evans and An Khe . During this time I managed to contact Lieutenants Charlie Griffin and Paul Tate—classmates from Spider D. I met other Aggies as well and visited with a friend from high school. In some ways Vietnam was a small world.

On April 7 we had a USO show set up near the airfield tarmac. This was the only USO event I witnessed during my year in Vietnam, and it saved my life. Before the show an Air Force captain who flew a recon aircraft in and out of our base asked if I would like to fly with him to Da Nang. He was going to a meeting but would be gone for only a few hours. I thanked him for the offer but told him I preferred to stay and watch the USO show. Neither the captain nor his plane ever returned. On his way back he had been asked to scout some sites in the A Shau Valley. Whether he was shot down of just crashed I don't know.

A few days later a C-130 landed with a contingent of the 101st Airmobile. Larry Kennemer, who had been on the *Newsweek* cover, was aboard. After several months in Japan recovering from his wounds, he said he just walked out of the hospital and caught a flight back to Vietnam and joined the 101st.

In early April the 1st Brigade of the Air Cavalry began moving into the A Shau Valley. The aviators had problems getting into the valley because the NVA had .51-caliber machine guns high on the mountains. A CH-53 "Flying Crane" was shot down on the first day of the operation. Limited helicopter support meant no hot chow for the ground troops during the entire operation, but still they captured several thousand rifles and many crew-served weapons. The 1st Brigade Commander promised each of his troops one of these rifles to take home as a war trophy.

Near the end of my tour a marine infantry company flew in from Khe Sanh, and the major in charge wanted his unit bedded down for the night before leaving the next day for an in- country R&R. I advised him to dig in across the road because it would be safer than staying in a tent or the terminal building. He replied that they had just left Khe Sanh, and he preferred to put his men in the transit tents. Later that night we received mortar and rocket fire that hit the transit area. The major used my landline to report eleven killed and several more wounded. I thought, "What a waste."

In early May an infantry company from the 2nd Brigade came through the airfield. Lt. John Dougherty, '65, was with them on their way to the Rockpile, north of Quang Tri. We visited for a while, and he joked that we should trade jobs. A week later the company came back through the airfield, but John was not with them. He had been killed several days after the operation began.

In late May I received instructions for my last big job in Vietnam. I flew to Saigon to secure authorization for two thousand captured enemy rifles to be taken home as souvenirs by soldiers of the 1st Brigade—including me. It took a while for the MACV Provost Marshal to process the large stack of paperwork, so I had time for classmate Paul Tate to show me the town.

When I had delivered the completed paperwork to Quang Tri, I worked to orient my replacement. After several delays I finally flew out of Cam Ranh to Japan and then on to McCord AFB, Washington. I arrived back in the United States on June 24, 1968.

Jeffery Murray (1973, Squadron 6 and H-2) 281st Aviation Company, 1968–69

During my tour I flew everybody from recon teams to high-ranking officers in all kinds of weather and combat conditions. My most interesting passenger was actress/comedian Martha Raye. I flew her many times to isolated camps so she could visit with the troops. She was one of the few Hollywood folks who truly supported the war and its warriors. She was gracious, friendly, talked all the time, autographed the inside of a few of our helicopters, and gave each of us her home address in Los Angeles, telling us all to stop by and stay a few days when we got home. I should have; she was a great lady. But I didn't want to take advantage. My one close-to-fame moment was when we shared a C-Ration lunch sitting on the skid of a Huey.

Jim Lanning (1964, D-1) 25th Infantry Division, 1967

It was a long, hot, steamy day on the coast along the South China Sea. Sand and more sand made walking difficult for my unit, Company C, 2nd Battalion 35th Infantry Regiment, 25th Infantry Division. We were weary and needed a break. At last we received orders to return to LZ Liz for security/command-post duty. This promised ice, better food, and a chance to take our packs off! Everyone in the company was excited by the news, and there was urgency to get moving. However, our route to LZ Liz ran through terrain that was like a patchwork quilt interspersed with huts, walking paths, hedgerows, rice paddies, and trees that limited our vision. We could not move quickly or safely because long-range sniper fire interrupted our movement. In an effort to subdue the fire from snipers, we placed artillery in the general vicinity of the line of march. We planned four different barrages roughly a thousand to fifteen-hundred meters apart along our eight-kilometer route. In accord with the company SOP, high-explosive rounds were never fired without first calling for a harmless smoke round to confirm the impact area. The first barrage was fired, and we quickly moved past its impact with negative sniper fire. As we advanced, the next barrage, or "stepping stone," was fired. At this point, our pattern seemed routine. However, all did not seem in order with the firing of the third concentration.

Because of the vegetation and terrain, we couldn't see the smoke round. The Forward Observer said he could hear the impact of the smoke round, but I didn't hear it. As a precaution, I asked for it to be fired again. This was done, and this time several others in my Command Group said they heard it. But I still did not hear or see the impact. There was mounting tension and grumbling among the troops because of the delay. The FO persisted: "Let's lay it in." I said that because we weren't in a real hurry, we would fire the smoke again in order to confirm our location. As our fire mission had no priority, we had to wait our turn. We waited.

Again the smoke fire round was fired. This time it was followed by an urgent radio message over the battalion-command net, "All units check fire! Check fire!" followed by the question if we had any idea where the smoke rounds were coming from that were landing at the edge of Company A's position. I asked for the transmission to be repeated and handed the radio headset to the FO. His confident demeanor changed completely, and he fell to his knees crying as he realized the gravity of what could have happened to Company A if he had followed the smoke with HE rounds. A check, double-check, and triple-check by the Artillery Fire Direction Center revealed an error in their calculations. It seems uncanny that this type of blunder could have happened with artillery normally reliable within 50 meters—yet the smoke rounds were impacting A Company six kilometers distant.

With a grateful Forward Observer we soldiered on to LZ Liz.

Mike Burroughs (1967, Squadrons 13 and 15) 553rd Reconnaissance Wing, 1969

My Crew 32 of the 553rd Reconnaissance Wing, based in Korat, Thailand, was flying a nighttime mission over North Vietnam. I was the CICO, in charge of the men in the back monitoring ground and air traffic. Our wing commander was in the front as the AC.

There was a great deal of turbulence, and visibility was about as far as the tip tanks when looking out the overwing windows. It probably wasn't much better from the cockpit. I was sitting at the forward galley table eating my in-flight meal and drinking a cup of coffee that I tried to keep from spilling.

Suddenly the aircraft went into rapid descent—a nosedive. It was one of those moments when you just freeze and feel the pucker factor increase. Shortly we leveled off, and crew members scrambled to find out what had happened. We had nearly hit a fighter aircraft head on. Fortunately for everyone, the fighter pilot's and our AC's quick thinking prevented a midair collision. The fighter climbed, and we dove.

To this day I am not sure why both planes were flying at the same altitude. Normally aircraft flying in opposite directions flew with a thousand feet of air space separating them to prevent this. Perhaps our flying in an orbital pattern, changing directions every few minutes, accounted for this problem.

When we landed back at Korat, it was morning and the sun was up. As we deplaned, the AC walked over to the nose of the aircraft, so I went over to have a look myself. The black paint on the nose was peeled. I doubted that it had been caused by the fighter aircraft's exhaust, but I didn't ask. All that mattered was that all of us were safely on the ground.

Tom Templer (1965, A-1) 11th Armored Cavalry Regiment 1968–69

Upon completion of the Armor Officer Basic Course at Fort Knox, Kentucky, I was one of the lucky ones who had orders to Germany. I was assigned to the 3rd of the 12th Cavalry, the Divisional Cavalry Squadron of the 3rd Armored Division, located in Budingen, Germany. During that assignment I was fortunate to perform a number of duties—Cavalry Platoon Leader, Troop Executive Officer, Squadron Maintenance Officer, and Troop Commander—a lot of OJT that would be very helpful when I got to Vietnam. The Divisional Cav Troops had APCs, tanks, infantry, and mortars, so I had a pretty good idea how to employ these forces. As a Cavalry unit, we were run ragged playing aggressor during training exercises for the rest of the Division elements. We also performed relief border duties for the 14th Cavalry Regiment. At the same time we were trying to maintain proficiency in Scout Tactics, Tank Gunnery and Armor Tactics, Mechanized Infantry Tactics, and Mortar Gunnery. And we had to maintain all weapon systems and the armor and wheeled vehicles assigned to the unit. All this proved to be a lot of fun for a butter-bar lieutenant, and it built character by making me keep a lot of balls in the air at the same time.

In Germany things really happened fast. I received orders to Vietnam and had just two weeks to get everything in order. I had been promoted to 1st Lieutenant and was commanding a Cavalry Troop. We did a quick change-of-command inventory. There were no equipment shortages, and all vehicles in the troop were combat ready. I sold my brand-new red MGB to a fellow officer and packed up what little personal property I'd been able to accumulate on lieutenant pay. Then I boarded a plane for the USA for a two-week leave in Crystal City, Texas, to see Mom and Dad before heading to Vietnam.

We flew into Bien Hoa in a big Saturn Airways commercial jet. As we approached the base it had an eerie look. The sky was filled with parachute flares. The light and smoke from the flares created ghostly images on the ground. Tracer bullets zinged all over the place. That is about the time the Saturn pilot came on the aircraft intercom and said "Welcome to Vietnam! The airbase is under attack, and we will be doing a short landing. There are military security troops on the ground, so take your instruction from them once we land."

Nobody told me anything about Tet 1968, but I was getting to experience it firsthand, and fast. The aircraft hit the runway and quickly came to a screeching stop. We exited in a hurry, but orderly. Air Force security forces led us in single file to bunkers about two hundred yards from where the plane landed. Occasionally I heard the thud of mortar and 122-mm rocket rounds and the whistle of outgoing counter-battery artillery. It was about 0100 or 0200, and it was dark with the exception of those eerie parachute flares.

I felt safe, however, as I had my trusty Browning 9 mm that I had purchased at Barbarros Sporting Goods in San Antonio before shipping out. Someone had told me I could get all the 9-mm ammo I needed from the Australian military forces operating in Nam.

All of us were dead tired, and being able to sleep sitting up in the bunker was a blessing. By first light things had quieted down, and there was no more incoming—just an eerie quiet. We left the bunker to board old blue Air Force buses that took us to the Long Binh Replacement Battalion. About thirty meters away, I saw about forty or so Vietnamese squatting blindfolded with their hands tied behind them. Some had wound dressing on their bodies. All were beaten and dejected, with their heads down. I asked one of the security personnel who these men were and he told me they were VC POWs that had been captured inside the wire the night before. We were lucky that we managed to get off the airplane without injury and to survive the night in the bunker without incident.

I was anxious to get to the replacement battalion and onto my assigned unit to learn what my duties would be. My orders read that I would be going to the 1/4 Cavalry, the Big Red One Divisional Cavalry Squadron. While I was home on leave, I had Mom sew on some First Infantry Division patches so I would have my uniforms "fit to fight" once I arrived in country. But, as I would soon find out, sewing on those patches was a waste of time. The next day I was called in to see a captain who worked at the replacement battalion. He told me my orders had been changed. I would be going to the 11th Armored Cavalry (Blackhorse) Regiment and to get ready ASAP as the regiment was sending a vehicle to pick up replacements.

A short time later an awful-looking 5-ton truck pulled up. The vehicle had one fender blown off, no canvas over the bed, broken troop seats, and a front bumper that looked like a pig's tail, all curled up, on one side. I could faintly make out the number 11 on the other side of the bumper. The truck was covered in old red laterite dust and had sandbags on top of the hood and two deep in the cargo area. The only good-looking thing about that ride was the well-cleaned .50-caliber machine gun attached to the ring mount. The sergeant in charge of the vehicle yelled out, "Everyone going to the 11th Cavalry get on board."

I climbed on the truck with about a half-dozen other replacements. That dang truck didn't have any shocks either. I wondered who was responsible for vehicle maintenance in the 11th ACR. But there was one thing about that 5-ton that I did like: it ran like a scared wolf!

A short time later we pulled up to a field-command post consisting of four M-577 Command Tracks, a briefing tent, and several large sleeping tents for 11th ACR headquarters personnel. The accommodations were scant but adequate. The Regiment had recently arrived at what was called Widow's Village, located in front of the US II Field Force Headquarters. The 11th ACR had been called back from conducting reconnaissance-in-force operations around An Loc and Loc Ninh to reinforce US defenses around Long Binh and Bíen Hoa against the Tet Offensive.

I reported to the personnel officer, who, after reviewing my records, assigned me to the Regimental S-4 Shop. I hoped my prior Squadron Maintenance Officer assignment would not be noticed, but the S-1 had to make the assignment quickly. As Assistant S-4 I was responsible to get food, fuel, and ammo to the 11th ACR troops fighting in the field—and to do it immediately.

Several weeks later, after the Tet Offensive had wound down, the S-4 reassigned me as Regimental Maintenance Officer. That required me to brief the Regimental Commander every night on the status of all assigned combat vehicles, visit each Squadron Maintenance activity, expedite repair parts for combat and maintenance-recovery vehicles, conduct periodic visits to our direct-support maintenance and our supporting maintenance shop headquarters, and participate in other support activities as determined by the S-4. After I had worked in the S-4 shop for about nine months, the Regimental Commander asked if I wanted to command an armored cav troop. There was a catch: I would have to extend my tour in country another eight months. I responded "yes."

On October 10, 1968, I assumed Command of E Troop, 2nd Squadron, 11th ACR. The squadron consisted of three line troops (E, F, and G), one tank company (H), and a headquarters company. Each line troop had twenty-four M-113 Armored Cavalry Assault Vehicles (ACAVs) and three M-106 4.2 inch Armored Mortar Tracks. In my headquarters I had an M-113 ACAV Command Vehicle and an M-577 Command, Communications, and Operations Track. Each ACAV had a crew of four, and was armed with a .50-caliber heavy machine gun and two M-60 7.62-mm machine guns. The ACAV Line Troop bristled with weapons, and each ACAV was loaded with extra 40-, 7.62-, and 5.56-mm and .50- and .45-caliber ammunition, claymore mines, and bunker-busting and mine-detonating explosives. The ACAV crew could fight from the track or, when required, dismounted.

In January 1969 we were operating in an area fifteen miles east of Lai Khe, near the 1st Infantry Division. During January 1969, E Troop performed a number of missions, including a large cordon-and-search of a village in support of other 2nd Squadron units; six reconnaissance-in-force missions (making contact with the enemy twice while clearing two large enemy base camps); twenty effective mounted and dismounted night-ambush patrols; daily hasty road clearing and convoy-security missions; and two "pile on" operations in support of other 11th ACR units in enemy contact.

In late January and early February, after completing a week-long Rome Plow Security Operation (jungle clearing), we closed our night defensive position at FSB Hawk and moved to FSB Jim, sharing security operations with H Company.

February 3, 1969, started as a typical day for my E Troop Cavalry troopers. At first light we sent out one platoon of eight ACAVs and an attached Tank Platoon of five M-48A3 Tanks. Their mission was to clear approximately twelve kilometers of roadway hastily and to post strongpoints to ensure road security during convoy operations. One ACAV platoon was assigned the mission of ready-reaction force for convoy security elements or for other friendly forces operating within our AO. The remaining ACAV platoon was to perform a much-needed vehicle-maintenance break (change engine oil, grease suspension, replace damaged road wheels and tracks, and clean all crew-served weapons). Generally these maintenance operations took four or five hours.

While these operations were going on, an artilleryman—and fellow Aggie (Capt. Mario Macaluso, Class of 1965)—came to the FSB to discuss fire-support plans for FSB Jim and for our troops conducting operations in the AO. We also had some unexpected visitors, several Donut Dollies. These dedicated women visited the units in places like Bien Hoa Air Force Base or Long Binh, but to have them come out to the boonies, to a place like FSB Jim, was a special treat. During this time I also occasionally saw the F Troop Commander, Capt. Tom McAdams, Class of 1964. A short time later, on February 28, 1969, he was killed in action.

By 1300 things began settling down at the FSB. Our visitors were departing, and platoon maintenance operations were just about completed. It was time to start preparing for night-ambush operations, issuing the operating orders, and making sure fire-support plans were coordinated with E Troop mortars for illumination and with the Troop Fire Support Officer for 155-mm howitzer battery support. Two weeks earlier one of our platoons conducting a mounted ambush killed several NVA resupplying an enemy base camp under the cover of darkness. The previous week a mounted ambush captured an NVA soldier. That soldier was sent to the Regimental Headquarters for interrogation and had been returned to E Troop to provide further intelligence about the enemy operating in our AO.

At about 1400 all heck broke loose on the Squadron Command Net. They ordered my troop and H Company to conduct a "Pile-on" operation in a wooded area approximately four kilometers northwest of FSB Jim. The Regimental Air Cavalry Troop Aerial Rifle Platoon was in heavy contact with an NVA force in well-fortified bunkers surrounded by a network of trenches in which were several machine guns. I gave my two ACAV platoon leaders a quick FRAGO consisting of general direction of movement from FSB Jim to the contact area and the order of march. A helicopter flying over our column would guide us to the contact area. I had the lead ACAV, and one of my alternate radios was set to the designated Air Cav frequency so the helicopter above could provide direction assistance if needed. As the column of ACAVs departed Jim, the lead platoon leader's ACAV track got caught in the perimeter concertina wire. I moved into his position behind the lead ACAV in the column. There was no time to wait. He could join us later. We needed to get to the contact ASAP. There were cavalry troopers pinned down. We were hurrying to the sound of the contact.

When I jumped on my ACAV, I took the NVA POW with me. Normally I had a driver, a Vietnamese interpreter, and a cavalry soldier manning one of the two M-60 machine guns. The interpreter manned the other M-60, and I controlled the .50-caliber machine gun. My troop was the lead element in the armored column, and the Air Cavalry Troop Commander in the helicopter overhead kept shouting over the radio for us to hurry up. We were moving as fast as possible across the brushy, rough ground, but from the air the terrain looked pretty smooth. I felt like telling him to come down and ride in my ACAV. Then he would realize we were going at maximum speed. I didn't want any of my ACAVs to blow an engine or transmission or throw a track. We would need every bit of the combat power we could muster when we reached the contact. After a few minutes the Air Cavalry Troop Commander seemed to understand that we were moving as fast as possible. He quit prodding us to hurry and let us do the business of moving our armored forces to the contact area.

When we neared the wooded area where the contact was ongoing, we broke out into dry rice paddies. I deployed my troops from our column to a frontal-assault-line formation facing the wooded area. Just as we got on line, the Air Cavalry Troop Commander radioed to hold the formation. Fast movers and additional artillery had been called to soften up the area before we assaulted. And tanks were en route to provide additional suppressing fire. I got on my command net and told our cavalry troopers to get down inside their ACAVs as an air strike and artillery were on the way. I hardly got the words out of my mouth before fast movers streaked in dropping HE bombs. The artillery fire shifted to pound possible enemy egress routes. I was glad I had told the troops to get down inside their ACAVs: the air strikes and artillery came in close. Mud and debris from the strike landed all over the top and on the trim vane of our ACAVs. The fast movers made several passes before the Air Cavalry Troop Commander gave us the all clear and the order to attack the wood line.

The air strikes and artillery had knocked down a lot of trees and set off small fires that were still burning. As we began our assault on the woodline, amazingly we still received AK-47, machine gun, and RPG fire from the entrenched NVA. From our assault line we opened up with every crew-served weapon: seventeen M-2 .50-caliber machine guns and thirty-four M-60 machine guns. It was well-aimed chaos brought to bear on a determined and well-entrenched enemy. The tanks arrived and joined in the fray taking out targets in the woodline and along the right flank while our Troop was on the left. I had several cavalry troopers dismount and place grenades and small-arms fire inside bunkers as we advanced through the complex. From prior experience we knew that you had to have a methodical approach to clearing bunkers. If you went too fast and did not neutralize each bunker, the NVA would pop up and fire RPGs into the back of your ACAV, wounding or killing the crew and catching the fuel and ammunition on fire. The Aerial Rifle Platoon fell in behind the tanks to neutralize the bunkers as the tanks advanced in the assault. Using conventional armor formations in Vietnam may have been unusual to some units, but not to the 11th Armored Cavalry Regiment, especially when methodically clearing large bunker complexes in "Pile on" operations.

We continued to assault on line until we came to a major trench. Facing my ACAV, only a few yards away, were an abandoned NVA machine gun and an RPG launcher. The machine-gun barrel was smoking, and there was still an ammo belt in the receiver. RPG rounds were scattered nearby. Apparently the NVA machine-gun and RPG crews had departed the area hastily—likely because they were in the kill and beaten zones of our .50-cals.

My ACAVs and the tanks halted near the trench line as the troops on the ground continued to neutralize the bunkers we had just rolled over. To my left I saw cavalry troopers pulling NVA prisoners out of the trench and one bunker. The NVA POW riding on my ACAV jumped out the back of the track and ran over to the NVA prisoners. It was obvious he knew them. He was yelling at them and kicking at one of the prisoners. I quickly put a stop to that. From the interpreter on my ACAV I learned he was mad at the prisoners for not surrendering earlier like he had done. The Americans weren't so bad after all.

We continued to clear the complex, taking prisoners and collecting AK-47s, light machine guns, small-arms ammunition, RPGs and launchers, and all sorts of military equipment. The Regimental Commander and Air Cavalry Troop Commander landed nearby and moved to my ACAV for a situation report. As I was talking with the Air Cavalry Troop Commander, the Regimental Commander took his CAR-15 and started blasting away at some of the canteens and metal plates scattered at the bottom of the trench. I politely reminded him that I still had troops manning the machine guns in the ACAVs to our rear and did not want them to get itchy fingers when they heard the firing to their front. Because a lot of low brush and blown-down trees obscured their view, they might think it is enemy activity and open up.

I had been in Vietnam and in the 11th Armored Cavalry Regiment for fifteen months. During that time I served under four Regimental Commanders—one wounded and evacuated, one killed, one who completed a six-month command tour, and the commander on the ground in front of the ACAVs. I can't remember what he said to me, but he did stop firing.

Assisted by an infantry platoon that had been airlifted in, we continued clearing the bunkers and trenches. As evening set in, we all moved out of the bunker complex and established a night defensive position in the dry rice paddies. Our "Pile on" had been a success. There were eighteen dead enemy soldiers and seven more captured. Unfortunately the Aerial Rifle Platoon lost one of its finest soldiers in the initial contact.

Paul Dresser (1964, E-2 and Corps Staff) 5th Special Forces Group, 1967

I was the executive officer and then the commander of a Special Forces A Team in IV Corps. My camp, A-413, had been built by the Seabees and was the only high, dry ground around during the wet season. I'm not much of a "show and tell" guy, so I'll let my letters home and later articles in my hometown newspaper tell my story.

The February-March 1967 edition of the *Texas Aggie* included letters from several of us serving in Vietnam. Mine said:

> This is a hell of a war. . . . The truce doesn't mean much out here—only that we cannot initiate offensive operations. And I have about eight good ones planned, starting tomorrow. . . .
>
> The Viet Cong have maintained domination in this district since 1954. The guerrilla VC farm and fish by day and fight and booby trap by night. These people are highly motivated, well trained, and ingenious in the arts of ambush, camouflage, and deception.
>
> I put up a basketball goal the other day, and my troops love it. Tell Shelby (A&M Coach Metcalf) I have some All-Stars for his team. Of course the average height is five-foot-two, but we have some good shots. It takes about 122 players for a game here—100 for security and the rest for the teams.

My tour in Vietnam ended after four months. A booby-trap explosion knocked my NCO unconscious and left me with head and chest injuries. I was able to call a helicopter and was evacuated to a hospital in Saigon and then transferred to better facilities in Japan. By April I was at Fort Hood and was given a thirty-day convalescent leave to my parent's home in Corsicana.

Ed McDaniel (1965, D-1) Naval Intelligence Liaison Officer—Quang Ngai, 1969

On the afternoon of December 24, 1969, I departed Quang Ngai city and drove up Highway 1 to the Chu Lai Combat Base with the objective of being one of very few US Navy representatives at the Officers' Club festivities that night. If I say so myself, I did a fine job of representation. Before the evening was over I could lay claim to having launched a champagne-propelled cork across the room, hitting an Army captain squarely in the forehead. I fared far less well later in the evening during a Sumo-style contest with an Army artillery lieutenant who turned out to be a former Michigan State football tackle.

Arising the next morning, I made my way to the coastal side of the Chu Lai base, where the USN maintained a four-man advisory group on an RVN Navy Coastal Junk Base. Upon my arrival, one of the USN officers handed me a small gift box and said "Merry Christmas." Opening the box, a "care package" from an unknown organization in the US, I found the usual items—small packets of health-care sundries, hard candies, a magazine, and so on. In addition the box contained a pair of balled-up sweat socks.

As I sat there, with a cotton mouth and splitting headache from the previous night, I wondered why the hell someone would send a pair of socks. After all, I could get socks, underwear, cammies, and such through Army and Marine supply channels. But then, for some reason, I unrolled the socks—and discovered their real purpose: to hide a miniature bottle of whiskey. Wrapped around the bottle was a note from a small VFW post in eastern Kansas wishing me a Merry Christmas.

My first reaction was that more alcohol was the last thing I needed at the moment. Besides it was available at the PX for almost nothing. And people were not supposed to send us booze through the mails. But that reaction quickly faded when it sank in that far away, in Kansas, a group of vets had come up with a way to surreptitiously get a small drink to one of the troops in Vietnam. As I thought about their planning, their efforts, and their empathy, I developed a sense of profound gratitude and a feeling of comradeship. Many citizens were decrying US involvement in the conflict and openly denigrating the participants, but a group of WWII and Korean vets, who likely had endured far greater deprivations than I, had found a way to say thanks to younger military brother.

To date I have never received, and it is difficult to imagine receiving, a better gift than the acknowledgement and gratitude of a fellow veteran—especially when it seemed my efforts were unappreciated and even considered unwarranted by vocal segments of the US population.

Bill Morgan (1968, A-1) 9th Infantry Division, 1969–70

On May 25, 1968, the Texas A&M Class of 1968 stood together at G. Rollie White Coliseum and took the oath of office to support and defend the Constitution of the United States of America. We had become 2nd Lieutenants and Ensigns in our respective branches of service. I received my Army commission in the infantry, and one month later I found myself in the Infantry Officer Basic Course at Fort Benning, Georgia. This was followed by the Airborne training to jump and glide to the earth under a parachute canopy. Then I attended Ranger School—nine weeks of the physically, mentally, and emotionally most intense and demanding training the Army offered. Earning my Ranger Tab was one of my proudest accomplishments. In November 1968, my training complete, I was off to my first assignment with troops . This Stateside assignment lasted barely five months. In May 1969, at the age of twenty-two, I boarded an airplane at Travis AFB, in California, en route to South Vietnam.

Upon my arrival in country I spent two days filling out the inevitable stack of forms and other in-processing. Finally I learned that I was assigned to the 9th Infantry Division in IV Corps, the southernmost area of South Vietnam. The following day I boarded a 5-ton truck for a long ride in a convoy along the banks of the Mekong River to the 9th Division headquarters at Dong Tam. There I received two more days of orientation before being sent to my unit.

My experiences in Vietnam really began when I received orders to the 6th Battalion, 31st Infantry. The Battalion Adjutant informed me that A Company needed a new platoon leader and I was going there. A Company operated out of a forward fire base named Ranger. Early the next morning, I met Captain "Nic" Nicolini, my company commander, on the helicopter pad. Nic was old school, a seasoned veteran, on his third tour in Vietnam. At first I don't think Nic was sure what to think of his new "Shave Tail," but he was short officers, so he gave me the 3rd Platoon. I wasn't too sure of my standing with Nic either. It didn't appear that we had much in common. He grew up in New Jersey, enlisted right out of high school, came up through the ranks, and earned his commission through OCS. He chomped on cheap cigars and cigarettes and sprinkled his speech with colorful language, often using "Mother" as a prefix.

However, it soon became apparent that Nic knew how to lead a rifle company and how to fight the VC.

At the 3rd Platoon area I met S.Sgt. Dean Hess, the Platoon Sergeant. Dean was a smart, efficient NCO who had combat experience and obviously was concerned for the welfare of the men in our platoon. During those months in A Company I learned a lot from Dean Hess about being a good combat leader.

Our platoon's mission was to take back control of a large area of the rural countryside that the VC held west of our fire base. If we were successful in forcing the VC to abandon the area, it could be "pacified" by establishing a security cordon provided by ARVN and then using civic-action projects to help local peasant farmers improve crop yields and water quality and having medical assistance teams treat their maladies and diseases.

To accomplish our mission of forcing out the VC, we employed helicopters and "brown water" Navy boats to transport us to our AO. When we used boats, we normally rode in Navy Tangos, which resembled the small craft used to land GIs on the islands of the Pacific during World War II. The advantage of using boats was that we could enter our patrol area from where the enemy did not expect us—the river. The downside was that the boats moved slowly and offered tempting targets for enemy gunners to launch RPGs and leave or hide before we could react. To help protect us, PBRs (small, flat versions of the famous PT boats of WWII) provided a lot of firepower when we came into contact with the enemy. Not all PBRs were configured alike. Some had mounted twin M-60 machine guns; others had .50-cal. machine guns, automatic grenade launchers, and occasionally a mortar. Some were equipped with powerful flame throwers called Zippos.

The preferred mode of transportation to the AO was the helicopter. The UH-1 Huey was fast, delivered us close to our patrol area, and often had Cobra gunships flying alongside to provide cover until we were safely off the LZ. The downside was that every VC within five kilometers of the LZ heard us coming long before we got there. They had plenty of time to prepare an ambush on or near the LZ or to hide their weapons and resume farming until we had passed through their village.

My platoon executed many long foot patrols to find the VC, often staying out in the field for several days tracking what we thought was an enemy unit. When we found the VC, we had small firefights to kill or capture them. Most often, however, we moved through the rice paddies and slogged through the mud and slime of the Delta with very little to show for it. Most of the time we walked out of FSB Ranger to a predetermined area, where we moved along the rice paddy dikes and into the treelines that provided the only available cover and concealment.

When a Special Forces Camp south of Tan An came under attack, Nic radioed to tell me that 3rd platoon would be picked up by Hueys and sent in to reinforce the camp and repel the VC attackers. He then gathered the rest of A Company and inserted by helicopter a little later to bolster our defenses. The battle lasted until the first light of dawn, when the enemy withdrew. This was my first major fight as a platoon leader, and we battled the VC successfully. After this mission, Nic and I had a much improved respect and affection for each other. I had proven myself to my company commander as well as to myself. Our respect and friendship continued throughout the rest of my tour. Nic would later serve as an usher at my wedding back in The World.

After four months in A Company, I was selected to lead the Battalion Reconnaissance Platoon. Lt. Col. Gerry Carlson, the Battalion Commander, assigned Recon the mission to "find the enemy and start a fight so we can pile on." This meant we were to go farther out and stay longer in the field to make contact. Once we engaged the enemy, the Battalion would reinforce us with additional units to carry on the fight. All the guys in Recon were experienced in the field before volunteering and being selected for the platoon. A soldier in the Recon could leave and return to a line unit whenever he wanted. Likewise, I could have a soldier removed from Recon for no reason other than "incompatibility." We were an elite unit that had the toughest missions in the battalion. The platoon usually operated as widely dispersed six-man teams outside normal artillery-support range. To survive and accomplish the mission we had to trust each other completely

Recon had "Big John" Thompson as platoon sergeant—a tough, professional NCO who always had my back. He joined the Army out of high school to avoid the deprivation and discrimination that come with the life of a black sharecropper in the rural South. "Big John" was a large man with a no-nonsense air about him. When Big John barked an order, no one dared disobey. Compliance was always immediate. This was due, in part, to the respect in which he was held and in part to his ideas on discipline. He did not believe that any soldier in Recon should receive the Army's formal judicial or nonjudicial punishment for most infractions.

Whenever a Recon soldier got out of line, Big John personally took care of his punishment. If we were in base camp, Big John had the offending soldier fill sandbags on the berm or forced him to service the platoon latrine by burning the nasty waste buckets. If the offense occurred while we were in the field, John took away the offending soldier's weapon and gave him an entrenching tool to carry. This was a terrifying prospect for anyone on a long patrol out of range of any friendly help. Thirty minutes of walking point was the usual sentence. This was a very effective disciplinary technique that had to be used only a few times and never on the same man twice.

One of our operations involved following intelligence from battalion that the NVA had set up a training base near the eastern edge of the Plain of Reeds. While we were searching a clearing within a dense stand of nipa palm, one of my scouts observed something that looked out of place. He saw a spade mark in the soil where there were no other signs of digging. After further examination we discovered a hidden tunnel entrance and uncovered a group of enemy soldiers hiding inside. We captured them, their weapons, and their documents and sent them back to Division for interrogation. The documents later revealed that this was part of the group that the NVA were training. We had stumbled on the training base that Carlson had sent us to find. The best part of the mission was the tub of beer waiting for us when we got back to the base camp. It was cold and tasted great—compliments of the battalion commander.

Many patrols later, we were again searching for the enemy near the Plain of Reeds when our point man stepped on a booby trapped artillery or mortar round. The explosion killed or wounded the first four men in the file. As the third man, I was among the wounded. All I really remember is that I had just turned back to the front after giving instructions to my radio operator and then there was a bright flash, everything went dark, my ears were ringing, and I was looking up at Big John's face. He was telling me that "Doc" (our medic) said I would make it and that the Dustoff would be landing in a few minutes. I next remember being taken off the Dustoff at 3rd Surgical Hospital and being prepped for surgery. My next clear memory is recovering at an Army hospital in Japan.

I sustained wounds to both legs, my wrist, and my hip. The upper portion of my left ear had been severed from my head, but fortunately the surgeons at 3rd Surgical had sewn it back on. Because I was wounded in the head and ear, I was evacuated to a hospital with the resources to help my recovery—the hospital at Camp Zama, Japan. While in the hospital at

Zama, I witnessed more courage that I had ever seen. All the patients on my ward were combat casualties. Some had been blinded, others had lost limbs, and still others had suffered burns. In spite of their wounds, self-pity was not allowed—a philosophy enforced by peer pressure from the other patients.

After the evening meal, the guys occasionally would organize "chariot races" around the ward. The guys who could walk (even though blind) were drafted to push the guys confined to wheelchairs in a race around the ward. The races were organized into heats. As one of only two officers on the ward, I was a judge. The wagering was heavy, with guys betting on their favorite "chariot." The other officer, a helicopter pilot, recorded the bets. The standard wager was dessert from the next evening meal. Nothing proclaims victory as well as a slice of freshly baked apple or cherry pie. When one's section of beds was betting on him to win the race, he had no time to feel sorry for himself or to dwell on what he had lost.

After seven weeks of recovery in Camp Zama, I returned to my unit, where I was assigned as the S-3 Air (Air Operations) on the Battalion Staff. My job was to coordinate daily helicopter-assault missions and USAF and USN air-support missions and to fly as observer on dawn and dusk helicopter patrols. In April 1970 the battalion participated in the invasion of Cambodia with the mission of securing the southern end of the Ho Chi Minh Trail at Batu. The Delta Company Commander was wounded during the initial fighting and Lieutenant Colonel Carlson radioed to have me ready on the helicopter pad. He picked me up and dropped me into D Company's patrol base to take over until a new company commander could be brought in.

I faced this new assignment with mixed emotions. As a career soldier, I was professionally flattered and personally thrilled to command a rifle company in combat. The real truth is that I had about forty days remaining before my DEROS, and I was scared that I wouldn't make it home on time or, possibly, at all. I was engaged to be married upon my return, and I didn't know how to tell my fiancé I wouldn't be coming home as planned. Fortunately an experienced captain was found and, a few weeks later, arrived to assume command of the company. He flew into our company base around noon, and we spent the afternoon and one long evening going over the tactical situation, the current operation, and upcoming plans. I introduced him to the company officers and senior NCOs. The First Sergeant and Executive Officer took over the transition from there. When the resupply chopper flew in the next morning, we gathered, shook hands, and saluted each other, and I hopped aboard. Next stop—The World!

I survived my year in Vietnam, albeit a little worse for wear. Too many of our classmates didn't. I have never laughed so much, cried so much, or prayed so much as I did during my tour. I made lifelong friends. The lessons learned and the struggles endured beside the heroes with whom I served helped shape me into who I am today. I will always feel deeply honored to have been part of such a great group of Americans.

Tom Gardner (1967, Band) 119th Aviation Company, 1970

Like many Aggies, I took an extra year to graduate. After commencement and commissioning, in May 1968, I worked in construction before going on active duty in October. I attended the Artillery Officer Basic Course at Fort Sill, Oklahoma, the Rotary Wing Basic Course at Fort Wolters, Texas, and the Advanced Rotary Wing Course at Savannah, Georgia. Upon graduating from the Advanced Course I reported to Vietnam, where I joined the 119th Aviation Company (Assault Helicopter).

On September 15, 1970, I was flying a UH-1C escorting an unarmed O-2 fixed-wing aircraft in a search-and-destroy mission near Dong Tre. During the earlier hours of the morning the Dong Tre airstrip had taken extensive damage from B-40 and 122-mm rockets fired from the southeast. As we approached the suspected enemy location, we began receiving small-arms fire. We went in at low level firing rockets and miniguns. After we made numerous additional runs, the enemy fire decreased as they began dispersing in the covering foliage.

As we broke off our gun runs against the old target, we began receiving fire from a new location. When we rolled in to attack the new target, we were met by even more small-arms fire. Our rockets set off several secondary explosions that blew dirt, shrapnel, and other things against our aircraft. We suffered no serious damage, but we had to break off our attack when we ran low on ammo and fuel. After a quick flight to the airfield to resupply, we returned to continue the assault against what now appeared to be a complex of buildings, bunkers, and foxholes.

We maintained our gun runs until the return fire ceased. A ground assessment credited us with a body count of thirty and fifteen structures destroyed. My copilot and I each received a Distinguished Flying Cross for the fight. But for lots of similar incidents there were no awards. The only proof of these battles remains in the recollections—war stories—of those of us who were there.

Homer McCall (D-1, 1966) 29th Support Group, 1970

I don't really have much of a story about Vietnam except that I credit Jimmy Huggins, Class of 1968, for saving my life. When I received orders for Nam, I was assigned to the 101st Airborne Division stationed at Phu Bai, about as far north as you could go without crossing the DMZ. When I arrived as a Signal Corps officer, they stuck captain's bars on me. I could just see my life ending right there because I would have a big target on my back.

While at the 90th Replacement Battalion at Long Binh waiting transportation to the 101st, I contacted Huggins, a friend from Lufkin, who was already in country. Supplies had priority over troops for flights north, so I spent about five days just waiting for transportation to Phu Bai. During this time, my buddy Jimmy contacted one of his friends in the assignment section of USARV Headquarters, and on the very morning I was to board the plane for my flight north, orders came down reassigning me to the 29th General Support Group at Long Binh.

I spent my whole tour in the 29th. I know I was one of the lucky ones, because I never had to face some of the bad stuff a lot of guys did. For that I thank my God, Jimmy Huggins, and his friend at USARV.

Mike Feighny (1965, D-2) 313th Radio Research Battalion, 1970–71

I graduated from A&M in 1965 and then went to law school at the University of Texas before I went on active duty as a Military Intelligence officer. I served as a MI captain with the 509th RR Battalion in Saigon from June to August 1970 and then was the S-2 for the 313th RR Battalion in Nha Trang from August 1970 to June 1971.

Nha Trang was not a real hot spot, but we got shelled by "Nha Trang Charlie" a couple times a month. On Sunday, August 30, 1970, at about 0900, one of our vans, along with ten of our soldiers, was hit—one KIA. I ran to the site and told the MPs to let the emergency vehicles in. They came in and evacuated the wounded. At 1100 my boss called and told me I shouldn't have let the vehicles into the secure area—but a few hours later I learned I had been put in for a medal for helping with the evacuation.

When off duty we'd go to a bar in Nha Trang called the Nautique. It was off limits after the curfew that began at 10:00 p.m. When the MPs and Quan Canh raided the place, the GIs would hide behind the bar in a secret room.

Being an MI officer, I had a "Jesus Pass," which authorized me to be anywhere, anytime, and I traveled all over the Central Highlands. There was a scheduled Caribou flight that went from Nha Trang to Pleiku and An Khe. Once while I was taking off from Pleiku, incoming rounds began landing on the runway. The Caribou pilot just kept going, and we took off safely. Another time I was on a C-130 flight from Da Nang to Nha Trang. It was monsoon season and raining hard, so hard that water was leaking into the aircraft. An ROK unit from Nha Trang was on board. The pilot announced he was diverting the plane to Saigon. The Koreans held a vote and voted to go to Nha Trang. They sent someone who spoke English to tell the pilot. He announced that, regardless of the vote, the plane was going to Saigon. We went to Saigon. The next morning I went out to the airfield to discover that the plane had already departed for Nha Trang with all the Koreans. So I had to make my own way back to Nha Trang.

Another time I was stranded in Quy Nhon overnight. The next morning I went out to the airstrip. The people at the control tower told me that a U-21 taxing on the runway would stop for me. I ran out to the plane, climbed aboard, and found an ROK two-star general—the Commander of the Korean Division assigned to I Corps—looking at me. He said in perfect English, "Good morning, Captain. How are you?"

I said, "Fine."

In the back of the plane was a woman dressed in traditional Vietnamese attire with huge rings on each finger. There was no introduction. When we arrived at Nha Trang, a band was playing. The general said, "They're here for me. The plane will taxi around to the back of the hangar and let you off."

That's what happened. The plane taxied to the rear of the hangar, and the Vietnamese lady and I got off the aircraft. This was among my first experiences with Koreans. I didn't know that eventually I would marry a Korean and spend more than twenty years in Korea as a JAG officer and a DAC attorney.

Bill Beall, (1968, Band) Detachment B-43, 5th Special Forces Group, 1971

I graduated from Vietnam rather than Texas A&M. A combination of grades and not wanting to miss the war caused me to leave after three years of marching in E. V. Adams's Maroon Band. I was not drafted but rather volunteered for the army and Special Forces. After Special Forces and other training I ended up as the medical specialist with the Special Forces Group, Detachment B-43, in Chi Lang (Seven Mountains), in the Delta Region of South Vietnam. Our mission was to train and lead light-infantry battalions of the Royal Cambodian Army, the Khmer Serei, for redeployment to their home country.

On February 25, 1971, Sgt. John Duboise, the team's communications NCO, and I accompanied the recon platoon of the 3rd Cambodian on a night ambush as a part of a combat-training exercise. We moved the platoon of twenty Cambodians until after dark and then occupied a rice paddy with scrub-brush treelines and dikes on all sides that overlooked a buffalo path we had previously scouted. We set up typical fields of fire for a lineal ambush—the main body spread along the buffalo path with left and right flanks and rear guard inside the small rice-paddy dikes The Cambodian platoon leader set up his command post on the opposite side of the rice paddy from me and Duboise.

Line ambushes are triggered by the soldiers on its flanks. If the enemy comes from the right, the soldier at the left end of the line initiates fire. The ambush is never initiated from the center. On this occasion there was an immediate glitch in the routine. The Cambodians lost radio contact with their battalion headquarters and were forced to move back and forth across the rice paddy to use our American radio. Overall, however, it was just another ordinary night in the life of training the Cambodians in Vietnam. We wrapped ourselves in our camo ponchos on the ground facing out, and Duboise and I took turns being on alert while the other slept.

I was not happy with the recurring traffic back and forth across our position as the Cambodians used our radios—but it became so routine that late in the evening I assumed a group of soldiers approaching was the Cambodians. Another look revealed that it was actually a squad of Viet Cong and that they were inside our platoon position. They were so close that I could see the white stitching on the pockets of their black pajamas, their brown canvas knapsacks, and the AK-47s with thirty-round magazines they were all carrying.

I knew immediately that the crap was about to hit the proverbial fan. What to do? Roll over on my back to bring my Car-15 to bear? Stay still under the camo and hope the darkness covered me? Both actions were fraught with risk. Then Duboise woke up and moved. The VC were as surprised as we that they had walked into our position. They began to respond. Their second in line squatted down and hissed to his point man to stop. The rest of the VC squad initiated their immediate-action drill, all squatting and facing alternate directions—which meant half were looking at us. Our interpreter and I instinctively rolled away from each other and grabbed for our weapons. At the same time, Duboise, who was unaware of our visitors and had been drinking from his canteen turned to see what the commotion was all about.

The VC opened fire on full automatic and sprayed the three of us with lead. My body shook and jerked from the impact of the rounds. Duboise was down with critical wounds. Our interpreter lay mortally wounded. I returned fire and saw several VC go down before they faded into the darkness. The Cambodians were in utter chaos and began firing wildly as they too began to disappear into the darkness. I remember thinking that their wild fire might very well hit me and Duboise and thought, "Please, please don't throw grenades." In the calm after the VC and Cambodian soldiers had "escaped" into the night and in spite of not being able to stand because of my wounds, I crawled to the PRC-25 radio to call for help. The Duty NCO at the commo bunker back at Chi Lang, 25 kilometers away, received the message and alerted the camp. Unfortunately, because army helicopter units in our area were being redeployed, none were available for evacuation support. With no air assets available, a frustrating wait began for the isolated SF camp—as well as for Duboise and me.

I administered IV fluids and morphine to Duboise as we discussed the seriousness of our wounds. Our future didn't look good. We agreed that this appeared to be "the end." Duboise expressed the wish that he could have a final chance to say some things to his mother. All I wanted was a radio call from Chi Lang saying help was on the way. Our situation suddenly got worse. There was a rustle in the brush about 25 meters away, and a soldier appeared pulling another under his arms. I hailed him in Khmer, and he responded by setting his VC buddy on the ground and shooting me one more time. I returned fire, and he fled into the jungle.

Finally, three hours later, two Marine Huey gunships and a Navy Seawolf Cobra responded to the urgent-support request from Chi Lang. Captain Purdy, the detachment commander, along with six SF soldiers climbed aboard. One of the soldiers was Sgt. Robert Reed, longtime friend of both Duboise and me. Reed would later write about much of this story filling in details I was not aware of or have forgotten. He was also a senior medic and carried his aid bag to help.

We were extremely happy to hear on the radio that help was on the way, but we were both fading fast. Duboise later told me he thought, "Well, at least our bodies will be extracted and sent back to the States."

Neither of us was ready to give up just yet. I retrieved and turned on our hand-held strobe lights. We looked like a pair of reclining Statues of Liberty, and each time the strobes blinked, marking our position for the approaching choppers, we also marked ourselves as targets for any VC still in the area. When the choppers reached our location, one of the Marine pilots hollered at Purdy and Reed, "Make the pick-up quick. Any sign of problems, and we're out of here!"

Tracer fire arched up from the jungle as the choppers neared. Despite the hot LZ, a chopper landed about 150 meters from us. Purdy began helping me while Reed began to assess Duboise's condition. The prognosis was not good. He was shot through the chest with multiple rounds. It was difficult to determine the difference between entry and exit wounds. Several of the Cambodians reappeared out of brush to help carry us to the choppers. Purdy remained on the ground to reorganize the platoon while Reed accompanied us abroad.

In the air Reed continued to administer aid. He determined that Duboise, and possibly I, could not make the long flight to the 3rd Evacuation Hospital north of Can To alive, so he directed the pilots to set down at the B-43 base camp. There he did a "cut down" to increase IV fluid and blood flow into Duboise. Army dustoffs finally arrived, and we were loaded aboard for transport to 3rd Evac. Reed accompanied us as he continued to treat our wounds. Again, I recall little of this and know the details only from what Reed told me later. I was conscious enough, however, to hear a doctor say, "His blood pressure is 60 over nothing" just before they rolled me into surgery.

Reed went to a nearby hanger and fell into a deep sleep. He did not see either me or Duboise until he tracked us down twenty-five years later to see it we had survived. We had a wonderful reunion at a Vietnamese restaurant in Tampa, Florida. I remained in Special Forces after eighteen months of recovery and rehabilitation and retired after twenty-two years of service—including two and a half years in Vietnam. Both Duboise and Reed left the army after their tours. Reed later became a contract medic for US Forces in Iraq and was killed in Uzbekistan.

Mike Richardson (1965, A-1 and 1st Brigade Staff) First Marine Air Wing, 1969

The war in Vietnam was not going well in 1968. A major escalation of the conflict during the Tet Offensive in January caught our government and military by surprise. Nor were they prepared for the backlash that followed. Demonstrations and protests were common across the country as students and others marched against the war. Still others marched for civil rights. Tension and violence were common. In April Martin Luther King was assassinated.

President Johnson's popularity plummeted, and he decided not to seek a second term. Robert F. Kennedy entered the race on the Democratic ticket, but in June he was assassinated. Richard Nixon ran as the Republican with a promise to end the war in Vietnam, and he became the country's 37th President. By the end of 1968—in that year alone—over 16,500 of our nation's finest would lose their lives in that God-forsaken country called Vietnam.

I was aware that all these things were going on, but my life was all about flying airplanes. I had joined the Marine Corps the previous year and had entered the Naval Air Flight Program. With luck and a lot of hard work I had also been selected to fly jets when I finished basic flight training out of Pensacola, Florida. From Pensacola I was assigned basic jet training in Meridian, Mississippi. From there it was back to Pensacola for Carrier Qualifications and Gunnery and finally to Kingsville, Texas, for advanced jet training.

It had been my dream to be a military pilot since my days as a student in College Station. I had been a skydiver on the Texas A&M Parachute Team and had fallen in love with the sights, sounds, and even the smell of aviation. One day we had planned a nine-man jump from three planes flying in formation. It was on that day—seeing the beauty of those other airplanes wingtip to wingtip, so close that I thought I could reach out and touch them—that I knew flying had to be in my future.

So in October 1968 I was designated Naval Aviator # 27184 and earned the right to wear my wings of gold. My mom came down from Dallas to Kingsville to pin them on. For me that was the best day of my life and the one accomplishment I am most proud of.

A few weeks later, after some leave at home and travel time, I reported to Cherry Point, North Carolina. There I began the process of becoming not just a "Naval Aviator" but a real Marine Pilot. In flight school I had been told that it normally takes about a year to become fully qualified in any new aircraft before being sent to Vietnam, so I was eager to meet my new squadron mates and start the process.

It didn't take long to find the flight line and locate my squadron's hanger. All I had to do was look for all the airplanes. What a sight it truly was! As I entered the hanger looking for the operations office to present my orders, I was brimming with both excitement and apprehension. With a warm welcome aboard and a big smile the operations officer said, "Great to have you here, Lieutenant Richardson. We have your orders for Vietnam!"

I was sure he had mistaken me for someone else. I pointed to my shiny new wings and reminded him that I hadn't even qualified on my new aircraft. He said he understood, but a replacement pilot was needed, and because I had just walked in the door and was not married, it was my lucky day. He also told me that everything would work out just fine, that I would have top priority on all training and aircraft availability.

Everything happened just as he said. "Needs of the service" dictated that I be ready. I might not have felt fully qualified, but if they told me I was qualified, I was confident that there would be no obstacle I could not adapt to or overcome. Just five months later, in April of 1969, I was on my way to my new squadron in the Republic of South Vietnam.

The first leg of my flight was on a Continental Airlines military charter that took me first to Okinawa. Most of us on board were going for our first tour, but some were returning from R&R or maybe to their second or third time in country. The flight was subdued. Most on board were deep in their thoughts of what the next year might bring. It was late in the day when we arrived in Okinawa, and I was looking forward to a shower and getting out of my uniform. After checking into the Bachelor Officers Quarters, I was pleasantly surprised to run across an old friend from my early days in flight school. He and several others had been assigned to fly helicopters after primary flight training. The helicopter program was a little shorter than the jet program, so I knew many of them were already in country. We had dinner together, and I learned that he had been in Japan for almost two months recovering from burns received from having been shot down in his CH-46 after inserting troops into a hot LZ. For his actions he had received a Purple Heart and a Silver Star. He could have returned home after his recovery, but instead he chose to return to his unit and in his words "go back and finish the job."

Early the next morning we left Okinawa on an Air Force C-141 for Da Nang, which would be my home for the next year. On the ground I reported to the processing center on Freedom Hill, also called Hill 327. Located just west of the airfield, it was best known for its huge PX. The processing center was just a large nondescript metal building. Inside was an elevated platform with a lectern. Facing the platform were a lot of folding chairs, and along the side were a number of desks where clerks were busy answering questions, processing paperwork, and helping new arrivals find their units.

Because I knew the squadron I was to be assigned to and where it was located, I thought this whole exercise was a colossal waste of time. Still, after two years in the Marine Corps I had grown used to the concept of "Hurry up and wait." Noticing other pilots milling about, I joined them in conversation, hoping they might know more than I did about what we might expect.

After a while a Marine captain walked to the lectern and, after getting everyone's attention, began a standard "welcome to Vietnam speech." He appeared to be as bored as we were, and because there was no working sound system, we could understand only a small portion of what he was saying. In any event, my new friends and I had been up since zero dark hundred. Whatever breakfast we had eaten seemed a long time ago, and we were hungry. We were a lot more interested in finding something to eat than in listening to whatever the captain had to say.

Not long into his speech, we heard a loud explosion somewhere off in the distance. The captain paused, looked off to the side for a few seconds, and then continued. After four or five minutes, we heard another explosion. The captain stopped again. I wasn't concerned; it seemed far away. But this was my first day in country, and the captain's expression told me something was not right and certainly not normal. He told us all to take a break, and he would be back.

He returned a short time later and said that the explosions were coming from our own bomb dump and that we should immediately find the nearest bunker and take cover. My new friends and I welcomed the break but did not feel any need for great haste. We were still hungry and wanted to find something to eat. Leaving the building, we were pleasantly surprised to find a mess hall just a short distance away. Unfortunately it had been evacuated. No one was there to serve us. We could see that everyone had left in a hurry. Tables were thrown all about, chairs were toppled, and glass was all over the floor from broken overhead light fixtures.

Despite the damage, this still was a mess hall, so surely there was food somewhere. Because no one was there to help us, a command decision was made to serve ourselves. Scrounging around the area behind the normal serving line, we found no sandwiches, but we did hit pay dirt with the discovery of my favorite dessert—peach ice cream! In short order we found bowls and spoons, and after scooping copious amounts into our bowls, we proceeded to sit and enjoy our afternoon treat. As far as we were concerned this was just another normal day. We were not long into this tasty diversion when we were interrupted by another large explosion. The window screens were blown in, and overhead panels and what was left of the fluorescent lights came raining down on us as we were blown to the floor. Not being the brightest Aggie/Marine around and being more than a little irritated at this inconvenience, I picked up my chair and started picking broken glass from my ice cream as I stubbornly proceeded with my meal. About that time a Marine sergeant burst through the door yelling, and even though my ears were still ringing I believe there were more than a few profanities and something about some idiots needing to find the G.D. bunker.

Sensing there was some truth to what he was saying, we put down our spoons and walked out the door, heading toward where we thought the bunker would be. Passing by the processing center, we all stopped and commented on how the bomb blasts had pushed out the sides of the building, separating the metal from the frame. I was pointing at the destruction when another blast blew the wall completely off and knocked us down for the second time that day. I received a small cut on my arm. After wiping the blood away, I laughed. It was only my first day, and already I had earned a Purple Heart.

I knew that God loves small children and stupid Marines, but even I now understood that I was pressing my luck. The bunker was not far, so we made our way there and ducked in. Designed for twelve to fourteen people, it was about two-thirds below ground and had a frame and metal cover supporting several layers of sandbags. It was more than adequate for our protection and, fortunately, was not too full. We were safe but still had no idea how long we might be there or what options we might have for getting off the hill. The rumor was that Viet Cong sappers had penetrated the bomb dump and that we could expect more attacks. In truth no one really knew what the hell was going on.

The explosions were now coming more frequently, and from time to time we heard large chunks of shrapnel hit the side and top of the bunker. I had never experienced the overpressure of a large bomb blast. The vibrations pulse through my body, and after an hour or so it definitely started to get on my nerves. Across from me sat a Marine grunt who obviously had just come out of the field. He still had on his flak jacket and helmet, and he was more than a little dirty. He probably was there to process home or maybe for a little in-country R&R, but the thing that impressed me is that all the explosions didn't seem to bother him one bit. This must have been nothing compared to what he had seen during his combat tour. Next to him was a young, slender Vietnamese girl maybe eighteen years old. Her dress was clean and tidy compared to the large, very dirty Marine. Probably she had been working in the mess hall, but now she found herself in a dark, musty bomb shelter not knowing what would happen next. The grunt had put his arm around her, thinking he might offer her some comfort, but from the look in her eyes she was more afraid of him than of what was going on outside. She didn't have to wait long for something to change. It was about to get even more exciting.

About the time we decided we were stuck with nowhere to go, a Marine popped in yelling he had a truck and it was time to get the hell out of there. There was no argument. We scrambled out as fast as we could, and sure enough there was a truck. A one-ton flatbed with stake sides, it had more than enough room for all of us, so we all jumped aboard. We were barely on when the driver popped the clutch, skidding the back tires, and off we went. I'm sure the driver was trying to impress us with his high-speed driving skills, but about the second time we made a sharp right turn, the stake side collapsed and several of us started to slide off the truck with it. The woman screamed, and the men all yelled at the driver. Fortunately we were able to grab the person next to us, so no one went over the side. At this point I was more afraid of the driver than of bomb shrapnel.

Finally the truck slowed down. We had been delivered to China Beach, best known as an in-country R&R center—later as the name and location of a popular television series. Several hundred like us were milling about. There was little to do but wait, but someone eventually brought sandwiches and water, and we made ourselves as comfortable as possible because we would be spending the night on the beach. The danger seemed to have passed as there were no reports of other attacks, but the fireworks show continued. As day turned to night, it was like the Fourth of July back home. If I had had a lounge chair and a beer, it couldn't have been a better show. As it was, I was tired and dirty and thinking how good a hot shower would feel. It would be the next day before I could finally check into my squadron.

Late in the evening someone made his way down the beach asking if any of us were officers. When I answered in the affirmative, he directed me to a small group standing near a jeep. In just a few minutes we left the beach and I was given a small room with a bed and running water. (The enlisted troops slept on the beach.) Still, sleep did not come quickly. Going over the events of the day, I wondered what to expect in the year ahead. If all my days were as eventful as this first day, I had one hell of a year to look forward to.

Jim Lanning (1964, D-1) 25th Infantry Division, 1966–67

Every Aggie who served in Vietnam has a story to tell. Unfortunately, some cannot relate their own experiences. It is the responsibility of us who survived to remember and stand for them.

The Corps of Cadets was the crucible in which were forged the standards and values we carried into the military and our later lives. Every fish class was welcomed by harassing sophomores eager to exhibit their privileges as upperclassmen and the somewhat detached seniors, who were masters of all and already looking forward to lives after A&M. The real men of influence and the ones who instilled the Aggie spirit and way of life were the juniors. And so it was in my Corps company—D-1. When I joined Spider D as a naive, scared cadet in the fall of 1964, one junior who greatly influenced my fellow fish and me was Thomas Henry Ralph Jr. of Clifton, Texas. Tom Ralph was the kind of upperclassmen we all hoped to be some day.

Upon graduation, in 1962, Tom accepted a commission in the US Marine Corps. A few years later he was in Vietnam for his first tour. In 1968 he was back in Southeast Asia for his second as a captain in command of India Company, 3rd Battalion, 27th Regiment, 1st Marine Division. On May 16, India Company air assaulted into a landing zone near the hamlet of Le Nam on Go Noi Island as a part of Operation Allen Brook. The remainder of the battalion was scheduled for insertion the following day.

On the morning of the 17th, before the rest of the battalion arrived, India Company approached a dry river bed with a heavily wooded treeline. Without warning the unit came under attack by an NVA battalion firing mortars, machine guns, rocket-propelled grenades, and small arms from well-concealed positions. An intense battle followed. Owing to a lack of airlift assets, reinforcements did not arrive to assist India Company until late in the afternoon. By then Tom Ralph, two of his lieutenants, and twenty-six other Marines lay dead. One of these casualties, PFC Robert C. Burke of Monticello, Illinois, posthumously received the Medal of Honor—the youngest recipient of the war at eighteen years of age—for his bravery that day.

News of Tom's death saddened all of us who had been privileged to know him. It also reminded us that we who had answered our country's call to the profession of arms risked far more than hardship and family separation. Our mortality was on the line.

I thought of Tom often over the years, but not until nearly a quarter-century after he was killed did I learn more details about his death. On May 11, 1994, the *Clifton Record*, Tom's hometown newspaper, published the following:

> Dear Editor:
>
> This letter is 26 years late. Even now, putting these words on paper is emotionally painful. My purpose in writing is to let the citizens of Clifton know the story of one of their own, a young man, a hero of large proportion (even by Texas standards).
>
> In early March of 1968, I was a freshly minted infantry Second Lieutenant of Marines assigned to India Company, Third Battalion, 27th Marine Regiment.
>
> Our area of operations was in an area called "Death Valley"—a very appropriate name. The company commander was Captain Thomas H. Ralph, Jr.
>
> Captain Ralph was serving his second tour in Viet Nam, and was wise to the situation and things necessary to keep his Marines alive. He was successful. Our casualty numbers were the lowest in the battalion.
>
> Though we never forgot the protocol of rank, we became very good friends. We enjoyed making "digs" at the other's alma mater—he attended Texas A&M, while I came out of the Virginia Military Institute.
>
> Moreover, he was my mentor, letting me learn by doing. He let me make non-fatal mistakes while precluding my making fatal ones to myself or my men. If anything, Tom was one of the fairest men I have ever known.
>
> For instance, after 12 to 14 hours of fighting in the jungle in 125-degree heat, men still had to remain awake on guard that night. Being mere mortals, some would fall asleep. This "crime" was punishable under the Uniform Code of Military Justice with six months in the brig, six months forfeiture of pay, and a bad conduct discharge.
>
> Instead of this punishment, Tom simply assigned the sleepy Marine to two days' work in the morgue. He got back a grateful Marine who never again fell asleep on guard.
>
> In this, and in ways too numerous to recount, Tom became one of the most popular leaders to his men of any other I knew in my Marine Corps career.
>
> Tom was a smart leader. On many occasions he simply "out-thought"

and defeated the foe. This went a long way towards gaining the respect of his troops. They trusted him, and never questioned an order. Extra steaks and beer while in base camp always raised morale. I never knew how he managed to provide those things.

I could expound in great lengths about the qualities that made Tom a great man and friend, but this is not a book. You'll just have to take word of someone who was there.

It's time to describe the true mettle of the man.

On 17 May 1968, the company was on patrol in an area which higher command had neglected for some time. At approximately 10 a.m., India Company, with 146 men, ran headlong into a North Vietnamese regiment with an estimated 2,000-plus men.

It's not my purpose to tell a war story, nor should you be asked to read the details of this one. It was brutal, but the company did what Marines have always done—fought with everything they had.

Flying bullets sounded like the inside of a bees' nest, punctuated by the explosions of grenades, mortars, and artillery. Tom was all over the field—directing, comforting, fighting, leading. He was always at the weakest point, shoring it up.

Somewhere close to 1 p.m., a bullet creased my head over my left eye. I did not fall, but stood unconscious in the line of fire. From I don't know where, Tom ran to me, knocked me down, and attempted to drag me to some cover.

The bullets that killed him were meant for me.

They say that laying down your life for another is the full measure of a man. In that sense, Tom is a giant!

I owe Tom a great debt. I spent another three years in Viet Nam, attempting to repay that debt. It has, however, taken me these 26 years to realize that I can never repay that debt.

I have thought of Tom Ralph every day since that hot day in May 1968. This May 17, would you think of him, too?

Thank you.

M. N. (Chip) Chafey
Major, USMC, (Disb. Ret.)
Carlsbad, CA

Jeffery Murray (1973, Squadron 6 and H-2) 281st Aviation Company, 1969

On the 21st of January 1969 we were on standby to support several Recondo teams in the jungle outside our compound. We got a call for extraction of a team in contact with one wounded. We ran to our aircraft, where S.Sgt. Marvin A. Gies of the 5th Special Forces Group Recondo School briefed us on the mission and then hopped in back as the recovery sergeant. Giles added that he was leaving for Hawaii the next morning on R&R and that his wife was already there waiting.

We took off, got to altitude, and contacted the team. They popped smoke, gave us a direction from the smoke, and we dropped down to pick them up. We flew on the heading they gave us, eventually slowing down to hover over the dense trees. S.Sgt. Gies suddenly shouted on the intercom, "Stop, they're right below us."

We hovered, and as I looked back at Gies at least seven rounds came up through the bottom of the aircraft. Gies rose up and turned over to a half sitting position with a gaping hole in his neck and blood shooting everywhere. SP4 Alan Johnson, a new door gunner but trained in what to do, immediately came to Gies's aid, applying pressure to the wound. I told the AC who was looking forward and had no idea we had been hit that we needed to head out of there in a hurry, and I then called Nha Trang tower and told them (not asking) that we were over flying their runway with a casualty and landing at the hospital pad and they had better clear the traffic. Our commanding officer kept coming on the radio net to ask what we were doing. We replied that we had a wounded man and that it was bad. We had S.Sgt. Gies on the pad in three or four minutes, but with a hole in his jugular vein as well as one in his chest, he did not survive the night.

We flew back to the 281st area, exchanged our aircraft for one that was not shot up, and with the same crew returned to the area of operations. In the interim another aircraft was shot out of the same hole. An Air Force Huskie with a hoist had extracted the most seriously wounded of the Recondo team. It was now our turn to go down and pick up the remainder of the team. We hovered over the pickup zone. (It was surrounded by jungle and too small for us to land.) Other helicopters covered our flanks with 7.62-mm rounds by the hundreds interspersed with an occasional rocket. The fire was so close that a piece of shrapnel came in from somewhere and ripped a hole in the knee of my Nomex trousers.

We got the first group out on a McGuire Rig and landed back at base. A second bird did the same, pulling out the remainder of the team.

The mission was considered successful. But S.Sgt. Gies lost his life, and he left a wife awaiting him in a paradise of a vacation spot only to receive notification that he would not be coming. War is hell, and life sometimes sucks.

Charles H. (Butch) Gregory (1964, F-2) 525th Military Intelligence Group, 1967–68

On May 22, 1964, I graduated from Texas A&M and was commissioned a 2nd Lieutenant in the Military Intelligence branch of the US Army. My commission carried a standard two-year active-duty military-service obligation. Rather than enter active duty immediately, I obtained a deferment to attend law school, which I did at the University of Texas in Austin.

I entered active-duty service on April 10, 1967. As a law-school graduate, I was eligible for a branch transfer to the Judge Advocate branch of the Army, but such a change required a three- or possibly four-year active-duty obligation. And I wasn't interested in doing Army legal work. As a result I chose to remain in the Intelligence branch. In the wisdom of the Army, all Intelligence branch officers were required to complete the Infantry Officer Basic Course at Fort Benning, Georgia. After Benning, I went to the Intelligence Officer Basic Course at Fort Holabird, Maryland. These two courses were the full extent of my Army training. Before completing IOBC at Benning, I received notice that my first permanent assignment would be to an unspecified posting in Vietnam. Before leaving Holabird, I received orders to Vietnam and to report to Oakland Army Terminal on August 9, 1967, about four months to the day from when I entered active duty.

I actually departed the US from Travis AFB, California, on August 12, 1967, which meant my DEROS was August 11, 1968. After nearly twenty-four hours in transit, my flight arrived at Long Binh military post, in Vietnam, where I spent two days at the replacement depot awaiting a specific assignment—the 525th Military Intelligence Group. Ultimately I ended up in the 519th Military Intelligence Battalion, which provided personnel to several headquarters area commands.

My initial assignment in country was to CICV, a brainchild of Gen. Alexander McChristian, the previous G-2 of MACV. General McChristian's vision of CICV was a central intelligence center where American and Vietnamese intelligence personnel worked collaboratively. In reality, however, little collaboration took place. The different sections were located side by side, with connecting doorways, but there was virtually no interaction. At CICV, we accumulated large amounts of information, but much of it was historical and of little immediate value at any given time.

I was assigned to the Research and Analysis Section of CICV, which existed to research a number of different areas in response to requests from the field. A few months after my arrival, the concept of collaboration was scrapped and the American parts of CICV were combined with similar groups at US headquarters. The combined R&A Section did similar work. One early project that I participated in required that I spend a short time at the forward headquarters of the 1st Infantry Division at Lai Khe, in III Corps. At Lai Khe, the 1st ID was testing a new device called "the sniffer." Sensors were attached to the skids of helicopters that were flown in a gridded pattern over an area to collect data. The sensors detected high levels of ammonia, indicating possible enemy-troop concentrations. When such readings were detected, a force would be inserted into the area in an effort to establish contact. That would be followed by a search-and-destroy operation. During my short time there, we got one strong reading. A battalion was deployed, and it encountered a regiment-size enemy force.

Another R&A Section effort was to study rice supplies and movements in all of South Vietnam. The enemy food supply consisted largely of rice. Commanders of major US field groups periodically became interested in finding and interdicting the rice supply. A lot of information was gathered, but trying to cut off the rice supply was like trying to catch the rain. Rice was just too pervasive to be located and cut off.

The Tet Offensive of late January 1968 brought an increased urgency to the US military effort. About six weeks after Tet, I was transferred to the Current Intelligence Section of MACV. Unlike R&A, current intelligence was just that: anything older than a few days to a week was history. I was assigned to the Targeting Section, which worked up missions for B-52 aircraft strikes. There were ten strikes daily. Each day targets were presented to two general officers, who selected the strikes. During my first month, all our targets were in support of the embattled Marine force at Khe Sanh. Once the siege of Khe Sanh ended, strikes were directed at other targets around the country. I continued to do targeting work, concentrating on the I Corps region during the remainder of my tour, which ended June 25, 1969, when I left Vietnam for a three-month temporary-duty assignment in Bangkok, Thailand. After Bangkok I was assigned to a basic-training brigade at Fort Bliss, in El Paso, Texas, where I remained until completing my active duty service on May 22, 1969.

Bill Vasser (1964, Squadrons 9 and16) 480th Tactical Fighter Squadron, 366th Fighter Wing, 1968

I served in Vietnam with the Air Force in 1968 as a weapons-systems officer, better known as the GIB (Guy in Back), on an F-4 Phantom and again in 1972 as a forward air controller, flying an O-2A. All total, I flew 101 missions over North Vietnam and 110 over South Vietnam.

My first tour I was with the 480th Tactical Fighter Squadron of the 366th Tactical Fighter Wing. I was well aware that Air Force studies dating back to World War I showed that if you survived your first ten missions, you had a 90 percent chance of surviving your tour. I also knew that if you are shot down, your odds of being rescued drop off drastically if you are not picked up in the first hour. And getting shot down after dark narrowed the chance of rescue to near zero.

After several months I had successfully completed fifty missions and was often assigned newly arrived front-seat pilots. We weapons-systems officers were known as back-seat pilots, among other names. We operated the weapons systems, radar, navigation, and radio communications. We got to say only a few things, such as, "Nice landing," "I'll buy the first round," and "I'll take the fat one."

I don't consider the following a "war story," but it is the one I remember best. It is more a "five beers later, I got one better than that" story. On April 21, 1968, I volunteered to sit day alert as Gunfighter 02 to insure that I would have the evening off to attend the Texas A&M Muster at the Da Nang Air Base Officers Club. My front-seater was a newly arrived pilot who had flown only two previous missions. Major Webster checked out our F-4 to be sure it was properly loaded at the max weight of 58,000 pounds with two drop tanks, four sidewinders, four sparrow air-to-air missiles, and six Mark 82 slick 500-pound bombs. Our 20 Mike Mike gunpod hung centerline.

Once satisfied with our plane, we cocked it in place so we could make our five-minute scramble time. We were to be relieved at 6:00 p.m., and I was starting to count down the hours when, just before 4:00 p.m., the scramble horn sounded and we ran to our cocked F-4D. As I was strapping into the back seat, I was a little disappointed that we were getting scrambled so late and thought to myself that it looked like I would miss Muster, as missions last about 1.3 hours and maintenance and mission debriefing 2-plus additional hours. A minute later we roared—more like lumbered—down the runway.

At our weight it took a bunch of runway to get up to nose-rotate speed, 182 knots, and off the ground, at 200 knots. We used a good eight thousand feet and then staggered out over the hooches at the end of the runway with both burners roaring as we got up to a decent flying climb-out speed of 300 knots.

As soon as we joined up, on lead's wing, we got vectors and target info from the airborne control agency. We were scrambled to knock out a 37-mm gunsite on a mountaintop that was firing at C-130s flying supplies into Khe Sanh. Several other flights had taken their turn at the target site with no luck. An A-4 had been hit earlier that day. We took our turn dropping our bombs with marginal success. They shot at us as we dropped our bombs all around the peak. It would take a direct hit to knock out the hilltop target. At least they stopped shooting after we turned away. I think they just ran out of ammo, or else it was nearing their 5:00 p.m. quitting time. Nonetheless, we chose not to get in a gun battle with them with our 20-mm Gatling gun.

Because we still had our two thousand rounds of 20 Mike Mike ammo, Gunfighter 01, our lead, checked in with the airborne command center, and they looked for a target in North Vietnam. They said they didn't have any, but an F-105 pilot came up on the radio and said he had just chased some trucks down a road that ran North-South just east of the mountain range to a park site north of the DMZ. So off we went.

I wasn't too happy about where we were going. That area had a lot of guns—it must have been some general's or senator's R&R area. It was off the beaten resupply route and hard to get to, as it was surrounded by mountains. Our lead found the suspected truck park and rolled in and sprayed the area with a long burst of 20 Mike Mike. Being an "old head" of 120 missions, he rolled in at the normal 13,000 feet, but fired at about 9,000 feet and pulled off. I watched his tracers hit somewhere in target area. I can say with certainty that they did "fall" to the ground somewhere in North Vietnam, but that is about all. He then called, "Off. Two, it's your turn." It was now a little after 5:00 p.m., and I remembered that it was not cool to get shot down after dark.

My aircraft commander had only two previous missions. I was the old head GIB with thirty North and fifty total Vietnam missions. I was supposed to keep him safe. I ran through our "personal safety brief of best place to head if we get hit" with him. I advised him that with our northwesterly attack heading, it would be best to head for the mountains due west (not very populated, rough terrain, and heavy foliage with trees and lots of places to hide) and not try to make the coast, some twenty miles to the east across flat, heavily populated open land and rice paddies.

We rolled in from 13,000 feet in a 45-degree dive. As I called altitudes, I calculated our bottoming-out level. As we went through 6,000 feet (our firing altitude), we did not fire. "Hello," I thought, "pull the fucking trigger!"

I called out "5,500, fire!" and then (much louder) "5,000, fire!" I was starting to get very concerned that this would be my last mission. At 4,500, I called out the altitude and added, "Shoot and pull!"

I was sooo happy to hear the grrrrrrr of our 20-mm Gatling gun spitting out its 100 rounds a second. Major Webster must have thought he was at a stateside gunnery range and would walk a line in the woods with our 20 mm. He did a very good job—a nice "S" pattern in the wooded area. Unfortunately nothing blew up.

It takes 2,300 feet to pull out of a 45-degree dive at 450 knots. I figured that a two- or three-second burst put our nice white belly about 1,000 feet above the ground. (I cannot imagine the idiot who thought a white belly, of all colors, would be hard to see. You can spot it fifteen miles away against a blue sky.) We bottomed out of our dive, in great .50-caliber range and very accurate 37-mm range—and there were a lot of enemy guns shooting back. Heck, even kids with slingshots had a good chance of hitting us.

Our Lead must have woke them up or caught them at the 5:00 p.m. shift change. You know how government workers are at 5:00 p.m.—running for the exit. They probably had to stop and run back to their guns, because they were really pissed off when we pulled off target. As I watched our red tracers go down, I saw their big red 37-mm fireballs and a bunch of .50-caliber white tracers coming up. It was like being in the middle of a Fourth of July fireworks display. We were the lone duck on opening day. As we bottomed out at about 1,000 feet, I heard that sickening sound of tin foil crunching and tearing, the screeching of metal turbine blades grinding and scraping on something they shouldn't, as a couple 37 mms found us. We took one close to me in the left air intake—I could see pieces of shrapnel sticking out of the top. Another round hit our left wing, knocking down the left landing gear.

I think we took another hit, but I'm not sure where. Anyway, two were enough to ruin our day. Since we were in a hard pull off right, we were heading north when we actually got hit. There was no way with the damage we had sustained to turn back to the west and the safety of a mountain bailout. That would require turning into our left dead engine and damaged left wing. I sure hated to see the nice safe mountains disappear behind us. When I looked east to the ocean there was nothing but sand as far as the eye could see. Heck, I couldn't even see the water we were so low.

As I was still looking around for tracers, Webster told me all the failed-systems lights were on, that we had a fire in the number 1 engine, and that he was shutting it down. Lead called and said, "You're burning from the intakes back."

Well, la de da, that was real comforting, since that was where I was sitting. Lead could have said all kind of nice things, like they are not shooting at you any more, or head some direction, or, more importantly, jettison your external stores. Or he could have asked about our status. But no, he tells us we are on fire and right where I am sitting. I think we knew that!

I am not sure how he could tell anything because he was so far away. The other aircraft is supposed to pull up close to assess what he can about battle damage. I guess he kept his distance because he did not want to get hit if we blew up or got shot at again since we were such a nice target.

Fortunately no one else bothered to shoot at us, even though we were really low, about 2,000 feet (a real duck-shot target drone), slow, at 250 knots, and, streaming a big smoke trail, as our poor old dying Phantom struggled to get us to the ocean on one engine in full afterburner, and our left main gear dangled in the breeze like a broken leg. Guess they didn't want to waste any more ammo and were just waiting for us to fall out of the sky. All they would have to do was line up with the smoke trail and pull some lead. Or else they thought we were trying to bait them to shoot. But I really think it was just because it was after 5:00 p.m.—you know, quitting time. They didn't want to get their guns dirty and have to re-clean them and then get home late for supper.

Major Webster and I went over the standards of what was wrong—number1 on fire and shutting down, number1 hydraulics at 0. Lots of warning lights, probably thirty of a possible fifty. My radar was out. I gave Webster our position so he could send out a Mayday. Lead scrambled rescue choppers and other fighters with ordnance. As I pulled my seat belt extra tight, stored stuff out of the way, checked my six-shooter, ammo, survival knife (like I was going to start a war, John Wayne style), getting ready to eject, and looking at nothing but sand as far as I could see, I thought the war was over for us. The bad guys would catch us fairly quickly in the rice paddies. Hopefully we wouldn't get shot or beat up too badly.

The thought crossed my mind that a US Air Force Manual states, "It is generally inadvisable to eject directly over the area you just bombed."

I was not looking forward to this, but somehow we kept lumbering along. Webster was doing an excellent job keeping us airborne with all the things wrong. There was not much I could do other than offer encouragement and suggestions and keep a sharp eye out for someone wanting to claim a shoot-down to start firing at us. There was no way we could dodge any gunfire.

After the initial hit and sorting out what was wrong, we just casually talked about the aircraft status and how it was flying—which was not very well. The most severe problem was the hydraulics that operated the flight controls. We had lost PC number1 (left wing) flight-control hydraulics. Backup flight-control hydraulics were failing because of the hit in the gear wheel well. PC number 2 (right wing) flight-control hydraulics were still good, but they too were losing pressure. Somehow, though, that old Phantom was hanging in there, refusing to fall out of the sky.

Webster maintained 250 knots and a steady climb. We were up to about eight thousand feet when we hit the coast. Just as we crossed the beach and went feet wet (over the water), we lost all electrical power and my ability to talk to the front seat. It sucked not knowing if he could signal me to eject or would just eject me, I had to sit in a ready position.

The way the F-4 is set up, the front seater automatically ejects the back seater when he pulls his ejection handle. We had no intercom communications. We did have hand signals, but they're hard to see with the GIB having to look around the pilot's ejection seat. Or there might not be time for a hand signal. Bottom line, you get only a couple of seconds to see that hand signal or the eject light, and then, one way or another, you are gone.

When we made it over the water, I felt confident we would be rescued and started to go back over my stuff. I had just made new maps and had my camera with some neat pictures in it of the guys getting awards. I thought—funny what you think about in such a situation—they would get really mad if I lost their pictures. After a minute of trying to figure out how to hold onto the camera when we ejected, I decided to remove the film and leave the camera behind. Trying to hold on to a camera and maps while ejecting at 20 Gs into a 400 mph air stream didn't seem like a really smart idea. So, very reluctantly, I stashed my camera out of the way. Then, giving thought to my maps, I figured I could tuck then inside my flight suit. It had taken me hours to make them. I had to be quick, because the eject light might come on at any time.

Then I had a couple of minutes to just enjoy the ride and look at the ocean as we cruised south along the coastline. We passed Tiger Island, right on the DMZ line, so I knew we were pretty safe now. I started to wonder how far Webster was going to go before we bailed out. The closer to home, the better. I looked ahead toward Da Nang AB and saw it was socked in with weather. At first I thought he was going to try to get all the way back. We had gotten up to 15,000 and were still trucking along at 250 knots when we spotted a group of five navy ships in a circle. I thought that was weird.

My thoughts returned to the airplane as it started to wobble and dip a wing. I thought we were going to circle the ships before bailing out, and then the number 2 hydraulics system, the last of our flight-control hydraulics, lost all pressure, and Webster lost control. As the aircraft began to roll, Webster hit the eject button. I was looking at the ships below when I saw the eject light and reacted instantly without thinking. I reached for the "D" ring ejection-seat handle between my knees and pulled. The ejection seat is supposed to fire within a nanosecond of pulling this handle. That nanosecond seemed like forever as I sat there thinking, "What the shit have I done now?" and looked around the cockpit one last time wondering, "Is this baby going to fire?"

About that time, the ejection fired, catapulting me up the rail—the F-4 seemed to disappear below me like a roller coaster in reverse. There was a lot of wind noise, and I bounced around a little in the seat. I couldn't see anything. The next thing I remember was looking down at this circle of Navy ships between my knees. I thought that was pretty cool and wondered if the seat would work as advertised. I planned to sit in the sucker until I could see men on the ship before trying to separate from the seat manually. I remained in the seat for a minute or so as I descended from 16,000 feet to 10,000 feet when I heard things whirling, hissing, and clicking as the seat belts and my attachments were cut so I could separate and get kicked out of the seat. Next I felt a jerk as the main chute opened. As I checked my chute, I thought, "This is pretty neat, but I wouldn't want to do it again."

I continued to check everything and also looked around for Webster. I couldn't see his canopy but could see Lead circling. I got out my radio to tell the world I was still alive and said, "This is Gunfighter 02 Bravo."

Lead replied, "Shut up Vasser, we're working your rescue."

"Well, pardon me," I thought, "I am just the guy who got shot down!" Nothing like being put on hold when you are just hanging around under a parachute. I went back to watching the ships, listening to my rescue on my survival radio, and looking for Webster.

I noticed that I was heading for one ship in particular—which turned out to be the USS *Cleveland*. My chute was not steerable, but I discovered that I could twist and pull the straps to point it in certain directions. At first I thought I was going to be Joe Cool and land on the helo pad in the back of this ship. I tugged on the chute risers to head in that direction. As I neared the ship, though, I realized that I didn't have good control of my descent rate and that I might hit the side of the ship by coming in low or be dragged off the ship even if I hit my mark. Neither option seemed good. In a near-panic I managed to turn the chute so that I drifted down parallel with the ship about a hundred yards off the left side. When I saw all the sailors taking pictures of me, I waved at them. I almost forget to deploy my water wings and dinghy in the excitement.

I hit the water just in front of the *Cleveland* thinking it would be a hell of a thing if they ran over me. As I bobbed to the surface, an LSD landing craft pulled up and there was a "Hello" shouted from above. A helicopter also hovered nearby.

The LSD pilot looked like he didn't have any clothes on. (Later I learned he had been sun bathing when he got the scramble notice.) I waved off the helo since the LSD seemed a better option and climbed into my dinghy. As the LSD pulled up next to me, I couldn't figure out how I was going to get up its seven-foot side. My concern was answered when a sailor with arms like Mighty Mouse's came aside. He held on to the side of the landing craft with one arm, grabbed my extended arm with the other, and then lifted me, soaking wet with all my gear, out of the water and threw me onto the deck above. With my wet gear I must have weighed more than two hundred pounds. I was impressed!

On deck I discovered three more sailors, a very large cake, and a barrel full of beer. I thought this rather strange, but what a way to get rescued! They asked if I would like a beer, and I replied, "Well, don't mind if I do."

Another LSD picked up Webster. We boarded the *Cleveland* together.

On board we learned that this was the first anniversary of the amphibious transport's launching and this was her maiden voyage/combat tour. She had been on station since November for a nine-month tour. The ship was having a "down day" to celebrate the event. They were having a huge steak fry on the back of the ship, and the LSD had picked up the celebratory cake from a larger vessel. Most of the crew was on deck taking it easy, while several of their LSDs were in the water. They were not allowed to drink beer on the ship, so they put the beer on the small craft and took several crew members at a time on a "fishing brew" tour around the ship. As a result, they had lots of their small boats in the water and were able to pick us up with very little problem.

They had seen our aircraft trailing smoke and watched it crash into the sea. Comments from crewmembers included, "Hey, that is really cool."

About that time they also saw our parachutes and thought that was a neat air show for them. Our rescue was the most significant event for that crew during their long cruise. Several of the sailors' hometown newspapers related the story that so and so from the ship had "personally" rescued us and was a hero. They got a big kick out of that. One guy was asleep through the whole thing, but he "rescued us" per his hometown newspaper.

The next day Webster and I heloed back to Da Nang AB, where the chopper pilot asked where we wanted to get out. We made a quick decision and headed for the Jolly Green Giants pad at the midpoint of the taxiway. We figured we could get a lift from a crew van back to our squadron pretty easy from there. A fuel truck happened by, and we jumped on board. As it turned out, the entire squadron, the Wing Commander, and everyone else with a jeep or car was running around trying to find out where we were. Of the last six planes shot down, we were the first crew to get rescued. When they got the word that we were on the fuel truck driving across the tarmac, they came from everywhere with lights and sirens going. What a way to return!

From then on, no one wanted to fly with me. I was known as Magnet Ass. I had gotten hit by small arms a couple of times before our shoot-down and several times after, but I was never aware until after we landed. Later my Phantom took a 37-mm hit—I did notice that one—that knocked out an engine. We had to limp home on one engine from quite a ways up north. After that the name really stuck.

When I rounded up my Aggie buddies back at Da Nang and asked for my $5 back for our Muster dinner, they told me my excuse for missing Muster was not good enough because I made it back, and they knew I would have wanted them to drink up the $5 celebrating my rescue.

Over the years I have maintained contact with the *Cleveland* by attending their reunions. I also pay my respect to my A&M classmates and fellow Vietnam squadron members who were killed in the war: a plaque in my office notes their names under the heading "Freedom is not free. All gave some; some gave all."

Mac Phillips (1969, D-1) 101st Airborne Division, 1971

When I joined the 101st Airborne Division after my old unit, the 1st Cavalry, stood down and went home in early 1971, I assumed command of a rifle platoon that was a total mess. Months before, hit by "friendly artillery," they had suffered nine dead and nine wounded. My company commander, Capt. Martin Niskanen, was a top-shelf commander and became a good friend. He gave me carte blanche to get the platoon functional. After a few days of observing, I replaced my platoon sergeant and promoted several soldiers into leadership positions. Soon we were an effective fighting unit.

Near the end of my tour, I was out of the field and working in the Brigade TOC. One day I was ordered to deliver some papers to my old battalion in the jungle. While waiting for a chopper to take me to Camp Eagle, I wandered around the perimeter. To my surprise I came across Kent Mills, who had been a year behind me in Spider D back in College Station. As I recalled the grief I had given him when he was a fish, my first reaction on seeing him was, "Uh oh, he's got loaded M-16 in his hands." I was very happy when he smiled and began a friendly conversation. After only a few minutes, my bird returned and I was lifted out of the jungle.

It wasn't until 2001 that I heard anything more about Captain Niskanen and Kent Mills. My old boss and fellow Aggie at Brigade, Maj. Robbie Robertson, called me after seeing my name in one of the Former Student publications. We talked a while, and I asked if he had run into Capt. Niskanen after the war. After a brief silence, he said, "Mac, I guess you never heard. Capt. Niskanen and one of his platoons were all killed in a Chinook crash in November 1971, after you went home."

I felt like someone had sunk a knife deep in my chest. I asked which of the platoons had been in the crash, but he wasn't sure. A few days later, knowing Mills had been in country when the helicopter crashed, I contacted him. The news could not have been worse. Kent said it was my old platoon that went down with no survivors. He even had a picture he had taken of the men loading the Chinook. He and his men were due to be lifted out next, but bad weather canceled their extraction.

I later learned that the chopper had gone down in the vicinity of Hai Van Pass en route to Da Nang. The pilot apparently developed vertigo and flew full speed into a mountainside. It took more than a week to recover the bodies. Since learning about the crash, I have visited the Vietnam Veterans Memorial Wall in Washington, where I found the names of many of my old platoon as well as Texas Aggies.

Larry Sommers (1968, C-1) 4th Infantry Division, 1970

My infantry platoon of about thirty-five men in Vietnam was an eclectic group. It was a lot like my fish buddies, who showed up wide-eyed and clueless in 1964 at an A&M where upperclassmen didn't like us until a year later.

One man in my platoon was the equivalent of the class clown. His nickname was Ding-A-Ling, and he always had a joke to tell or a way to pick up everyone's spirits. One day we were humping through really hilly jungle in the Central Highlands, making a long move to secure a landing zone so that some general could fly in and visit the troops. Everyone was dragging, so during a brief stop Ding put two heavy rocks in his ruck. He told me and the platoon that he was doing this so that when he got to the LZ and took them out, he would really feel great because his load was so much lighter. We couldn't help but smile, and everyone's spirits were lifted.

After arriving at the LZ, Ding pulled out a bright red braided belt he had bought at a Montagnard village a couple of weeks earlier and wrapped it around his waist. We had no clue why, but we soon would learn. The general landed an hour later amid fanfare and hurried activity. He made his rounds, and when he got to Ding he saw the red belt. "What's this?" he asked.

Ding replied, "Our unit's called the Red Warriors, and I'm honoring all red warriors."

I was doing all I could to keep from losing my military bearing. But when Ding took out the rocks he had been carrying and said, "Sir, here's a souvenir for you from Vietnam," I lost it. The general didn't know what to say, but he held on to the rocks as he moved on. I glanced at the rest of the platoon to see them burying their faces—laughing so hard they were crying.

Some time later, during an intense firefight, Ding earned a high-valor medal when he pulled to safety two wounded men who'd been pinned down by enemy fire . Upon receiving his medal, he said, "Was no big deal."

But it was a big deal, and so was he.

Bruce G. McKenty (1970, B-2) 1st Cavalry Division, 1972–73

I flew with F Troop, 9th Cavalry—the last Air Cavalry Troop from the 1st Squadron, 9th Cavalry, 1st Cavalry Division, to serve in Vietnam. It stood down and went home in February 1973, after the ceasefire was in place. F Troop and three other air-cavalry troops were about the only active US Army combat forces in Vietnam from about mid-1972 until we went home. There were US advisors (combat forces) and combat service support units around the country but no others who engaged in combat activities on a daily basis. The Air Force, Navy, and Marine air assets were still active, but no other US military units were on the ground. The big difference for F Troop and other air-cavalry units was that when we got into trouble, there was no one on the ground to help out. If shot down we had to rely on our organic assets for rescue.

On December 3, 1972, we had an early breakfast and grabbed our C-rations for the rest of the day, to be consumed at the airstrip at Lai Khe. The team put together was one UH-1H (C&C), three UH-1Hs with the Browns (ready reaction team of ARVN Rangers), four AH-1Gs (Cobra gunships) and three OH-6As. Because enemy activity in the area around the Cambodian border was heavy, we usually flew heavy pink teams (two AH-1Gs and an OH-6A plus the UH-1H C&C). Our mission was to recon the area between Tay Ninh city and the Parrots Beak on the Cambodian border to find, report, and destroy the NVA supply line from Hanoi.

We had worked this area, on and off, for the past several months. It was always the same thing. We kept reporting activity, which increased every day, but nothing ever happened. Oh, every once in a while the Air Force FACs would give us a pair of fighters to drop some 500-pound bombs or napalm for our viewing pleasure—CBUs were also fun to watch. The NVA and VC must have thought we were just putting on an air show for them or maybe were there for some good old antiaircraft target practice. As it turned out that day, it was the latter. The first team out refueled at Lai Khe and headed for the AO. It consisted of the command and control UH-1 (piloted by Maj. George Hewlett and 1st Lieutenant Jefferies), a pair of AH-1s (one flown by CW2 Bobby Rinehart and me; the other crewed by CW2 Bob Monette and 1st Lt. Danny Buda) and an OH-6 (flown by WO1 Wally Lundwall). We headed for an area just east of the Razorback Mountains, northwest of the Michelin Rubber Plantation. The Cobras, led by CW2 "Buffalo" Bob Monette, made a couple of slow and low passes (trolling for the bad guys) and then put the little bird on the deck. The Cobras then began their racetrack pattern at about 1,800 feet, bobbing and weaving, just below the cloud layer.

Things were fairly quiet, and then "ka-boom!" A loud explosion violently shook our helicopter. A SA-7 missile had hit us in the left engine door destroying our engine and rupturing fuel lines, hydraulic lines, electrical cables, and such. The engine and transmission areas were immediately enveloped in flames. We began an emergency engine-out auto-rotation. The fire burned through the rear firewall into the cockpit, which filled quickly with flames, toxic fumes, and smoke from the burning aircraft components. We had no outside communications. We felt isolated. The AH-1G is a closed-cockpit aircraft, and the canopies should not be opened above 60 knots. The minimum airspeed for auto-rotation is 80 knots. At about 1,200 feet above the ground, our flight controls began to freeze up from the loss of hydraulic fluid and because fire was fusing the control tubes in the transmission area, leaving us very little control of flight direction or rate of descent. Unable to breathe, we opened the front canopy, which immediately sucked the fire through the entire cockpit, enveloping us in flames. We both unbuckled our seat belts and shoulder harnesses. Jumping without parachutes at about a thousand feet meant certain death, but it seemed better than burning to death. Then we opened the rear canopy, and the flames were sucked out through the right rear of the cockpit. Able to breathe again and not burned badly, we decided to ride it out. We quickly rebuckled our seat belts and shoulder harnesses. By this time we were about eight hundred feet above the ground and had no control over our vertical rate of descent, which was increasing. The ground was closing fast. Finally we began a deceleration move with our cyclic, and both of us put every ounce of energy we had into pulling up on the collective to slow our decent—without much success. We hit the ground at between 40 and 50 knots, in an extremely uneven, small clearing. Our skids collapsed, and our rotor blades cut off the tail boom. Bouncing about twenty feet in the air, we flipped upside down, landing on the canopy. The fire continued and began to cook-off ammunition from the bay and the wing stores. Knocked unconscious, I was hanging upside down and covered in blood from my injuries. With the helicopter in flames and ammunition exploding, Bobby Rinehart, who had gotten out, returned to the aircraft to pull what he thought was my dead body from the burning aircraft. As he cut me out of my seat belt and shoulder harness and started dragging me away from the burning aircraft, I started to come to. He realized I was alive, grabbed me, and we started running from the pursuing North Vietnamese. If Bobby hadn't wanted to keep my dead body from burning up in the aircraft, I would still be there today. We finally reached the C&C rescue helicopter in a nearby clearing. Major Hewlett wasn't leaving without his boys, and thanks to some heroic actions by "Buffalo" Bob Monette and Wally Lundwall, who kept the bad guys away, we were picked up and flown to the 3rd Field Hospital in Saigon.

Rinehart suffered severe burns and lacerations and was eventually evacuated to the States. I had minor burns, lacerations, a fractured skull, and three broken vertebrae. After release from the hospital, I was medically grounded due to my fractured skull but eventually assumed command of HHC, 12th Combat Aviation Group, for the remainder of my tour.

Frank Bonvillain (1967, D-1 and B-1) 173rd Airborne Brigade, 1969

My helicopter lifted off from battalion headquarters and gained altitude as we headed out over the South China Sea. It was a gorgeous day, albeit hot, but then every day in Vietnam was some variant of hot—hot and raining, hot and dry, hot and humid, or simply hot as hell. You got used to it. The sky was, well, sky blue, the water below, turquoise. Whenever possible, flights leaving Battalion Headquarters flew over the water. It was much safer than going over land, where the enemy had extra chances to shoot at us. He had plenty of chances as it was. Bringing down a helicopter with ground fire was hard, but when it happened there seldom were any survivors. So we flew over the South China Sea despite its being several kilometers out of the way.

Within a few minutes, we turned west and were flying over rice paddies. They were greener than the greenest shade of Ireland's shamrocks and stretched for miles until they met mountains, about fifty kilometers inland. Each paddy was about half the size of a football field and was separated from its neighbors by earthen dikes a few feet higher than the irrigation water and wide enough for one person to walk along with ease. I was raised in Brazoria County, Texas, the largest rice-producing county in the US, so I knew a little about growing rice. However, I had never seen anything like this. There was no machinery to help plant or harvest or irrigate the crop. None. This was strictly a manual operation.

The men and women were dressed in their black pajamas and cone-shaped straw hats. I could see them busily working the rice or transferring water from one paddy to another by means of large, straw buckets with two strands of long thin rope tied to each side. Using the ropes, two women would swing the buckets in rhythmic arcs between two paddies, adding water to one while draining it from the other. I found out later it was much more difficult to do this than it looked. And it was hard work. However, it seemed these women could do it all day long.

Scattered throughout this vast maze of paddies were small hamlets where the people who worked in the fields lived. Fewer than twenty families lived in most of these hamlets; some may have been larger but not by much. There were no shops. The people walked or rode bicycles to small towns (some as far as twenty kilometers away) to get necessities.

Every so often I spied structures that actually looked like houses, certainly not mansions in our sense of the word, but large and made of concrete, block, and brick. At one time they must have been beautiful. I never knew for certain, but I believe these houses were remnants of French occupation and were the residences of French expatriates who managed rice production in the region. Now they were run down and abandoned, their tile roofs caved in, paint peeling, and glass windows broken. Relics of a failed foreign policy, and to a sociologist or anthropologist possibly a sign of the steely determination of these people we supposedly were here to help.

We flew over large flat areas raised a few feet above the paddies, hamlets, and dikes and bordered by a few twenty- or thirty-foot-high coconut palms. Here women lay the harvested rice to dry on large circular mats. They shook the mats until the kernels separated from their hulls and then left them to dry overnight.

Despite traditional aviator concerns over ground debris getting sucked into rotor blades or the engine upon landing, my chopper landed directly in the middle of five drying mats, effectively blowing an entire day's work all over the village. So much for maintaining good relations with the locals.

I was going to join an infantry company as a platoon leader. Aboard the chopper with me was part of a weekly battalion supply run. This included a bundle of clean fatigues, C-rations, and a medium-sized box (called an SP) of candy, cigarettes, gum, writing paper, envelopes, and other personal-care items. As soon as the chopper skids touched ground I jumped off and three men from the platoon pulled off the various supplies. Within five minutes the bird was gone.

I was not new to Vietnam, having spent the first portion of my tour in a Ranger Company—a great assignment but not necessarily good for my career. In the 1960s, Regular Army officers wanting to make the Army their life career were told to stay away from what now are called Special Operations Units. These were thought of as the kiss of death for advancement. Their ranks were filled with former NCOs and enlisted men who had gone to OCS and officers (even some West Point graduates) who did not plan on making the Army their career. They tended to be wild and crazy and did outlandish things. There may be a need for such units, but a Regular Army officer should stay away from them—or so we were told.

At the time I wanted someday to be a general. Therefore, commanding a traditional infantry rifle platoon was critical—and all the better that it was in the famed 173rd Airborne Brigade.

On the ground I was directed to my new platoon command post, where I met my platoon sergeant. He was a tall, slender, black man about thirty-five years old. Confidence, experience and professionalism oozed from every pore of his body. This was his second tour in Vietnam, and he was everything a platoon leader could want in a platoon sergeant.

Infantry Officer Training at Fort Benning, Georgia, had been good, but Benning was still teaching World War II tactics and doctrine. As for Vietnam, if anyone knew how to fight a guerrilla war, they were keeping it a secret. When it came to Vietnam, we were told, "Check with your platoon sergeant, follow his guidance until you get your feet on the ground. He will give you the real dope." That was great advice if you had a good platoon sergeant. But good platoon sergeants were scarce; the supply could not keep up with the demand. "Seasoned" was quickly becoming a term defined as a first tour NCO with four months in country. To have a platoon sergeant who was on his second tour and who knew his business was a godsend.

We shook hands, introduced ourselves, lit cigarettes, and sat down with canteen cups of coffee to talk. My first question was about the landing-site selection. It seemed unusual to me that, with all the available open space, it was in the middle of an area used by the villagers. Perhaps there was a reason I didn't understand. After all, I had been on the ground all of fifteen minutes. "Nope," he replied. "The boys just like to have some fun every now and then. Breaks the monotony."

"Wonderful," I thought to myself. "That's a hell of a way to show that we're 'the good guys.'"

After our talk I introduced myself to the platoon, explained what I expected of them, and said my primary mission was to insure they all made it home alive. My platoon consisted of sixteen men, the platoon sergeant, and me. According to the manual, an airborne rifle platoon should have forty-two men, but that was rarely the case. I don't believe any platoon in Vietnam ever had forty-two men present for duty. I was lucky to have sixteen; I never had more than twenty-five; nor did any other platoon in my company. Men were getting wounded or killed or were leaving at the end of their tour faster than replacements could be trained and delivered.

Over the years my unit had seen some of the harshest fighting in Vietnam. However, our designated combat role had recently changed. Someone in Washington had come up with a policy called "Pacification." And with this doctrine came the phrase "winning hearts and minds."

In brief, the idea of Pacification was to work "with the people" not "against them." We were to show the Vietnamese that Americans were there to help keep them safe from the Viet Cong and the North Vietnamese Army, enabling them to make the political decisions they wanted to make, not those forced upon them. We were not to hide behind sandbags and concertina wire, seeing the locals only when patrols went tearing though their hamlets, villages, and towns scaring the hell out of everyone on the good days and burning their houses and destroying their crops on the bad, sometimes (not often, seldom on purpose) killing them along with the VC.

Pacification was carried out something like this: A battalion moved its companies into towns, villages, and hamlets with each platoon responsible for a sector. Acting as security guards, the platoons lived among the Vietnamese and the two groups got to know each other. As the song goes, "To Know Me Is to Love Me." As the mission progressed, each platoon also worked hand in glove with a South Vietnamese platoon assigned to the same sector. Working together and playing together for success.

However, it didn't quite work out that way.

Headquarters memoranda and briefings on the goals and objectives of Pacification touted the anticipated success of the mission. I never read them. But I know how Pacification translated to the soldier on the ground: failure. It sucked. I don't believe it worked anywhere. It certainly didn't work for us.

We were not trained for the Pacification mission. There was no objective to take, no ground to seize. There was no enemy sighting to check out. There were no "hunter-killer" missions. Nor were there any "cordon and searches." Instead, squad-size patrols (five or six men) walked around their assigned area hoping to draw fire or perhaps find booby traps or weapons caches. At night they established ambushes. Normally we didn't find anything or see anybody. Our main purpose was to be seen by the villagers and give them a sense of security—monotonous duty at best.

Our secondary mission was to train our Vietnamese counterparts. That didn't work any better than mixing with the civilians. No one in my platoon spoke Vietnamese, and very few Vietnamese—including their officers—spoke English. Few of my soldiers, or my superiors for that matter, had taken a class, received a briefing, or read a book on Vietnam or its people. "Cultural awareness" was a term yet to become part of the military lexicon. In short, we had no idea who these people were, how they thought, how they fought, what they considered important, or what they wanted and expected out of the war. We knew nothing and could not talk to them to ask them questions.

The Pacification policy cost untold American lives, and any military leader whose eyes were open could see that it was a failure. It not only cost American and Vietnamese lives, but it also influenced junior officers who later would become leaders of our military and government. When American soldiers invaded Afghanistan and then Iraq, they relied on the same pacification policy. It failed in Vietnam, and it's no surprise that it failed in Afghanistan and Iraq. I don't understand why it was even attempted. You would think we would learn from history.

On my second day as platoon leader everything changed with a radio call from the company command post. I was told a helicopter was coming in to pick up my platoon sergeant and that he should have all his gear packed because he was not coming back. I had no idea what was going on, but sure enough, in about an hour a helicopter landed and picked up the platoon sergeant I had been so happy to have. I did not see him again until after the war.

No one got off the helicopter that took him away. I made the senior sergeant the acting platoon sergeant and then got on the radio and requested permission to go to the CP and talk to the company commander, Capt. Richard Lewis. Permission was granted. I had met Captain Lewis a few days before at battalion headquarters. He was a relatively new company commander but was on his second tour in Vietnam. A West Pointer from Virginia, he was a professional soldier and a pretty nice guy. I was not looking forward to this meeting. The four-kilometer walk was not particularly dangerous, but I had not expected my first patrol to be a trip to the command post to ask where my platoon sergeant had disappeared to. I set off to find out what the hell had happened. Except for tripping and falling into a damn rice paddy, the trip was uneventful.

Captain Lewis said he was as surprised as me by the departure of my platoon sergeant. It seemed that the outgoing platoon leader had been asked to take over the battalion reconnaissance platoon for his remaining two months in Vietnam. The recon platoon was a hot-shit platoon usually led by the "best" lieutenant in the battalion. It was unusual for someone with only two months remaining to be asked to return to the field. Normally an officer pulled from a field assignment remained on the battalion staff until his departure. This gave him cross-training as a staff officer. More important, it increased his chances of staying alive long enough to get on the "Freedom Bird" for home.

The lieutenant had agreed to take the job on the condition that he could have his old platoon sergeant. The battalion commander concurred, and just that fast I was minus one hell of a good platoon sergeant. Captain Lewis promised to give me the next senior NCO assigned to the company. In the meantime I was to "make do." I really had no choice, so I picked up my rucksack and headed back to my platoon.

Upon returning, I got everyone together and explained what had happened and why. I told them we would "soldier on" and that I had full faith and confidence in the new platoon sergeant. I did not note that going from squad leader to platoon sergeant within the same platoon is always difficult. One day you're "one of the guys," the next you're the head NCO. Some men handle the transition well; others do not. Despite his junior rank and limited time in country, the young sergeant transitioned well. We sent out two short patrols that afternoon—both were uneventful. Thus ended my first full day as an infantry platoon leader. I did not sleep as well the second night as I had the first.

On my third day, I decided to do something that the platoon had never done—go into the hamlet. According to my NCOs the platoon had never actually gone into the village proper; they just patrolled around it. The previous platoon leader thought his job was to keep this hamlet (as well as several others) "safe." He did not place a high priority on getting to know the locals.

I thought it would be a good idea to go into the village and visit with the people. My understanding was that this was part of the mission. When in the hamlets, we were supposed to be "friendly" to the people. We were to get to know them, and they would get to know us. I also thought that on our first visit we should take gifts. The only problem was we had no gifts.

I understood that when the battalion commander visited a town or village, he brought a ton of goodies. But that was the battalion commander. We didn't have anything, and I seriously doubted that the company had extra candy or tobacco either.

The only thing we had to give away was C-rations; however, the C-rations were all we had to eat. They weren't very good, but they were better than rats or dogs. C-rations were developed in World War II and had been used throughout the Korean War as well. Of course, our C-rations weren't left over from those wars. America would never send its boys out to fight feeding them food left over from World War II. Just because the stuff tasted like it was twenty-five years old did not mean it was!

C-rations consisted of four or five cans: a main food item such as beans and weenies, perhaps a can of cheese and crackers, peanut butter, cookies, fruit, and condiments such as salt and pepper. Each carton also contained four cigarettes, a pouch of powdered juice, and a chocolate bar.

About the only thing the chocolate bar was good for was to melt in a cup of hot water to make cocoa. You couldn't eat the damn things. Even the Vietnamese kids hated them. As soldiers moved through the larger villages, they would throw these chocolate bars at the kids. If a child got hit, it was like getting hit by a rock. For sure we were not going to win friends by giving out chocolate bars.

Then I remembered the SPs. They had candy, cocoa, a powdered fruit drink, chewing gum, and cigarettes. The cigarettes usually were unfiltered Pal Malls, Lucky Strikes, or Camels, but at least they didn't taste like leftovers from World War II. We could give away the C-ration cigarettes and keep the ones in the SPs and still have plenty of smokes. Great idea! We would take some of the candy and other items from the SP box and distribute the goodies to the adults and kids. This was textbook pacification—winning hearts and minds. Hell, I might even get a medal.

No one was keen on the idea of going into the village, but they didn't complain. Most soldiers were ambivalent about the Vietnamese. They didn't especially like them, but neither did they hate them; they just didn't care one way or the other. Officers, NCOs, and privates alike came to Vietnam not knowing or caring the first thing about the Vietnamese people. Unless someone had shown them a map while in basic training, many soldiers didn't even know where Vietnam was located.

Of course, not everyone was that uninformed or unconcerned. Each battalion had an S-5 (Civil Affairs Officer) who dealt with the locals. Some even spoke Vietnamese or at least had an interpreter. The S-5 worked with community leaders to build schools, distribute books and other educational materials, and provide medical support along with other assistance. Basically, though, he was a voice crying in the wilderness. Most GIs—officers and soldiers alike—just didn't care. They only wanted to finish their tour of duty in one piece and go home. Period. End of story.

The hamlet nearest to my platoon was a short walk away. Except for a grass hut or two obstructing our view, we would be within sight and sound of the platoon CP and defenses during our walk through the village. This was not to be a patrol. This was simply "taking an apple pie to visit the next-door neighbors." I understood this; we did it in Texas all the time.

In my previous position, with the Rangers, I had never seen a Vietnamese up close, at least one that was not trying to kill me. We had different SOPs in that assignment. Despite a meeting with the battalion commander and two meetings with Captain Lewis, we never discussed unit SOPs. This was because they were pretty basic infantry stuff. There were no complicated "Rules of Engagement." If someone was shooting at you, you shot back. The idea was to stay alive. If you had to cheat a little, or a lot, to do so, no one said a word. No VC or NVA was stupid enough to drop his weapon and raise his hands, knowing that to do so merely offered a better target. If he turned and ran, he would just die tired.

When on patrol, a person carried certain things: rifle, ammo, water, smoke and fragmentation grenades, and a first-aid pouch. Later I would make a list of items to be carried on patrol as part of my platoon SOP, but at that time, I assumed everyone knew from experience what they should take with them. Moreover, this was not a "patrol" in the true sense of the word; we were just "visiting the neighbors with an apple pie." We planned to be gone about thirty minutes and never to be out of sight of the CP. I saw no sense in loading up like we were hitting Omaha Beach. Besides, if you filled your ammo pouches with rifle magazines, where would you put the candy?

I was not used to wearing the typical steel helmet worn in infantry platoons. In my Ranger unit we wore a soft hat or simply tied a bandana around our head. This was zero protection, but you looked really cool. At twenty-two years old you consider yourself invincible. You won't get killed. The other guy will, but not you. Looking cool was much more important than safety.

My new platoon sergeant and the majority of the platoon remained at the CP. I took only five men plus my RTO, a seventeen-year-old black kid named Perry Irby from Spartanburg, South Carolina. Irby was always talking about his hometown and would begin by saying, "Spartanburg is in the Piedmont section of South Carolina." A devout Christian, he had his Bible and high-school yearbook in his rucksack wherever he went.

One of the nicest young men I had ever met and the first black man with whom I had any real close contact.

My venture into the village didn't last long. Just inside I handed a bag of jelly beans to a small child then everything went black. When I recovered consciousness I was face down in the dirt. I didn't really see stars; I just could not focus my eyes. My head hurt like I had been hit with a baseball bat, and my ears were ringing. I wiped my head and looked down at my hand. It was bloody. Mother of God! I had been shot in the head. Bullets were flying everywhere, and I had no idea where I, my RTO, or the squad was. All I knew was that I had been shot in the head. (But the advantages of wearing a helmet were becoming very clear.) My RTO grabbed my shirt and dragged me to a clump of brush. My vision cleared enough for me to see that one of my men had also been hit and was bleeding badly. I could see a bone of his left leg sticking through his fatigue pants, and it also looked as though he had been hit in the stomach. His eyes were open. He was shaking uncontrollably, but he was saying nothing.

"Is anyone else hit?" I asked my RTO.

"Only Morales," he replied.

Lying in the dirt not far from me was the man who had tripped the booby trap. All that was left of what once had been a man was a crumpled heap. I must have been knocked down when a part of his body or possibly his helmet hit me. The blood in my hair was his. Other than being dazed and extremely scared, I was okay. There was no time to focus on the body. If I didn't do something quick, we all would be just as dead.

In combat there is "cover" and there is "concealment." "Cover" stops bullets; "concealment" hides you—you hope. It is best to have both; we had little of either. Our concealment was limited to the base of palm trees and thatched huts. You could hide behind the huts, but you were exposed the moment you stuck your head out to return fire. Nothing in the entire hamlet would stop an AK-47 round—except one of us. It was not a good position to be in. The platoon CP was different. They were in fighting positions already dug, and one side of the perimeter was along a rice paddy that protected it. They were returning effective fire, but we were not. We were stuck.

We were huddled near the hamlet's north edge with open rice paddies to our east and the hamlet on the other three sides. There was no better concealment or cover than where we were. Returning to the platoon CP, on the other side of the hamlet, was too difficult and risky—especially carrying a dead body and a wounded man who, in my estimation, was in no condition to be moved.

Bullets continued to cut through the palms and thatched huts. Everyone hugged the ground except one man who was putting a tourniquet on Morales's leg. Bullets sound different depending on whether you are in front of the barrel or behind the trigger. There was a zinging sound overhead, but I couldn't see any muzzle flash and couldn't tell where the rounds were coming from. The firing was coming from the hamlet, but I had no idea from just where. What only a moment ago had been a bustling village full of men and women busy with their daily lives and children playing and begging for candy was now a ghost town.

Knowing that soldiers under fire were prone to fire at anything that moved, I shouted, "Don't shoot unless you have a target; don't just start firing into the village." I called the CP on the radio. My platoon sergeant said they were under intense fire, but no one had been hit. He knew that moving toward us would be deadly. There really was not much he could do for us. I told my RTO to raise the company CP on the radio. Captain Lewis got on the radio immediately and said he had heard the explosion from the booby-trap and also the rifle fire. I explained that the platoon was split, I had one killed and one wounded and that we were still under sporadic fire from an unknown number of the enemy. I conveniently left out the fact I had left my CP with no medic, little ammunition, and (although I did not know it) no smoke grenades. I told him I needed an immediate Medivac.

This was not the time for Lewis to ask why I had not notified him I was going on a patrol—something every unit was required to do when they left their CP. That question would come later, assuming there was a later. I turned my attention back to the situation at hand. The firing had slowed considerably. Like us, the enemy probably were conserving rounds until they could see a target.

My mind raced. "Dear God, how did I get us into such a position?" So much for my display of dynamic leadership right out of the box! Not yet three full days with my platoon, and I had one soldier dead and another seriously wounded. I don't believe I had spoken to either man in the time I had been on the ground. I was told later that the dead man had been with me on the patrol to the company CP, but I didn't remember him. I did recall Morales. He was the biggest of four Hispanic soldiers in the platoon. He smiled a lot. I didn't know either man's name until my RTO told me.

I looked over at Morales. He was still alive, but you didn't have to be a medic to know he was badly hurt. He must have been near the soldier who tripped the booby trap. The tourniquet had stopped most of the bleeding from his leg but the bone was still sticking out. A soldier was now placing a pressure dressing on his side; possibly some shrapnel or a bullet had hit him in the torso. Fortunately he had passed out, but his body was still shaking. Regardless, Morales required a Medivac. We all needed to get the hell out of there.

The radio came alive; it was the Medivac chopper wanting to know our position. I took the radio handset, identified myself, and asked for an estimated arrival. The company CP had given the pilot the coordinates to our hamlet, so he already knew our general location. The pilot said that he was only a few minutes out and could see the platoon CP, but he couldn't see my location. I explained that we were on the north side of the village about seventy-five meters from the CP and that we had one dead and one seriously wounded. I also said we had been under heavy rifle fire from the hamlet but that it had stopped.

I knew the pilot's next statement before he said a word, "Pop smoke, and I will come get you." I just hoped to keep my job if anyone heard my reply, "Roger. I don't have any smoke. But we are no longer taking incoming rounds, and we are right next to an open field that will make a decent landing area. As soon as I hear your chopper blades someone will move to the open area and you can key off them. That's the best I can do."

Silence . . . for what seemed an hour. "Roger" was the one-word reply. Then I heard the chopper blades overhead. I knew he would come in. I also knew I would be the main topic of discussion in the Medivac Officers Club for weeks to come.

Most dustoff pilots were Warrant Officers. Warrant Officers are "specialists." Yes, they are officers, but as they liked to say, "not real officers." A Warrant Officer does one specific job in the Army: fly a helicopter, supervise supplies, manage a maintenance facility—any one of a number of important jobs. The Army has a lot of them. However, the Warrant Officers that infantrymen came in contact with in Vietnam were helicopter pilots. All helicopter pilots I ever met were crazy but with balls the size of cantaloupes. The only difference between a regular helicopter pilot and a Medivac pilot was that the Medivac pilot's balls were even bigger. They did have one thing in common: Warrant Officers thought all Lieutenants were idiots. And I was doing nothing to dispel that belief.

As I heard chopper blades, I turned to the soldier who had placed the pressure bandage on Morales. "Want to be a hero today? Go bring that chopper in."

I received a one-word reply that under other circumstances might have been considered insubordination, but the soldier ran into the open field waving his rifle. "Okay, I see him," the pilot radioed. "We are on short final and coming in. Try to make sure no one shoots us."

As soon as the helicopter landed, the soldier who guided it in went to the far side of the LZ. I sent the remaining two men to the chopper for a stretcher, leaving my RTO and me with Morales. When the men returned with the stretcher, they had a medic. He stuck an IV in Morales's arm and directed the two men to place him on the stretcher. As they moved to the chopper, I touched the medic's arm. He looked at me and shrugged. "Don't know. He's lost a lot of blood and it looks like he has internal injuries. But we'll have him to a hospital in fifteen minutes."

They hurried Morales onto the chopper. It was in the air and gone as fast as it had come in. The entire operation had taken less than ten minutes. I notified Captain Lewis that the dustoff was successful. The four remaining men came back to our makeshift perimeter and waited. Five minutes. Ten. Nothing. It was over.

I called my platoon CP. The firing on their position also had ceased. No causalities. I told my platoon sergeant to leave four men guarding the CP, move the remainder of the platoon toward my location, and bring a body bag. I then called the company CP and notified them that the enemy firing had stopped and that I was going to consolidate the platoon on my position, recover the dead man's remains, and return to the platoon CP. Once back at the CP I would request another chopper to take the body home. I did not want the body bag to remain with the platoon overnight—very bad for morale.

The fight lasted less than an hour, probably closer to thirty minutes. Adrenalin had steadily pumped through my body since I had been hit on the head. Now I was drained. The rest of the platoon arrived. We picked up the dead soldier and moved back. It was difficult for me to walk even the few meters to the CP.

During the entire firefight I never saw the enemy. When I was with the Rangers we found irregulars (VC) and North Vietnamese soldiers often. But that was a different mission and different circumstances. In all my time with a rifle platoon (almost a year) unless we were in a pitched battle we seldom saw the enemy. It was like we were fighting ghosts.

There were many more firefights, more booby traps, and more ambushes. But from that day on I insured that my platoon was prepared for whatever we encountered. I had learned my lesson the hard way. But I had learned it well. I also started wearing a helmet.

Two days later we were informed that the wounded soldier had died at the hospital. All I had wanted to do was deliver some candy to a few kids.

Gerald Madeley (1964, Band) PACAF Procurement Center Thailand, 13th Air Force 1971–73

By the fall of 1972 the US military air campaign Linebacker II was drawing to a close. The political climate in North Vietnam appeared to be changing, and some hope for a peaceful conclusion was being discussed. The 13th Air Force Purchasing Director tasked the Thailand Procurement Center (TPC) with the responsibility of negotiating contracts with South Vietnamese contractors to operate and maintain vehicles and also to operate a supply warehouse system at Tan Son Nhut Air Base, near Saigon.

Although my assignments at the TPC included primarily US contractors, I was assigned on TDY to the Purchasing Office at Tan Son Nhut AB. The negotiations dragged on for weeks, and I began to worry that they would not be completed by the deadline established for TDY personnel to depart Vietnam. Finally, the negotiations concluded, and the Contract Review personnel from the TPC arrived. They had to complete their reviews before the contracts could be signed. The reviews went well, so the four of us (captains) wrapped up our duties and headed to downtown Saigon to the Continental Hotel for a delicious French dinner. After the meal, I was handed a list of orders for Vietnamese ceramic elephants, the two-foot size known as BFEs (Big F****** Elephants) from TPC personnel in Bangkok. This was going to be a real challenge. The Contract Review team was leaving on a flight early the next day, and I was scheduled to brief the Tan Son Nhut AB Commander regarding our contract awards before leaving on a late afternoon flight to Bangkok.

The NCO of the office at Tan Son Nhut became aware of my dilemma and volunteered his service as well as his AF pickup truck. He also arranged for his Vietnamese secretary to accompany us to the “best elephant shop” in Saigon. She also would negotiate good prices.

The next day everything worked well until I suddenly realized that I would be driving a US Air Force vehicle through the streets of Saigon with a Vietnamese lady in the front seat, a load of ceramic elephants in the back, and an NCO riding on the bumper. Fortunately everything went smoothly. Even the guard at the Tan Son Nhut base gate just waved us on in.

All the elephants made the flight to Bangkok—except mine. (Having gone to all the trouble for others, I got two for myself.) Several weeks later I went out to Don Mueang Airport to pick up our Deputy Director. He had caught an embassy flight from Manila that happened to stop in Saigon. Due to the heat and heavy traffic in Bangkok, I was a little late getting to the airport. The embassy plane had parked on the far ramp, and there, barely visible at such a distance, was a Lieutenant Colonel in uniform walking along that hot ramp with a large briefcase in his hand and a large ceramic elephant under each arm for me.

We met later in the US, but I never got the courage to tell him one of the elephants arrived in my shipped baggage as a pile of broken ceramic.

John Erskine (1960, Squadron 2) 5th Special Forces Group, 1966

In 1966 the Special Forces A-Detachment that adjoined the village of Thong Duc was having a problem with the villagers, who were being intimidated by the local VC. In an effort to win the "hearts and minds" of the locals, we decided to put together a week-long "Medicine Show" and invite the villagers to come in and bring anyone who needed to be treated for an illness or an injury, especially the children.

The large turnout for medical treatment worked so well that three days later the VC retaliated by attacking the camp at night. We fought off the attack, killing many VC, and captured a lot of weapons and equipment. The Medicine Show turned out to be a huge success, and the VC were no longer a problem in the Thong Duc area of operations.

Many Special Forces A-Detachments worked closely with the Montagnard people. They were fiercely loyal to our SF teams, and they really hated the Vietnamese (on both sides), who treated them like second-class—or worse—citizens. As a Medical Service Corps officer I was frequently called upon to help Montagnard villages with health and sanitation issues. We held clinics for the children, improved water supplies, and helped educate them on waste disposal.

From repeated visits, many of the children got to know me, and on one of my visits a youngster who I guessed was fourteen or fifteen sat by a campfire with me. He had a notebook that we had given him for school, and he took a piece of charcoal from the fire and began to draw. Later, as I was getting ready to leave, he came over with our interpreter and offered me the picture as a "thank you." I was totally blown away. It was a charcoal sketch of me, and it was an amazing likeness. What a talent! The sketch is framed in my office today and is a constant reminder of some good times in Vietnam among the Montagnard.

George Isleib (1968, D-1) 101st Airborne Division, 1969

It had been just another day of humping rucks in the heavily jungled mountains of I Corps in the fall of 1969. I was platoon leader in an infantry company that was fighting heat, filth, insects, and occasionally the NVA. We had endured days of utter boredom interrupted by short periods of adrenalin-fueled contact with the enemy. The NVA were well dispersed in that area, and we had engaged several small units.

Now, in the late evening, we arrived at our night defensive position (NDP) on a heavily wooded ridgeline. It was always a relief to reach a night position, knowing we could be rid of our rucksacks and relax for a few minutes before preparing for the night ahead. On this evening, any relief my men and I felt was offset by the knowledge that it was our night to conduct ambush. Battalion SOP dictated that each company conduct two ambushes every night, but fortunately my captain knew what was best for his troops and reduced the requirement to one. At that time the company numbered around eighty souls, far less than the authorized strength. In that terrain and with the enemy troop strength in the area, we could not adequately support two ambushes.

I rotated ambush duty among my three squads, and on this night I decided to go along because the selected squad was more short-handed than usual. My radio operator wasn't thrilled, because he would be going with us as well. He was an outstanding troop, from New York State. I was his third lieutenant in the past six months, and we had become close friends.

As dusk settled, the eight of us started downhill to establish our ambush. Earlier in the afternoon I had selected a location along a trail that followed the foot of the ridgeline below the company NDP. We were only several hundred meters from the company, so that we could be supported by the main unit if the need arose. Our ambushes were simple affairs. We set up in heavy cover several meters off one side of the trail, placing Claymore mines along the entire area to our front and one aimed at our escape route, and then settled in within touching distance of one another.

Darkness falls rapidly in the jungle, and soon we were enveloped in inky blackness. We knew from experience that we would have to depend on our sense of hearing to alert us to an enemy presence. On that night things seemed unnaturally quiet, insect noises being the only sounds. I had decided to maintain a 50 percent alert status, with two-hour shifts and alternating men being allowed to get some rest. In truth, most of us slept poorly if at all while on ambush.

Night ambushes were a tricky proposition. Troop movement, especially at night, was confined to established trails that were negotiated single file. We might hear an approaching enemy force but seldom had any idea of its size. The decision to spring an ambush was really a crapshoot. We all were aware of an ambush several weeks earlier in our same area by another unit. The ambushers had heard approaching enemy soldiers in what sounded like large numbers. They decided not to execute the ambush and advised their company that they would "break squelch" (press the handset control) on the radio one time for each enemy troop that passed. They pressed it 126 times.

Call me paranoid, but my greatest fear was that the NVA would detect our presence by smelling us. I can assure you that on a number of occasions my unit had been alerted to the nearby presence of the NVA because we smelled them. The odor of the enemy is ingrained in my senses to this day. A combination of body odor, fish, rank tobacco, and wood smoke, generally it was easily detectable. I knew we emitted our own peculiar odors, and this was a real concern to me. Little did I know that our scent would be a factor later that night.

For several hours all was quiet, with nothing disturbing the normal night sounds. But that changed around midnight. Most of us were awake when we noticed a perceptible drop in the noise level around us. We also noticed a slight scent of carrion. I made sure everyone was awake, and we strained all our senses in an effort to understand the situation.

After several minutes we detected sounds of movement in the brush to our left. The noise appeared to be within fifty feet, and whatever was responsible began moving across the area to our rear at a slow but steady rate. I discounted the presence of NVA fairly soon and suspected the source to be an animal. A multitude of beasts were at home in that jungle, and most were harmless. We had seen wild pigs, deer, and monkeys on the ground and even elephants from the air, but this seemed different. About that time we heard the first animal sounds, and my blood ran cold. The noise wasn't a growl or a snort or even a loud purr, but more like a repeated "chuff." We were being stalked by a tiger.

We had all heard stories about tigers stalking or attacking humans, and I was damn scared. We knew there were tigers in the area and had even speculated on whether they might have developed a taste for human flesh after feasting on dead NVA. I was hoping we wouldn't be a test case.

I passed the word to everyone on what we faced and that we needed to remain quiet in case any NVA showed up. I did have everyone move to a central position, and we sat in a circle, back to back. We alerted the company about our situation and listened as the animal continued moving through the brush. I was running options through my mind but finally decided that staying where we were was the best bet. If we fired on the tiger, we would be forced to move away from the trail. In that darkness, I didn't want to take a chance on someone getting separated and becoming easy prey. Hand grenades were of no use because of the thick cover. We had no idea whether the beast had disturbed our Claymores, so that option was out. I decided that if any NVA appeared, we would not engage them unless we were detected. In the event the tiger attacked us, we would do our best to kill it.

After what seemed like hours, the sounds of movement stopped and normal night sounds began anew. I looked at my watch and saw that only an hour had passed, but it had been a long hour. We remained in close proximity for the remainder of the night, which passed in blissful quiet, although no one slept. At daylight we recovered our Claymores, returned to the company, and prepared for another day of humping rucks. One day shorter and thankful for it. My radio operator threatened to shoot me if I ever volunteered for another ambush.

(Later I did some research and found that two US troops were killed by tigers in Vietnam and that several more survived tiger attacks.)

Frank Supercinski (1964, A-1) MACV, 1968

My father was career Air Force, but my vision wasn't good enough for me to become a pilot, so I joined the Army ROTC at A&M. Shortly before graduation, in August 1964, I received my branch assignment as Military Intelligence. About this same time I was offered a Regular Army rather than a Reserve commission. Upon investigation, I learned that I would have to change branches to artillery, infantry, or armor if I went Regular. As a Regular officer I would have a three-year commitment on active duty versus two years as a Reserve. And rather than have a uniform allowance if I went Reserve, I would have to buy my own uniforms .

I was also told that if I accepted a Regular commission, I would have to report for active duty immediately upon graduation. If I went the Reserve route, I would be allowed to delay entry while I attended law school. It didn't take long for me to tell the interviewing officer, "Sir, if you don't mind, I think I'll go in as a Reserve officer."

I graduated from Baylor Law in November 1966, reported to Fort Benning, Georgia, for Basic Officer Training, and then went to Fort Holabird, Maryland, to learn to be an intelligence officer. Everyone in my class thought his destination upon graduation would be Vietnam, which had heated up significantly by this time. Instead, the Army sent half of us to stateside assignments and the others to Southeast Asia. I reported to Fort Bliss, Texas, but soon I too received orders for Vietnam. I had married while in law school, and our first child was born less than two weeks before I reported for deployment.

When I boarded my plane at Travis Air Force Base, California, for transport to Vietnam, I sat next to a full colonel. By coincidence, he was my boss when we got in country. I was assigned to MACV with an initial assignment to Phouc Long and then to Gia Rai as the Intelligence Officer, District Intelligence Coordinating Center. My responsibility was to help identify, locate, and neutralize Viet Cong leadership in the area.

Most of the information I gathered came from interviewing local villagers. Some came willingly—others not so much. The CIA and Navy Seals often swept through the area and brought in fifteen to twenty-five people at a time to be interviewed. Sometimes this revealed the identity of VC; often it did not.

The best information we gathered came from two VC leaders, ordnance and supply officers, who surrendered under the Chieu Hoi program. The program promised that they would not be jailed or punished but that they would receive monetary rewards for weapons and equipment they brought in or whose location they revealed. In response the VC leaders claimed they knew where a vast store of arms and equipment was hidden in the jungle.

The local US commander teamed with the South Vietnamese District Chief to coordinate a plan to seize the weapons cache. Because we were near the coast, they coordinated the support of Naval gunfire with Air Force jets, and Army helicopter gunships to back up our ground troops. My job was to be in charge of the landing zone once it was secure. We went in surrounded by exploding ordnance from the ships at sea and the various aircraft in the sky. The mission was a total success with tons of arms and equipment destroyed or evacuated. We were extremely happy—as were the two former VC, who received large rewards.

For my role in the operation I receive the Vietnamese Cross of Gallantry. The English translation of the award narrative made it sound like I had been under heavy enemy fire and that I had fought back with a bayonet between my teeth and a hand grenade in each hand. It simply was not true. I was not stupid enough to do something like that.

In Vietnam I learned to do what I had to but to do it smart. My philosophy was that I would obey every lawful order but would do everything I could to survive. I would not take unnecessary risks, and I would not be a hero. I would keep my men as safe as possible.

During my tour I was fortunate to be under great commanders—US and South Vietnamese. And I got out in one piece. When it came time for me to go home, I jumped on the first plane. I never had any hang-ups about my service. I knew I was working with good people—they did what they had to do. I am glad I served my country. I am glad I found that I had the courage to serve. I love this country. We are the greatest country in the world.

Mike Burroughs (1967, Squadrons 13 and 15)
553rd Reconnaissance Wing, 1969

Early in my tour with the 553rd Reconnaissance Wing I was the Communications Information Control Officer flying EC-121Rs stationed at Korat, Thailand. One day my Crew 32 took off for what should have been routine mission over North Vietnam. Our AC was new and was getting a check ride from another lieutenant colonel.

As we took the active runway and increased our ground speed, the bird began to vibrate excessively. Clearly something was wrong. After we were airborne, we determined that we had not only blown a main landing tire on the left side but also had broken the landing wheel rim, a large chunk of which lay behind on the runway. Without the cushion of the tire, the weight apparently placed too much stress on the wheel.

Rather than RTB, we flew the mission with the full realization that sooner or later the old bird would have to land. The mission itself went without incident. Fortunately for us, two very seasoned pilots were in the cockpit. Both likely had been flying longer than I had been alive. Because the damaged wheel was on the left side, the AC had the crewmembers in the rear move to the right side of the aircraft to shift the weight. Our landing was rough, as was to be expected, but considering everything, it was quite decent.

Jim Lanning (1964, D-1) 25th Infantry Division, 1967

Three significant events influenced my time in Vietnam. The first occurred when I secured a slot at the US Army Ranger School in Fort Benning, Georgia. One prerequisite for acceptance was that I pass the Army Ranger PT qualification test. This test contained five events—run, dodge, jump; horizontal bars; low crawl; one-mile run; and hand-grenade challenge. Most considered the hand-grenade event easy points, but not me. My upper-body strength was excellent, but for some reason I could not throw a hand grenade twenty-five meters with enough accuracy to score the required points. I practiced and practiced but to no avail. Test time came on a Monday, and nothing changed—no points on the hand grenade. I returned to the barracks filled with despair. By late afternoon the public-address system began calling out the names of Ranger candidates who had failed the PT test and were going to their next unit assignment.

My name was not called. Beginning on Tuesday the "called names" tapered off, and by Wednesday the PA system was quiet. What had happened to my scorecard? Thursday morning at breakfast my Tactical Officer approached and sternly asked; "Did you take the PT Test Monday?"

I replied, "Yes Sir!"

He asked, "How did you do?"

I replied, "Good, Sir, except for a problem with the hand grenades. I didn't get any points."

The TAC continued, "Well, you know to qualify for Ranger School you must score at least 60 points on each event for a minimum score of 300 points."

"Yes sir, I know," I replied.

The TAC said, "I don't know what happened—we can't locate your PT Scorecard. It's lost. If you make the run tomorrow morning, I'll keep you."

I made the run. I was motivated and successfully complete the course, and I received my Ranger Tab. The PT test graders—"Old Army" veteran NCOs—don't make mistakes. To this day I don't know what happened to the scorecard.

A second hand-grenade story highlights how difficult it was to stay alive or not be maimed on the battlefield. Soldiering occurs within extreme parameters of heat and cold. In Vietnam the heat was accentuated by thirst, humidity, and adverse terrain. From my personal observation of a rifle company for a year, only a few survived a 365-day tour without terror and bloodshed.

For example, one afternoon because of the heat we took a rest break in the vicinity of trees scattered around an area that had survived both bombing and the passage of tracked vehicles. During this interval a replacement Artillery FO arrived. After the initial greetings and without thinking like a combat veteran, he moved to a small patch of shade twenty meters from the command group. There was an explosion—the world stood still. A series of screams followed. The new lieutenant had sat on a booby-trapped hand grenade. He was quickly evacuated, but he died within the hour—his first afternoon of combat.

Even at twenty meters, the concussion of the blast slammed me and my radio operators backward. Reeling, I caught my fall with my left arm. Out of the corner of my eye I saw another booby-trapped frag grenade, within twelve inches of my head. Under my armpit a tension-tight tripwire was attached to an empty C-ration can covering the spoon of the grenade. Removing the C-ration can from the grenade would have released the spoon, which in turn would have released the firing pin. Detonation that at that range certainly would have killed me. With help from one of my soldiers, I gingerly neutralized the booby trap.

The detonation of the first grenade had sent shrapnel in all directions. Several of the company command-post group—PFCs Larry Prater, Frank Honderich, and Jim Phillips and Lt. Roger Cole—suffered minor cuts. One life was taken and several others nearly lost owing to a new lieutenant's misfortune. Using tweezers, a skilled medic extracted one small fragment from my neck. When he took out forms from his medical kit to register the wound for a Purple Heart, I said no thanks. My superficial wound paled beside what had happened to the new man. I never even got a chance to know him. To this day, I am proud of that medal I did not receive. We formed up and continued our job of combat. The old FO, who thought his field time was over, arrived on the next helicopter to resume his duties.

My third hand-grenade incident took place along the South China Sea near the hamlet of Yinh Hien 2. When a significant contact developed there, our rifle company was committed. Our first clue to the magnitude of the battle was not long in coming. A small group of women and children moved in our direction. Obviously they anticipated an exchange of death in the hamlet and did not wish to be part of it. We didn't hinder their departure. Doing so would only have taken time and further divided our force. Dispersion and control of the unit was excellent.

As we advanced, my command group followed my 2nd Platoon led by Lt. Devalis Ruthledge. Ruthledge relayed his estimation that contact was imminent. Lt. Gary Myers, 3rd Platoon Leader, reported that he was in a perfect field-manual position to the south overlooking possible escape routes. All continued calm in our area, but we could hear rifle fire about two hundred meters to the west. Where was the enemy? We were not long finding out. From nowhere a lone enemy rifleman popped up and ran frantically through the 2nd Platoon toward the command-post group firing his weapon. Our Artillery FO, Lt. Bill Farmer, responded by advancing toward the enemy soldier in a standing position and firing his CAR-15. They met face to face. The enemy fell literally within a couple of meters of Farmer's smoking gun. We in the CP group remained spectators as Farmer rummaged through the slain soldier's personal effects.

Myers jubilantly reported that his platoon had killed nine enemy soldiers fleeing from the contact area. A search of those bodies produced a number of weapons and other equipment, including whistles that the NVA used to signal movement while in contact.

The dead soldier at Farmer's feet may have been a sacrificial lamb, because as we continued in the direction from which he had advanced, we came under intense attack from close quarters by well-directed small-arms and automatic-weapons fire. Taking the nearest cover, graves in the hamlet burying ground, we returned fire. I estimated we were facing a reinforced platoon a scant twenty meters away. The initial advantage was the enemy's as he occupied a camouflaged interlinking trench system. Our godsend was the graves, but they were only twelve to fourteen inches high. Grenades would be catastrophic. Ruthledge reported by radio that he had suffered at least one dead and that his platoon was hard pressed just to return effective fire. Any maneuver at this point was virtually impossible. Aerial gunships were out of the question for close support; we were too close to the enemy positions. The abandoned village dwellings and vegetation around the hamlet greatly restricted visibility. The enemy definitely had the upper hand at this point—but not for long.

Sensing the urgency of the situation, Farmer moved forward, followed closely by Sergeant Finney, SP4 Nicholson, and two others. They entered one end of the extended trench system and methodically, one by one, eliminated enemy soldiers. The leader, Farmer, was severely wounded by fragments of an enemy grenade, but he continued to fight on in the trench. Farmer and Finney provided a foot in the door, and subsequently the 2nd Platoon was able to dislodge the enemy from their fortified positions. The action was a credit to Farmer.

During this time, my radios were useless. Because of the intensity of noise I just couldn't hear some radio transmissions. However, when word reached my position, ten meters to the rear, that Farmer was seriously wounded, I felt a lump in my throat. This man didn't have to take chances. As the FO he was there solely to communicate with the big guns for support. Because of the proximity of the enemy, a Medivac helicopter was not possible. In the absence of a helicopter and in an effort to evacuate Farmer and other wounded, I crawled a short distance to our flank and summoned a supporting APC from the nearby cavalry troop and led them back to where my FO lay on the hot sand. Using the APC, we moved Farmer and several others less wounded to a safe area approximately 400 meters to the rear and then evacuated them by air.

My short crawl to summon the APC had not gone unnoticed. PFC Robert W. Burgess later showed me a dead enemy soldier he killed who, after seeing my movement, was in the process of tracking me with his rifle. In fact, Burgess related, the VC had a finger on the trigger when he brought him under fire.

As the battle continued, two of the enemy who were well protected in the corner of the graveyard kept us busy with automatic rifle fire and grenades. One grenade knocked me from my feet and wounded the man next to me. An exchange of hand grenades ultimately neutralized the site. Ultimately the battle yielded thirty dead enemy and twelve captured weapons. This included seventeen dead in the trench system, nine from contact with the 3rd Platoon, and four within the hamlet itself. Our day's losses included PFC Gary Killian, age 19; PFC Joseph Ledesma Jr, age 20; and PFC Roland Rush, age 21, as well as nine wounded. PFC Stephen O'Shea died of wounds four days later. Lt. William H. Farmer, Jr. lived for nine days before dying of his wounds on 29 May 1967. We recommended him for the Distinguished Service Cross, but Corps Headquarters downgraded it to a Silver Star. I believe he deserved the Medal of Honor, and forty-eight years later we are working on the upgrade of his decoration.

Mike Richardson (1965 A-1 and 1st Brigade Staff) First Marine Air Wing, 1969

After a couple of months in country, I had a few days off the flight schedule at DaNang and planned to visit a good friend who was flying out of Quang Tri. Several of my flight-school buddies were also assigned there. When I learned that an H-53 helicopter left Da Nang every day to deliver mail and supplies to Quang Tri and that I could hitch a ride and return the next day, I figured it would be no problem to find my friend and classmates.

I met the flight crew for the H-53 in the line shack to introduce myself. Of course they asked why I wanted to hitch a ride, and when I told them my plan I could tell by the look in their eyes that I was about to hear bad news. They said my friend had been killed in a midair collision. Not to be deterred, and understanding the nature and dangers of war, I decided to continue my trip to find other friends. When I asked about an old Pensacola roommate, I was told he had been killed a few months earlier. And then the crew named another friend who had been killed.

By this time I felt I had been hit in the stomach. I thanked the flight crew for the info but no longer felt any need to go to Quang Tri. I had ten months to go in Vietnam, but never again would I find the need to visit a friend.

Jeffery Murray (1973, Squadron 6 and H-2) 281st Aviation Company, 1969

In May 1969 I was at An Hoa, where I flew Special Forces Delta and Roadrunner teams in and out of very dangerous country. After our arrival at the airfield, someone hired a bunch of hooch maids [Vietnamese women] to do our laundry. One day they all disappeared before quitting time, and a short time later we got incoming rockets. At midmorning the next day they again began to leave. Some of the troops grabbed one of them, tied her to a folding chair, and deposited her right in the middle of the runway. She screamed bloody murder as rockets began to fall. None hit her, but that was the last time we got incoming.

By late 1969 I had more than half my tour completed and lots of hours of flying behind me. Most of our missions were in the Nha Trang area, but we moved fairly often from airfield to airfield. One night when we were stationed near the village of Mai Loc supporting Special Forces, I wandered up the hill to the SF compound to see if they had a movie. I was fresh out of the shower, wearing only shorts, a t-shirt, and rubber flip flops. At the compound I got a beer and was headed toward the movie screen when something exploded about fifty meters away. I took off running as fast as my flip flops would let me and jumped into a hole, where I joined my crouching platoon leader.

"What are you doing?" he asked.

"Hiding from mortars I think," was my combat-veteran reply.

Calmly he said, "You're the standby pilot." In such a situation I was supposed to be on the flight line getting a bird in the air.

"Oh," was all I could say as I dropped my beer and took off jogging down the hill toward the flight line. I heard a faint whistle and then a thud as a mortar round landed not twenty feet from where I was jogging. Fortunately it was a dud. I ran through my tent to grab my helmet and then onto the flight line, where I strapped myself into the helicopter still clad only in shorts, tee shirt and flip flops. It turned out I was overdressed. My co-pilot had pants and a t-shirt, and the gunner was fully dressed, but the crew chief had run straight from the shower clad only in a really nice pair of flip flops, a towel, his helmet, and a lot of rapidly drying soap.

Off we went to defend our base camp, but it was dark. We saw no one and fired not a round. We did fly around enough to require refueling, so we headed to Quang Tri. We landed, taxied to fuel pumps, and started to get some gas. I was holding the fire extinguisher according to our refueling SOP but clad in underwear, flip flops, and a flight helmet. The crew chief, who was pumping gas, was as naked as the day he was born. And the gunner was providing perimeter security—meaning he had gone to take a leak. A Marine major managed to breach our security and surprised me with a tap on my shoulder. I turned around and was face to face with a field-grade Marine wearing starched fatigues and some funny hat carrying a clipboard. "What in hell do you guys think you're doing?" he asked.

I was down to maybe thirty days before completing my tour and feeling a little cocky, so I said the first thing that popped into my mind. "We're getting gas. What does it look like we're doing?"

He stared at me, did a 180 on his heels, and uttered one of my now favorite phrases: "Fucking army."

One day at Mai Loc we got called to do a sniffer mission, where they put a machine in the back of our Huey to seek out human activity by analyzing chemicals in the air. I was in one of the gunships that flew cover to react to whatever enemy we found. When the sensor picked up ammonia, that was supposed to indicate the presence of the enemy. More often it found elephants and baboons.

We were flying just off the ground in a dry stream bed when the sensor slick called out, "I have a tree house up here."

I zoomed right up there, turned the corner, and came face to face with a guy standing on the porch of this very well constructed tree house. I couldn't have been twenty feet away. I hovered, wondering just who was this guy out here in bad-guys land. Suddenly he ran inside, poked a rifle out a window, and squeezed off a round quicker than I could utter "WTF?" A round smacked right above my crew chief's head, which really pissed him off, but before he could do anything I recovered my wits and popped off a rocket that, not having to travel far, hit the tree house right in what would have been the doorknob had there been a door. That tree house went up just like something in the movies, with crap flying everywhere and most of it coming down through my rotors. It appeared that I was trying to shoot myself down. When the debris finally stopped falling, there was nothing left of that tree house except four stilts. I'm betting the guy inside had even less time than I did to ask himself "WTF?"

A short time later I completed my year in Vietnam and headed home. While waiting for our freedom bird, several of us sat in the club having a few drinks while a Vietnamese band played old rock and roll. Sentimental stuff. Just as they began to play the Animals tune *We Gotta Get out of This Place*, our plane's departure was announced. We stumbled toward the bus that took us to the tarmac, where we passed a long line of new guys just off the plane. They stared at us like we were holocaust survivors. Most of us were silent, just glad to be going home. A few in our queue hollered stuff like "360-what?" to the replacements, referring to the days they have left to rotate. I just kept walking; I was glad to be going home. The pilot fired up the engines, taxied maybe fifty meters and stopped. We had a flat tire. A fitting way to end my year in Vietnam.

Michael Lee Lanning (1968, D-1) 199th Light Infantry Brigade, 1969

By midsummer of 1969 I had been in country for several months—long enough to survive several exploding booby traps in the Delta south of Saigon and numerous firefights in our current triple-canopied jungle AO southwest of Xuan Loc. Along the way I had earned my Combat Infantryman's Badge and picked up patches of jungle rot and bamboo poisoning. I had also learned that, unlike the wars I had watched in theaters and on television back home, this war didn't have background music. Also unlike the movies, my platoon had nineteen-year-old sergeants who barely shaved rather than the grizzled vets played by John Wayne and Lee Marvin. But my men were experienced veterans, as good as any our country ever put on the battlefield.

In an intense battle on July 3, my C Company 2nd Battalion 3rd Infantry 199th Infantry Brigade supported our sister Delta Company in an attack against the bunker defenses of the 33rd NVA Regiment. In the fight nine Americans were killed and more than twenty wounded. One, Michael F. Folland of Richmond, Virginia, earned the Medal of Honor, and another, Capt. Jim Lewis, the Distinguished Service Cross.

The vast complex contained more than fifty trench-connected bunkers. Over the next six days, we searched the complex, finding large quantities of weapons, ammunition, explosives, food, and documents. There were so many bunkers and so much ammunition to be destroyed that a squad of engineers came in on the single-ship landing zone we had cut into the jungle.

By July 9, the engineers—and we infantrymen—had done our job, and orders came for the engineers to be picked up at the single-ship LZ. Then our company would march three or four kilometers eastward, to where a large natural clearing could accept sufficient choppers to fly us to Fire Support Base Blackhorse, where we could get a shower, clean uniforms, and hot chow. As the news circulated among the troops, morale—including mine—soared instantly.

In the early afternoon, a UH-1 dropped down into the small clearing, and the engineers hopped aboard. The chopper took off—straight into the trees. It made a half-turn to its left and fell to the ground. It didn't catch fire, but one engineer, pinned underneath, was dead, and another had a broken leg with the bone protruding.

A dustoff removed the casualties, and other choppers came in to pick up the surviving crew and engineers. Then another Huey arrived with a major aboard. I heard him introduce himself to my company commander as the accident-investigation officer. After a brief inspection of the downed bird, he said it was salvageable but that it would be the next day before he could get a CH-47 Chinook in to sling it back to base. We would have to remain on the ground for another night to secure the crashed helicopter.

Word quickly swept through the company. No one said anything, but no one welcomed the news. As the major walked back to his chopper, I noticed the Aggie ring on his finger. I introduced myself, and we spent a few minutes talking about our hometowns and A&M. Then I explained to him what we had been through to overrun the enemy base camp, how long we had been in the jungle, and how much everyone was looking forward to going to Blackhorse.

The major hesitated and then said, “Let’s take another look.”

After a few seconds at the crash site, he asked me if I knew anything about explosives. When I replied in the affirmative, he showed me the best location for a C-4 charge on the bird’s fuel tank. He then said that he had been wrong, that the chopper was not worth saving, and that what remained should be “destroyed in place.”

Two pounds of C-4 with a blasting cap and a long fuse produced an explosion that left nothing but a charred engine and transmission. The major flew away, we went to our pickup zone, and by dark we were enjoying a hot mess-hall meal and wearing clean fatigues. Left in the jungle were the remains of a million-dollar helicopter, a monument to the tradition of Aggies looking after each other.

Jerry Patterson (1969, H-1) 9th Marine Amphibious Brigade, 1973

I was peripherally in Vietnam at the very end—mostly on board the USS *Paul Revere* as a member of the 9th Marine Amphibious Brigade staff. I spent a little time ashore in Quang Tri, Da Nang, and Huong Dien. We got rocketed in Da Nang, and NVA 130-mm guns fired at the *Paul Revere*. That was the extent of my combat.

Aboard ship we had hot chow and clean sheets every night. Not much to write about.

Mac Phillips (1969, D-1) 101st Airborne Division, 1971

By the summer of 1971 I had been in the field more than eight months with the 1st Cavalry Division and then, when the Cav went home, with the 101st Airborne Division. Mentally and physically whipped, I welcomed the transfer to the 1st Brigade as its S-3 air staff officer. I did not have a clue what the job entailed, but I reasoned that as a veteran of more than thirty-five combat air assaults I would be able to figure it out.

When I arrived at Brigade Headquarters at Camp Eagle, I learned my major role was to coordinate all helicopter activity for the next day's missions. I went on duty at 1900 hours and a few hours later received the list of air assets for the next day. For the remainder of the night I allotted the assets while also serving as senior officer in the Brigade's TOC. The learning curve was steep and stressful, but at least I had a full stomach, clean clothes, and didn't have to squat in the jungle to take a crap.

I also learned quickly that I had an "ace in the hole" or a "guardian angel." Soon after I assumed my duties, a lanky officer speaking Texan and wearing an Aggie Ring came into the TOC. Maj. Robbie Robertson, Class of 1957, was the Brigade S-2, and he became my chief mentor and advisor. He advised me on ways to allocate the air assets, how to supervise TOC personnel at night, and how to present the daily morning briefing to the brigade commander.

Major Robertson took care of me in other ways as well. For example, he arranged a three-day courier mission. I caught a flight to Saigon, delivered an envelope of sealed papers to an office at the air base, and then had the remainder of the time to see the sights. I took a cab to what looked like the center of the city and got out at a large water fountain. Around the pool were a half dozen beautiful American girls being photographed. I thought I might be imagining things before a publicist came over and asked if I would like to take some pictures with some of "this year's Miss America candidates." Since few GIs in this area were in uniform, I guess he just wanted me as a "prop," but that was fine with me. With drool running down my chin, I stammered, "I don't mind, not as long as you can take some with my camera as well."

As the publicist introduced me to each girl, he told me what state she represented. One was Miss Texas. Among pictures I still have from my tour in Vietnam is one of me standing with “Miss Texas 1971.” Tough duty!

Near the end of my tour I applied for an R&R as I wanted to go to Thailand to visit one of my A&M classmates. Veerapun Putamonda—Tom we called him—had joined our fish class in Spider D and returned home upon graduation to be commissioned a lieutenant in the Royal Thai Army. Major Robertson came through once again, and soon I was on my way to Thailand. Tom’s father was a four-star general, and I was treated like royalty the entire week. We saw all the major sites, ate at the best restaurants, and had an absolutely wonderful time.

Many years later my son Jay, Class of 1999, took his family to Thailand after serving in the Marine Corps. Tom, now a four-star general himself and with his name on the General’s Plaque in the Sanders Corps Center, arranged for them the same tour I had gone on. Just another example of Aggies helping Aggies.

Hale Burr (1965, Squadron 7 and Corps Staff), 13th Tactical Fighter Squadron, 1968

One of my closest friends at A&M was Murray Wortham, Class of 1965. Our time as Ross Volunteers during our junior year created a close bond. Murray was fun to be around and always the life of the party. We frequently went to each other's southeast Texas home on weekends to get away from College Station. Then, between our junior and senior years, we drove together to Air Force ROTC summer camp at Webb AFB in Big Springs, Texas. After our graduation, he was a groomsman in my wedding and I was a groomsman in his. We and our wives lived in the same apartment complex while he and I attended Air Force pilot training at Laredo AFB. Then we both went to the same F-4 training class in Florida. But when we got follow-on assignments to Vietnam, it was to different units.

Unfortunately Murray was shot down and killed on 30 December 1967 during a mission over Laos. This was two months after the birth of his daughter (whom he never got to see in person). It was a loss I felt deeply then—and still feel today. I have gotten old, wrinkled, and grey haired, but Murray will always be twenty-four years old. I still miss him.

I survived my tour and returned to duty in the States. The Air Force had a personnel policy that no fighter pilot would be sent as a non-volunteer to Vietnam a second time until all eligible pilots had completed their first combat tour. After my tour in 1967–68, I felt very proficient in flying fighters and extremely confident in my pilot skills. During my first tour, fifteen of the forty-four in my original F-4 training class were shot down, and eight were killed. So our attrition rate was about one-third of the total class. Despite the odds, it was really easy to become addicted to the adrenaline rush of flying jet fighters and flying in combat. But that feeling isn't worth much if you don't survive.

It's difficult to explain the psychology of fighter pilots. We're self-assured overachievers, very aggressive, and competitive, with a strong will to win. These traits are what it takes to be successful in air combat. When antiaircraft tracers, enemy aircraft, or SAMs are flying, your training kicks in and you just react, especially if you've endured lots of realistic peacetime training. In actual combat you're in survival mode and have a heightened sense of alertness. Time seems to slow down in battle to where you're very aware of everything going on—as if it's in slow motion around you.

So I volunteered for a second tour. This was really tough on my wife, Barbara, because she knew personally quite a few young Air Force widows and wives of POW and MIA pilots, including Johnida Wortham.

I received orders to Udorn AFB, Thailand, where I was assigned to the 13th Tactical Fighter Squadron in late May 1969. After a couple days of base administrative in-processing, ground training, and getting over jet lag, I started flying combat missions once again. I didn't fly every day but averaged probably five missions a week—in Laos and occasionally over North Vietnam. We mostly attacked North Vietnamese positions along the Ho Chi Minh Trail. This was the road system that moved enemy troops and logistics from the North down into South Vietnam. We also flew a lot against the communist Pathet Lao forces in the secret CIA war for control of Laos. These missions were mostly dropping 500-, 750-, and 2,000-pound conventional "dumb" bombs and sometimes firing "Bullpup" cockpit-guided missiles.

In October 1969, after about four months in the 13th TFS, I was selected to become an F-4 Fast FAC. This was exactly the same mission that the O-2 FACs had that I flew in Vietnam a year before. The F-4 FACs marked targets with WP rockets for other fighters to attack. Our Phantoms were configured with a centerline 20-mm cannon, two WP rocket pods, and two 370-gallon external fuel tanks.

I really enjoyed these missions. We flew really low, usually well below 500 feet, and always over 500 mph. We had a saying, "Speed is life," and kept our air speed high because enemy air defenses were really dense in Laos and North Vietnam. If not flying at extremely low altitudes, we stayed above 4,500 feet to avoid small-arms and automatic-weapons fire. Of course you can't see much that high, so most missions were "down in the weeds," looking for targets. Our FAC missions lasted four to five hours with multiple air refuelings.

FAC duty was neither easy nor safe. From July 1967 until July 1970, forty-two Fast FAC jet fighters were shot down. That's a loss rate of 4.37 per 1,000 sorties flown—much higher than for any other type of aircraft during this three-year period. It's also the time frame that covers my tour as a Fast FAC. We knew the work was dangerous, but we didn't know the aircraft loss statistics—or care.

I did the FAC mission for a couple of months, and then the lieutenant colonel in charge of the program transferred to Europe. I was still a young captain, but the Wing leadership selected me to become chief of the Fast FAC program at Udorn. I was really lucky to be in that position at such a young age. This was one of my most rewarding assignments because I was leading a great group of warriors, including Capt. Dick Myers (later a four-star general and Chairman of the Joint Chiefs of Staff) and Capt. John Jumper (later a four-star general and USAF Chief of Staff). I don't think anyone who knew us as young, wild fighter pilots would have thought we'd ever become general officers. Later in our careers, I teased Dick and John that they rose to such heights because of the leadership skills learned when they worked for me as Fast FACs.

President Nixon's "Vietnamization Program," under which the South Vietnamese were to take over combat roles normally performed by Americans, enabled US forces to begin pulling out early in 1970. My DEROS was moved from late May to April 1—curtailing my tour by nearly two months. I was really happy to be going home early to Barbara and our two-year old daughter, Lara, in Texas.

As I approached the end of my combat tour, I, like others, counted the days until I would board my "freedom bird" for the trip home. In the last few weeks or days before our scheduled departure date, we said, "We're getting short." I knew several guys who got shot down in their last few days or weeks; they were very unlucky. The more combat missions you fly, the more you're exposed to enemy threats, and the more liable you are to experience something bad. The risk goes up with every mission you fly.

About four days before my departure, 7th Air Force headquarters in Saigon directed a big air strike against some SAM sites the North Vietnamese were building on their side of the border with Laos. (This was during the bombing pause over NVN, when we flew only reconnaissance flights to keep track of what the enemy was doing in the North.) Our wing at Udorn was tasked to attack these new missile sites. As commander of the Fast FACs, I was selected to be the mission commander and to lead the attack. The Frag order arrived late in the afternoon of March 26, and we immediately began planning the mission. Our Wing was tasked to provide twenty-four attack aircraft, with supporting aircraft from other Thailand bases, to destroy the SAM site. We worked until late that night coming up with the tactics for the next day's mission. We expected intense AAA fire because the North Vietnamese closely protected their SAM sites. On the morning of March 27, with the Wing Commander and the Director of Operations, I stood in front of the assembled twenty-four aircrews and briefed the mission.

Engine start, taxi, and takeoff were normal for the twenty-four F-4s carrying a mixed load of M-117 750-pound bombs and CBU-24s. We climbed out to medium altitude and air refueled on KC-135 tankers before heading into NVN toward the target.

We were lucky that the weather was clear with unlimited visibility. I dropped down to about 500 feet and moved about ten miles ahead of the bomber formation. This part of North Vietnam was mountainous and covered by trees. I pushed up my airspeed to over 500 knots and flew directly over the SAM site, which was camouflaged and hidden in the vegetation. I could clearly see the missile launchers, radar-control vans, and other assorted trucks on the ground. While lighting both afterburners, I pulled up immediately and climbed to about 10,000 feet while confirming the target to the incoming fighters. I rolled over in a looping 135-degree slicing turn back to mark the target with a white phosphorus rocket. During this time, three SAMs, which can fly at Mach 3 (nearly 2,300 mph) and up to an altitude of 80,000 feet, lifted off the ground in large dust plumes. My radar homing and warning equipment did not activate in the cockpit (indicating that no radar was locked on to my plane). I think the NVA (or Russian?) ground operators fired the SAMs optically. In any case I had three 5,000 pound SAMs flying up at my Phantom jet. I saw them and called out over the UHF radio frequency that all strike fighters were monitoring, "Falcon, we've got SAMs."

Listening to my audio tape recorder after I returned to base, I noted that the first three words were in a normal tone, but "SAMs" came out perhaps an octave higher. It was fascinating to watch these telephone-pole-sized missiles come up toward my aircraft. Our defensive maneuver against a SAM was a constantly changing flight path that kept the small wings on the missile moving and adjusting its flight path. Our hope was that the SAM guidance system would cause a large correction and overshoot instead of hitting the target—my aircraft. As I completed the roll in, one SAM went below me and two flew over my F-4 so close I could feel the turbulence. I fired two WP rockets into the middle of the target—which already had been made obvious by the large dust cloud caused by the missile launch among the green trees. As my white smoke rose from the ground, I called out to the first flight of F-4s, "Hit my smoke," and they rolled in on the target. I pulled up to get out of their way and noticed three white clouds where the SAMs exploded high above us. Then I watched the twenty-four F-4s drop their ordnance on the SAM site. It was fascinating to see the bomb impacts and explosions—and numerous secondary explosions—that billowed up where the SAM site had been. As the smoke cleared, an RF-4 recce bird came zooming over to take BDA photos of our attack results. I didn't feel any sorrow for the NVA troops that had just tried to kill me by launching the SAMs my way. Rather, I felt elated that I was still alive and that they probably were not. This was one missile site that wouldn't threaten any more American aircraft. Our return flight to Udorn was uneventful. Three days later I safely completed my final mission in my second Vietnam War tour for a total of 525 combat sorties.

Ray Dabney (1970, D-1) 1st Cavalry Division, 1973

Sometime during my junior year at A&M we received word that Robert H. Johnson (Class of 1969) had been killed in Vietnam. An infantry 2nd Lieutenant, he had stepped on an IED as they are now called. We called them booby traps. Because of that incident, Mike Waring, a classmate of mine, and I decided to take the Army flight test so we would not have to walk if we were sent to Vietnam.

After A&M graduation I attended the Infantry Officer Basic Course, followed by the Airborne School, both at Fort Benning, Georgia. Next came primary helicopter training at Fort Wolters, Texas, and then on to advanced helicopter training at Fort Rucker, Alabama. Shortly before graduation we received our orders. Mine were to Vietnam. I was both apprehensive and excited at reading those orders!

My family made the trip out to Travis AFB, California, both as a vacation and as a send-off to Vietnam for me. I flew Flying Tiger Airlines from Travis to Anchorage, Alaska, to Japan, and to Saigon (Tan Son Nhut Airbase).

The first indication that I was in a war zone was the dozens of illumination flares popping as we approached and landed at Tan Son Nhut. The next day we in-processed and received our unit orders. Mike Gustin (an Ohio State grad who had been my roommate in flight school) and I went over on the same plane and were assigned to the 120th Aviation Company at Long Binh. One night during our first week, VC sappers sneaked through the perimeter and blew up the ammo dump. What a display! Didn't get much sleep that night.

Most of our missions with the 120th were single-ship sorties flying advisors out to remote locations and the like. The exception was when Miss America and her escorts came over and we flew them around for two days.

Mike and I were with the 120th for about a month when we were transferred to F Troop 1/9 Air Cavalry squadron stationed at Lassiter Army Air Field, a short distance from Bien Hoa Airbase. Our daily missions at F Troop were to fly out to staging areas and then to fly search-and-destroy missions. Many of our staging areas were close to the Cambodian border in Tay Ninh Province. Those missions normally consisted of one LOH (pronounced "loach"), two Cobra attack helicopters, and one or two

UH-1s in the air at the same time. The LOH would fly low and slow, trying to spot VC positions, tanks, trucks, and such. When it found something or was shot at, it popped smoke to mark the spot, and the Cobras would roll in with rockets, chunkers, and miniguns. If the Cobras couldn't destroy the targets, we would call in Hueys outfitted with TOW missiles. If the TOW birds weren't successful, fighter bombers from the Air Force, Navy, or VNAF were requested. If the fighter bombers couldn't destroy the targets, B-52 bombers would be called. The B-52s would fly a cross pattern with the target coordinates at the center of the cross, three bombers crossing the target 90 degrees from another three. Usually we did the BDA the next day to ensure target destruction. These B-52 strikes out of Thailand were referred to arc lights because their bombs resembled the arc light of a welder as each line detonated.

I was primarily a UH-1 pilot but flew front seat in Cobras when needed. The back seat in Cobras, the Pilot in Command, fired the rockets. The front seat, the copilot, fired the chunker and the minigun. Hueys were armed with two M-60 machine guns manned by a crew chief and gunner. F Troop had Vietnamese Rangers assigned to Lassiter. Occasionally we inserted them at suspected enemy locations.

In January 1973, when the peace negotiators declared a ceasefire, Mike and I were assigned together to fly for the Four Power Joint Military Commission. We flew US personnel, VC officials, and other Vietnamese around South Vietnam. Some of those missions involved American POW releases. Others were to take people out to investigate violations of the peace, including the shoot-down of a US CH-47 Chinook helicopter after the ceasefire. It seemed strange. One day we were shooting at the VC; the next we were flying them around.

I returned to the US via the same route I had followed going out and went home to Texas and family for a thirty-day leave. My last duty station was Fort Lewis, Washington, where I served with the 2nd Battalion, 1st Infantry, 9th Infantry Division until my flight-school obligation was complete. I made captain eleven days before leaving the Army. I spent four years and eleven days in the Army and have no regrets. I cherish those memories.

Jon Beal (1969, Band) Marine Detachment, USS Oklahoma City, 1975

In April 1975 I was the XO of the Marine Detachment aboard the USS *Oklahoma City*—the flagship of the 7th Fleet—when we made an unscheduled departure from our home port of Yokosuka, Japan. We were not told where we were going until after a brief stop at Subic Bay, in the Philippines, for supplies. When finally en route to Vietnam, the Captain told us we would soon be eligible for combat pay and free postage.

When we arrived off the coast of Vietnam, we steamed around outside the seventeen-mile range of NVA artillery for thirty days waiting for something to happen. On April 30 we learned that Saigon had fallen to the communists. The next morning we were at muster at about 8:00 a.m. when the ship was called to general quarters. This meant that all hands were to report to their assigned battle stations. Radar had picked up hundreds of aircraft heading our direction. Fortunately, they had IFF responding Friend. A few minutes later our ship and the rest of the 7th Fleet were surrounded by helicopters filled with South Vietnamese military and government officials and their families.

That day about forty helicopters landed on our fantail helipad. There was room for only one at a time. Some we pushed overboard after the passengers and pilots disembarked. Most, however, flew off and were ditched in the ocean nearby by their pilots, who then were picked up by our rescue boats. At least twenty ships, including an aircraft carrier, took on helicopters. The Vietnamese machines, all Hueys, that landed on our ship went into the South China Sea. US Navy, Marine, Air Force, and Air America helicopters joined the evacuation, flying round trips all day.

I had read an intelligence message about the possibility of this mass exodus several weeks before, but I had the impression that it was a total surprise when the helicopters began filling the sky. We had prepared a landing party of forty Marines and fifty Navy volunteers to go ashore to assist in any evacuation, but we had made no plans for taking on the 240 refugees we now had on board.

The South Vietnamese were seeking and taking any means possible to escape the advancing communists. Several American Merchant Marine ships in Vung Tau, south of Saigon, loaded thousands of South Vietnamese and headed out to sea and safety. We received messages all day about their precarious position and slow progress.

A few days later we transferred all our refugees to a ship that took them to Guam. Their long war was over, and their country had ceased to exist.

J. Duncan Williams (1971, Band) 63rd Military Airlift Wing, 1973

I graduated from Texas A&M and was commissioned a 2nd Lieutenant in May 1971. I reported for active duty at Reese AFB, Texas, and began the standard route to becoming an Air Force pilot. After graduating from initial training, I was assigned to C-141 transports, attended the 141 school along with the standard survival courses, and began my C-141 career with the 63rd Military Airlift Wing at Norton AFB, California. Norton was one of three strategic-airlift bases on the West Coast. We primarily supported Southeast Asia but also performed airdrop missions. Airdrop consisted mainly of supporting the Army jump school at Fort Benning, Georgia, and dropping equipment at several drop zones in the California desert east of the Salton Sea.

As I look back on the many missions I flew as a copilot and later as an aircraft commander, some stand out as terrifying, some as enjoyable, and others as humorous. But one mission stands out above all the others. At the time this mission took place I was a copilot assigned to the 53rd Military Airlift Squadron, 63rd Military Airlift Wing based at Norton AFB. MAC was not the most glamorous assignment for a pilot. You couldn't turn upside down in your aircraft like the fighter pukes, and you didn't get to blow anything up like the BUFFs. All you did was go round and round the Pacific hauling junk to out-of-the-way places while playing a continuous game of cat and mouse with the ferocious thunderstorms that always seemed to be in front of us. You could always spot a MAC guy in any officers club in the Pacific. He was the tired fellow wearing a big watch and a sweated out flight suit trying to cash a check at the bar. We started calling it the "midnight airlift command" because we seemed always to be flying at night and trying to sleep during the day.

At that time (before aerial refueling on the C-141) the missions operated a little like the old Pony Express, only backwards. Unlike the real Pony Express, our mounts never got tired but we did. The airplanes continued on around the system, and every twelve hours or so a new crew took over while the old crew stopped to rest. Our crew had been flying around SEA for a couple of weeks hauling beer, boots, and household goods to all sorts of exotic places like Korat and NKP, and we were finally homeward bound. While we were in crew rest at Hickam AFB, Hawaii, I got a call from the aircraft commander telling me we were alerted for a Homecoming mission. This news was electrifying. Operation Homecoming was a big deal, and everyone wanted to get a chance to bring some of the POWs back. In spite of all the drawbacks associated with flying in MAC, Operation Homecoming missions made it all worthwhile.

The Homecoming process began with the POWs being flown from North Vietnam to Clark AFB, in the Philippines, where they were repatriated, given medical screening and treatment, and prepared for the trip home. From Clark they flew to Hickam AFB and then on to a stateside base near their homes.

We met "Balls 7" (C-141 67–0007) on the ramp at Hickam and took the final leg of the mission to Kelly AFB, at San Antonio. Shortly after takeoff the former POWs began to come up to the cockpit and chat. At first they came one by one, but as the hours wore on they came in greater numbers. Eventually we had standing room only in the cockpit, and everyone seemed to be really enjoying themselves. (Try that in an F-4.) It was my great privilege to meet Maj. Alton B. Meyer, Texas Aggie, Class of '60, who was one of the returning POWs.

Our call sign was, "Homecoming Air Evac 7 triple zero 7," and the ATC controllers gave us priority handling from when we entered US airspace until we reached San Antonio. As we went feet dry (crossed the coastline) over California, I announced on the intercom, "Ladies and gentlemen, welcome to the continental United States of America." A cheer went up throughout the aircraft, and the former POWs who were in the cockpit hugged each other and hugged us. What a great experience it was to play a small part in bringing home to their families and friends those men who had suffered so much for the country they loved.

The remainder of the mission was textbook: priority handling by ATC, a brass band welcome at Kelly AFB, and all the excitement and celebration associated with the homecoming. During the ceremony we stood out of the way with our aircraft and silently wished them well.

In 1998 the "Hanoi Taxi" (C-141B 66–0177), the first C-141 to go into Hanoi, came to Randolph AFB for the celebration of the 25th anniversary of Operation Homecoming. I was there doing my two weeks active-duty reserve time with the Air Force Office of Special Investigations, and the day before the celebrations, I got a chance to go aboard and talk to the crew. When I told them I had flown one of the Homecoming missions, they treated me like a king and gave me a tour of the aircraft. What a treat that was! The old C-141 looked, felt, and smelled just the way it had years before. That night in the BOQ as I contemplated my glorious military career, which was rapidly drawing to a close, I realized that participating in that single homecoming mission made it all meaningful and worthwhile.

APPENDIX A
Texas Aggies Killed in Vietnam

The names on this list are limited to those who actually died in Vietnam or its surrounding countries or waters as noted on the Vietnam Veterans Memorial. As with many issues of the Vietnam War, there is disagreement regarding actual dates. This list uses July 8, 1959, the date of the first American deaths in Vietnam, as its beginning and the fall of Saigon, on April 30, 1975, as its conclusion. Both hostile and nonhostile deaths are included. This list does not include those Aggies who died in training, in accidents, or from other means in the United States, Europe, Korea, or other locations. Home of record appears as listed by the Department of Defense. Date of death for those declared Missing in Action may vary according to declarations.

35 Hochmuth, Bruno A.	Marine Corps	Houston, TX	Nov 14, 1967
42 Holder, Leonard D.	Army	San Antonio, TX	Mar 31, 1968
44 Bonner, John S., Jr.	Air Force	McAllen, TX	May 31, 1970
48 Van Cleave, Walter S.	Air Force	Dallas, TX	April 22, 1969
51 Howison, Graham H.	Army	Bogota, TX	July 13, 1969
52 Campbell, William E.	Air Force	McAllen, TX	January 29, 1969
52 Fisher, Royal C., Jr.	Army	Baytown, TX	November 4, 1965
52 Tomchesson, Teddy J.	Air Force	Marlin, TX	May 5, 1968
54 Garcia, Heriberto A.	Army	Laredo, TX	November 8, 1964
55 Condon, Russell W.	Army	Humble, TX	May 22, 1965
55 Foster, Hadley	Army	San Antonio, TX	March 14, 1969
55 Mixson, Joseph G.	Marine Corps	Buna, TX	December10, 1966
55 Steel, Richard E.	Army	Texarkana, TX	November 4, 1965
56 Estein, Dalton M.	Army	Waco, TX	April 6, 1968
56 Kessinger, John M.	Army	Janesville, WI	July 2, 1967
56 McFeron, Ernest	Air Force	Edna, TX	May 16, 1965
56 Terry, Condon H.	Air Force	Dallas, TX	June 27, 1963
57 Fuller, William O.	Air Force	Houston, TX	August 26, 1967
57 Jones, Charles C.	Army	San Antonio, TX	May 1, 1967
57 Lewis, Tedd M.	Army	Dallas, TX	January 9, 1970
57 Mathis, Foy M.	Army	Gilmer, TX	January 29, 1966
57 Ramsower, Irving B., II	Air Force	Mathis, TX	March 29, 1972

57 Wyatt, Edward W.	Air Force	Houston, TX	July 28, 1969
58 Caston, James C.	Army	Weslaco, TX	August 10, 1965
58 Elledge, Don T.	Army	Mabank, TX	August 18, 1966
58 Johnson, Robert D.	Navy	Dallas, TX	September 1, 1967
58 McKnight, George P.	Air Force	Lafayette, LA	December 11, 1965
59 Blair, Donald D.	Army	Philippines	April 24, 1969
59 Goehring, Allen G.	Air Force	Tucson, AZ	November 14, 1970
59 Hawley, Donald R.	Air Force	Fort Worth, TX	December 17, 1965
59 Martin, John F.	Army	Watertown, NY	January 31, 1968
59 Smith, Allan L.	Army	Norman, OK	May 10, 1970
60 Coley, Billy J.	Air Force	Ennis, TX	December 20, 1963
60 Hartness, Gregg	Air Force	Dallas, TX	November 26, 1968
60 Kaase, Floyd W.	Army	Schulenburg, TX	May 28, 1967
60 Luna, Donald A.	Air Force	Houston, TX	February 1, 1969
60 Stone, Byron C.	Army	Houston, TX	August 20, 1964
60 Vrba, James M., Jr.	Army	Houston, TX	January 31, 1968
61 Whitehouse, Gregory K.	Army	Abilene, TX	March 6, 1968
62 Jones, William E.	Air Force	Fort Worth, TX	January 5, 1968
62 Ralph, Thomas H.	Marine Corps	Clifton, TX	May 17, 1968
62 Walker, Ralph B., III.	Army	Nacogdoches, TX	May 29, 1967
63 Allen, Charles F., II.	Air Force	Georgetown, KY	October 4, 1965
63 Dunn, Michael E.	Navy	Naperville, IL	January 26, 1968
63 Garner, Johnnie L.	Marine Corps	Bryan, TX	September 2, 1967
63 Graham, Dennis L.	Air Force	Greensburg, KS	March 28, 1968
63 Gutierrez, George, Jr.	Army	Harlingen, TX	September 1, 1965
64 Dehart, Donnie R.	Army	Houston, TX	April 29, 1967
64 Hottenroth, James R.	Air Force	Montclair, CA	October 15, 1967
64 Hubler, George L.	Marine Corps	Moab, UT	February 23, 1968
64 Lamb, Colin E.	Army	Caldwell, ID	July 3, 1968
64 Lowe, Donald W.	Air Force	Conroe, TX	February 3, 1972
64 McAdams, Tomas A.	Army	Liberty, TX	February 28, 1969
64 Mundt, Henry G., II	Air Force	Abilene, TX	May 8, 1969
64 Summers, Franklin D.	Army	Longview, TX	April 12, 1970
64 Thompson, Victor H., III.	Air Force	Houston, TX	March 15, 1967
65 Carroll, Wesley W., III.	Army	Houston, TX	January 27, 1970
65 Dougherty, John C.	Army	Terra Haute, IN	May 9, 1968
65 Jageler, Charles D.	Army	Gatesville, TX	October 9, 1969
65 Martin, Aubrey G.	Navy	Beeville, TX	July 19, 1969
65 Oman, Richard A.	Army	Georgetown, TX	April 27, 1968

65 Santos, Jose C.	Air Force	Brownsville, TX	November 13, 1968
65 Tijerina, Albert A., Jr.	Air Force	San Angelo, TX	March 1, 1971
65 Vann, Ronald B.	Army	Waco, TX	April 25, 1969
65 Wilke, Robert F.	Air Force	Milwaukee, WI	January 17, 1968
65 Wortham, Murray L.	Air Force	San Augustine, TX	December 30, 1967
66 Blake, Jack P.	Army	Beaumont, TX	December 20, 1968
66 Bush, Joseph K., Jr.	Army	Temple, TX	February 10, 1969
66 Callaway, Michael R.	Army	Bellaire, TX	March 21, 1968
66 Campbell, Clyde W.	Air Force	Longview, TX	March 1, 1969
66 Dimock, James A.	Army	Houston, TX	May 18, 1969
66 Kaiser, Larry K.	Army	Bay City, TX	April 30, 1970
66 Long, Carl E.	Marine Corps	College Station, TX	December 20, 1969
66 Neely, James E.	Army	Abilene, TX	August 23, 1969
66 Oates, Eugene C., III.	Army	Bryan, TX	August 4, 1969
66 Tubre, Stephen R.	Army	North Highlands, CA	August 31,1968
66 Welsh, Elbert A.	Army	Cadiz, OH	September 16, 1971
67 Connevey, Layne H.	Army	Pasadena, TX	September 4, 1969
67 Lewis, Converse R., III.	Marine Corps	College Station, TX	October 26, 1967
67 Matocha, Donald J.	Marine Corps	Smithville, TX	April 5, 1968
67 Russell, John E.	Army	Corpus Christi, TX	May 28, 1970
67 Russo, Michael P.	Army	New York, NY	November 8, 1967
67 Smith, Andrew D., III.	Army	Wakefield, RI	May 28, 1970
67 Ward, Neal C.	Air Force	College Station, TX	June 13, 1969
68 Arthington, Marvin S.	Air Force	Burkburnett, TX	Nov 27, 1970
68 Baldridge, John R., Jr.	Air Force	Memphis, TN	Nov 20, 1969
68 Boyd, Tom M., III.	Marine Corps	Corpus Christi, TX	May 13, 1968
68 Butler, James M.	Air Force	Pensacola Beach, FL	July 24, 1970
68 Harlan, Richard E.	Army	Dallas, TX	March 15, 1971
68 Johnston, Steven B.	Air Force	Muskogee, OK	January 4, 1973
68 Morton, James E., Jr.	Air Force	Memphis, TN	August 3, 1969
68 Noonan, Michael D.	Army	Amarillo, TX	July 4, 1969
68 Rinard, Kevin A.	Army	Waco, TX	April 24, 1971
68 Smith, Rayburn L., III	Army	Shamrock, TX	September 19, 1970
68 Taff, George T.	Army	College Station, TX	February 20, 1971
68 Woolley, James N.	Army	Odessa, TX	October 30, 1969
69 Cartwright, James H.	Army	Decatur, TX	January 8, 1971
69 Cowley, Jeffrey E.	Army	Freer, TX	April 15, 1971
69 Forrester, Ronald W.	Marine Corps	Odessa, TX	September 5, 1978
69 Johnson, Robert H.	Army	College Station, TX	May 12, 1970

69 Jones, Sanderfierd A.	Army	Hutchins, TX	March 5, 1969
69 Kildare, William T.	Marine Corps	Ogallala, NE	September 21, 1967
69 Mullen, Walter S.	Army	Brownsville, TC	June 5, 1972
69 Yates, David E.	Army	Chesapeake, VA	July 13, 1969
70 Anderson, Vincent C.	Air Force	Los Angeles, CA	September 26, 1972
72 Pannell, Phillip R.	Army	Plainview, TX	March 14, 1969

APPENDIX B

Texas Aggies Who Died on Active Duty during the Vietnam Era

Many Aggies who died while serving in uniform during the Vietnam War Era (July 8, 1959, to April 30, 1975) but who were not in the actual war zone at the time of their death are not included on the Vietnam Veterans Memorial. They died in training accidents, in air crashes, from disease, and in other ways while fulfilling their military duties. Their names do appear on the Texas A&M Corps Memorial. At least eight additional names on the Corps Memorial may be Vietnam Era vets, but neither the Sanders Corps Center nor the Association of Former Students has information sufficient to substantiate. The following include the class, last mailing address, and date of death of each.

35 Moore, Raymond A.	Alexandria, VA	April 7, 1968
36 Montgomery, Morris B.	San Antonio, TX	January 14, 1970
37 McInroe, Ben F.	Dallas, TX	November 10, 1969
38 Maxwell, Keith	Paris, TX	October 16, 1965
39 Garrett, Leonard E.	Fort Hood, TX	December 3, 1969
39 Schrank, Milton A.	Hamilton, TX	February 22, 1970
40 Morris, Kyle H.	Kirtland AFB, NM	February 7, 1964
40 Williams, Hugh R.	Bryan, TX	June 3, 1966
41 Hall, Clarence T., Jr.	San Antonio, TX	February 24, 1971
41 Schott, Ernest E.	La Grange, TX	January 12, 1965
42 Kulhanek, Bernard J.	Fort Sill, OK	May 7, 1966
42 Thompson, Roy H.	San Diego, CA	June 6, 1970
44 Andrews, William M.	Amarillo, TX	March 3, 1969
44 Cook, Sidney H., Jr.	Marshall, TX	August 30, 1970
44 McNeese, Frank J.	Round Rock, TX	July 23, 1972
44 Smith, Irvin D.	APO New York	November 13, 1969
45 Fowler, John H., Jr.	Minot AFB, ND	October 12, 1966
47 Turner, Jack E.	College Station, TX	August 5, 1960
49 Williams, Edward L.	Falls Church, VA	May 28, 1967
50 Golden, Elden W.	APO New York	October 6, 1968
50 Koller, John H.	Leroy, TX	May 13, 1968
51 Clark, Noble N.	Burleson, TX	May 26, 1972

51 Coslett, Roger J.	San Antonio, TX	September 11, 1969
51 Trochak, Frank L.	McAllen, TX	April 25, 1971
52 Pierce, Warren M.	Ellsworth AFB, SD	April 22, 1965
52 Royalty, James G.	APO San Francisco	December 9, 1966
53 Carr, Gordon W.	Dugway, UT	April 23, 1964
53 Cleghorn, Leonard V., Jr.	San Antonio, TX	April 30, 1960
53 McMahan, Billy M.	Austin, TX	August 18, 1965
53 Rawlings, Charles R.	Poteet, TX	April 2, 1971
53 Sutton, Ray B., Jr.	Midwest City, OK	July 18, 1964
54 Scott, Donald L.	Houston, TX	November 28, 1966
54 Vaught, Ralph R.	Odessa, TX	October 23, 1973
55 Jahns, Julius J.	Rosebud, TX	August 8, 1965
56 Biehunko, Ernest F.	College Station, TX	February 14, 1961
56 Patterson, Frank E.	College Station, TX	January 1, 1960
56 Tachibana, Richard M.	Ramstein, Germany	July 13, 1961
57 Smith, Rodney H.	Erath Co., TX	March 16, 1961
57 Smith, William J.	Palestine, TX	November 11, 1965
57 Smith, Allison F.	Alamogordo, NM	February 24, 1964
57 Stout, Ralph L.	Carswell AFB, TX	October 11, 1962
58 Eady, Arvin D., Jr.	Kermit, TX	August 9, 1959
58 Jenrette, James P.	College Station, TX	December 18, 1963
58 Roberts, Milton R.	Great Mills, MD	February 5, 1971
58 Spitzer, Joel S.	Tuscaloosa, AL	March 27, 1973
59 Hataway, James A.	Lufkin, TX	July 19, 1963
59 Isiminger, Garland J.	College Station, TX	March 28, 1965
59 Leidolf, Emil J., Jr.	Wichita, KS	March 12, 1974
59 Scott, Lynn P.	Granbury, TX	September 16, 1974
59 Smith, Edward H.	Lockport, NY	May 19, 1963
59 Stewart, Ronald D.	APO San Francisco	August 17, 1964
60 Cordell, William F.	McGuire AFB, NJ	June 25, 1965
60 Threadgill, Luther L.	Del Rio, TX	August 26, 1965
61 Ayers, Norman D.	Glendale, AZ	January 21, 1964
61 Thigpen, James C.	Alameda, CA	April 6, 1965
61 Walla, Gerald J.	Minot AFB, ND	January 20, 1969
62 Beakley, John	Langley AFB, VA	July 22, 1974
62 Hodges, Ted L.	APO New York	September 8, 1967
62 McAlpine, Robert E.	Taylor, TX	May 3, 1969
62 Reed, James L.	Texarkana, TX	August 24, 1965
63 Griffin, James R.	Vandenberg AFB, CA	September 16, 1965

63 Holt, William A., Jr.	Dallas, TX	December1, 1965
64 Korenek, Edwin J.	Hopewell, VA	July 14, 1968
64 Price, John B.	Victorville, CA	May 18, 1967
64 Rawls, Harlow W.	Corsicana, TX	February 24, 1969
64 Schnabel, James E.	San Antonio, TX	June 1, 1974
65 Hernandez, John R.	Houston, TX	September 14, 1965
65 Vick, Jerry Don	Hamilton, TX	August 6, 1969
66 Stevens, James R.	San Antonio, TX	October 2, 1970
66 Thornhill, John D.	San Antonio, TX	March 15, 1972
66 Whitson, John T.	Trinity, TX	April 4, 1969
67 Ebey, John J.	Citrus Heights, CA	March 13, 1969
67 Markham, William E., Jr.	Orange, TX	October 1, 1969
67 Tesch, John R.	Fort Walton Beach, FL	January 1, 1971
68 Garrett, Terrel V.	Dover AFB, DE	March 1, 1971
68 Ogdee, Jack E.	San Benito, TX	June 8, 1969
69 Halloran, William T.	Clovis, NM	March 21, 1973
69 Rockstroh, Henry J., Jr.	San Antonio, TX	June 19, 1970
69 Tillman, Robert H.	Grosse Isle, MI	October 16, 1971
70 Williams, Peter K.	Beauford, SC	May 8, 1973
71 Sargent, Tommy R., Jr.	San Antonio, TX	June 27, 1973
71 Spann, David H.	Fort Riley, KS	September 22, 1973
72 Bennett, John D.	Jefferson City, MO	October 14, 1972

Glossary

120-mm rocket A Soviet-made fin-stabilized 75.4-inch rocket with great destructive power. The use of launch tubes ensured greater accuracy, but the rocket could be fired from improvised launch sites. The NVA and the VC used it extensively in Vietnam.

A-1 (Douglas A-1 Skyraider). A single-seat attack aircraft that saw service between the 1940s and the 1980s. A piston-powered, propeller-driven anachronism in the jet age, it was the close-air-support workhorse of the South Vietnamese Air Force for much of the Vietnam War.

A-2 Company A-2, Texas A&M University Corps of Cadets.

A-37 (Cessna A-37 Dragonfly or Super Tweet). A light attack aircraft developed from the T-37 Tweet basic trainer in the 1960s and 1970s. It was introduced during the Vietnam War.

A-6 (Grumman A-6 Intruder). A twin jet engine, midwing, all-weather attack aircraft in service with the Navy and the Marine Corps between 1963 and 1997.

A-7 (Ling-Temco-Vought A-7 Corsair II). This carrier-capable subsonic light attack aircraft entered service with the Navy during the Vietnam War and later was adopted by the Air Force.

A4-E (Douglas A-4 Skyhawk). This single-seat, single-engine, delta-winged carrier-capable attack aircraft was the Navy's primary light attack aircraft in the early years of the Vietnam War.

AAA Antiaircraft artillery.

AC Aircraft Commander.

AC-130 (Lockheed AC-130 Spectre). Developed as "Project Gunship II" for the Air Force during the Vietnam War, this heavily armed, long-endurance, ground-attack variant of the C-130 carries a wide array of anti-ground oriented weapons integrated with sophisticated sensors, navigation, and fire-control systems. Unlike other fixed-wing military aircraft, it relies on visual targeting. Because its large profile and low operating altitude make it an easy target, it usually flies close-air-support missions at night. See C-130.

AC-47 See Puff the Magic Dragon.

ACAV See M-113.

ACR Armored Cavalry Regiment.

Aerial Port An airfield authorized for entrance into or departure from the country in which it is located.

Aero Rifle Platoon (Blues). See Pink Team.

Aero Weapons (Red) Platoon See Pink Team.

AFB Air Force Base.

Agent Orange The tactical-use chemical employed most widely by the US military in its herbicidal-warfare program, Operation Ranch Hand, during the Vietnam War. Named after the orange-striped barrels in which it was shipped, it was a mixture of two herbicides, 2,4-D and 2,4,5-T. The 2,4,5-T was found to be contaminated with 2,3,7,8-Tetrachlorodibenzodioxin.

AH-1 (Bell AH-1 Cobra). A two-blade, single-engine attack helicopter manufactured by Bell Helicopter and delivered June 1967. Originally it was designated UH-1H. The "A" for attack designation was soon adopted, and the Army applied the Cobra name.

AIT Advanced Infantry Training.

AK-47 (also Kalashnikov). A select-fire (semi-automatic and automatic), gas-operated 7.62-mm assault rifle developed and, in 1949, accepted by the Soviet Union. It remains the most widely used assault rifle in the world.

ALO Air Liaison Officer.

Americal Division The name of the 23rd Infantry Division (formed in New Caledonia during World War II) is a contraction of "America, New Caledonia."

Amtrak A small amphibious landing craft introduced during World War II as a cargo carrier for ship-to-shore operations, it evolved into assault troop and fire-support vehicles as well.

AO Area of Operations.

APC Armored Personnel Carrier.

Arty Artillery.

ARVN Army of the Republic of Vietnam.

ASAP As soon as possible.

ATC Air Traffic Control, Armored Troop Carrier. (See Tango.)

AWOL Absent without official leave.

B Athletics Texas A&M Corps of Cadets unit during 1950s.

B-40 (Bazooka 40 mm). See also RPG-7. Version of Soviet RPG-2 produced under license in Vietnam. Owing to its short range and inaccuracy, it was replaced by the more effective RPG-7.

B-52 (Stratofortress). A long-range, subsonic, jet-powered, strategic bomber capable of carrying a 70,000-pound payload, it was designed and built by Boeing in the 1950s and continues to be operated by the Air Force.

B707 (Boeing 707). A midsized, long-range, narrow-body, four-engine jet airliner built by Boeing Commercial Airplanes between 1958 and 1979.

Basic Basic Training.

BDA Bomb Damage Assessment.

BDI Bomb Data Indicator, Bearing Deviation Indicator. (See CDI.)

Beaten Zone An area in which maximum machine-gun fire is possible.

Blues (Aero Rifle Platoon). See Pink Team.

BOQ Bachelor Officers' Quarters.

Booby Trap A device or setup intended to kill, harm, or surprise a person whose presence or action triggers it.

Browns ARVN Rangers.

BUFF Big Ugly Fat Fellow (or Fucker). See B-52.

Bullpup The first mass-produced air-to-surface command-guided missile, deployed by the Navy as the ASM-N-7 in 1959 and as the AGM-12B in 1962. The weapons operator tracked the Bullpup by watching a flare on its rear and steered it using a joystick and radio signals.

Butter Bar 2nd Lieutenant The rank insignia is a gold bar shaped like a stick of butter.

BX (Base Exchange). A store operated by the Air Force Exchange Service to provide quality merchandise and services at low prices to active-duty military, National Guard and reserve members, military retirees, and family members. In the Army, the exchange is referred to as a PX.

C-1 Company C-1 Texas A&M University Corps of Cadets.

C-123 (Fairchild C-123 Provider). A four-engine turboprop military-transport aircraft designed as a troop, medevac, and cargo transport and built for the Air Force in the early 1950s. During the Vietnam War, the aircraft was used to spray Agent Orange.

C-130 (Lockheed C-130 Hercules). See also AC-130. A four-engine turboprop military transport designed and built by Lockheed (now Lockheed Martin). Capable of using unprepared runways, the C-130 was designed as a troop, Medevac, and cargo transport aircraft but has found other roles, including for search and rescue and as a gunship for airborne assault.

C-141 (Lockheed C-141 Starlifter). A jet-powered military strategic airlifter introduced to replace slower piston-engine cargo planes, it first flew in 1963 for the Air Force, and it remained in service until 2006.

C&C Command and Control.

C7-A (De Havilland Canada DHC-4 Caribou). A Canadian cargo aircraft with short take-off and landing capability, it was first flown in 1958. US and Australian Caribous, designated C7-A and C7-B, saw extensive service during the Vietnam War.

CAP (Combined Action Program, Combined Action Platoon, Civic Action Patrol). From 1965 to 1971 the Marine Corps placed fourteen-member rifle squads, each with a Navy corpsman, in or adjacent to rural hamlets, where they combined with older Vietnamese youth and elderly men to form local defensive units against VC and NVA incursions.

CAR-15 (Colt Automatic Rifle-15 Military Weapons System). A family of firearms marketed by Colt in the 1960s and 1970s. Colt later abandoned the CAR-15 concept but continued making the M16 for the military and the Colt AR-15 for law-enforcement and civilian applications.

CAS Close air support.

CBU-24 (Cluster Bomb Unit-24). An unguided, aircraft-delivered antipersonnel and antimateriel weapon consisting of a dispenser unit containing 665 tennis-ball-sized fragmentation bomblets that explode in a large semicircle on the target.

CDI (Course Deviation Indicator). An instrument used in aerial navigation to determine an aircraft's lateral position in relation to a course. If the aircraft is to the left of course, the needle deflects to the right, and vice versa.

CH-46 (Boeing Vertol CH-46 Sea Knight). A medium-lift tandem-rotor transport helicopter first used by the Marine Corps to provide all-weather, day- or night-assault transport of combat troops, supplies, and equipment during the Vietnam War.

CH-47 (Boeing CH-47 Chinook). A twin-engine, tandem-rotor, heavy-lift helicopter produced by Boeing Vertol in the 1960s. It is among the heaviest lifting Western helicopters and, with a top speed of 196 mph, was faster than other utility and attack helicopters of the 1960s.

Chamorro Indigenous person of the Mariana Islands.

Chieu Hoi ("Open Arms") Program An RVN initiative encouraging the VC and their supporters to defect during the Vietnam War. Those who took advantage of the program were called Hoi Chanh ("political returnees").

Chinook See CH-47.
Chunker See M129.
CIA Central Intelligence Agency.
CICO Combat Information Control Officer.
CICV Combined Intelligence Center Viet Nam.
CIDG (Civilian Irregular Defense Group). A US government program developed during the Vietnam War to create South Vietnamese irregular military units using minority populations.
CIM Combat Information Monitor.
CO Commanding Officer.
Cobra Gunship See AH-1.
COIN Counterinsurgency.
Colt .45 automatic (M1911). A single-action, semi-automatic, magazine-fed, recoil-operated pistol chambered for the .45 ACP cartridge, it served as the standard-issue sidearm for US Armed Forces from 1911 to 1986.
COMNAVFORV Commander Naval Forces Vietnam.
Corps Tactical Zone In the 1960s, South Vietnam was divided into four Corps Tactical Zones, each overseen by one of four ARVN corps with corresponding numbers. I Corps Tactical Zone was the northernmost zone, bordering North Vietnam. II Corps included the central highlands and contiguous central lowlands. III Corps was the region surrounding the capital, Saigon. IV Corps was the Mekong Delta region. In July 1970 the Corps Tactical Zones were designated Military Regions with corresponding numbers..
CP Command Post.
Crabbed (spoken of an aircraft). Turned, generally into a crosswind, so that it appears to be flying sideways.
CSAR Combat Search and Rescue.
CW2 Chief Warrant Officer.
D-1 through **D-3** Companies D-1 through D-3 in the Texas A&M University Corps of Cadets.
DAC Department of the Army Civilian.
DASC (Direct Air Support Center). The principal Marine Corps aviation C&C system and the air-control agency responsible for directing air operations in support of ground forces.
DEROS Date Eligible for Return from Overseas.
DMZ (Demilitarized Zone). An area within which any type of military force, such as personnel, hardware, and infrastructure, is banned.

Donut Dollies American women who, during the Vietnam War, volunteered to serve through the Red Cross in a program called Supplemental Recreation Activities Overseas. Armed with cookies and homemade entertainment, the women risked their lives daily to cheer up the troops.

DRVN (Democratic Republic of Vietnam). North Vietnam.

DSC (Distinguished Service Cross). The second-highest military award that can be given to a member of the Army (and previously the Army Air Forces) for extreme gallantry and risk of life in combat with an armed enemy force.

Dustoff See Medevac.

E-2 Company E-2 in the Texas A&M University Corps of Cadets.

E-6 US Army rank, staff sergeant.

E-7 US Army rank, sergeant first class.

E-8 US Army rank, first sergeant or master sergeant.

EA–6A With a full-spectrum receiving system integrated with high-power radar jammers, chaff-dispensing pods, and a state-of-the-art communications jammer, this two-seat, twin engine, carrier-capable aircraft was the premier US tactical ECM aircraft in the Vietnam era.

EC-121R (Military version of Lockheed L-1049 Super Constellation airliner). Nicknamed Batcats, these aircraft were based at Korat RTAFB, Thailand, where, between October 1967 and December 1970, they served as airborne relay stations to detect and transmit signals from seismic devices dropped behind enemy lines.

ECM Electronic Countermeasures.

F-105 (Republic F-105 Thunderchief). A supersonic fighter-bomber used by the Air Force during the early years of the Vietnam War. A two-seat Wild Weasel version was developed later to suppress enemy air defenses, specifically SAM sites, electronically.

F-2 Company F-2 in the Texas A&M University Corps of Cadets.

F-4 (McDonnell Douglas Phantom II). See also Fast FAC. An all-weather, long-range supersonic jet interceptor and fighter-bomber, it entered service in 1960 and was used extensively during the Vietnam War. The F-4E, first flown in 1965, was an Air Force variant with an M61 Vulcan cannon in its elongated nose.

FAC (Forward Air Controller). Aircraft that vector fighter and attack aircraft and support combat search-and-rescue operations.

Fast FAC See VR/TACA. In 1969, when proliferating antiaircraft defenses in Laos increasingly endangered slow FACs, the 469th Tactical Fighter Squadron, based at Korat RTAFB and flying F-4Es, was approved for Fast FAC duty.

Fast Mover Jet aircraft.

Flak (from German *fliegerabwehrkanone*, "flyer defense cannon"). Anti-aircraft gun.

FNG Fucking new guy.

FO Forward observer.

FRAGO or Frag Order (Fragmentation Order). An order used to make changes to an operations order without having to rewrite the original order.

FSB (Fire Support Base). A temporary military encampment widely used during the Vietnam War to provide artillery fire support to infantry operating in areas beyond the range of fire support from their own base camps

FSE (Forward Support Element). A 105-mm artillery battalion plus combat engineer, medical, and forward support (maintenance) companies attached to a brigade.

FWS (Fighter Weapons School). During the Vietnam War the Air Force and the Navy each had a fighter weapons school. The Navy Strike Fighter Tactics Instructor Program, popularly known as Top Gun, began as the Navy Fighter Weapons School in 1969. It teaches fighter and strike tactics and techniques to selected naval aviators and naval flight officers, who return to their operating units as surrogate instructors. The USAF Weapons School began as the Aircraft Gunnery School in 1949. In 1954 the school also began training fighter instructors and took on the title USAF Fighter Weapons School. In 1992, when the school began providing advanced training in weapons and tactics employment to officers of the combat air forces, it dropped "fighter" from its title and became the USAF Weapons School,

g-force (with "g" from "gravitational"). A measurement of the type of acceleration that causes weight. One g is 9.8 meters per second squared, the acceleration caused by gravity at Earth's surface. Consider the pilot. When flying straight and level, acted upon by only the force of gravity, he weighs, say, 165 pounds. If he were to pull back on the joystick, making his plane accelerate upward at 9.8 meters per second squared, the total gforce on his body would be 2 g, half coming from gravity and half from upward acceleration. His body is now generating a force of 330 pounds downward into his seat.

G-2 Command Staff Intelligence Officer.

G-3 Command Operations Officer and Company G-3 in the Texas A&M University Corps of Cadets.

Gatling gun See also Minigun. An early rapid-fire weapons and a forerunner of the modern machine gun. Its operation centered on a cyclic multibarrel design that facilitated cooling and synchronized the firing-reloading sequence.

GCA Ground Controlled Approach.

GIB Guy in back.

Gravity Weapon Iron bomb.

Grunt (also Ground Pounder). Infantry soldier.

Guard (also Aircraft Emergency Frequency). A frequency on the aircraft band reserved for emergency communications for aircraft in distress.

H-2 Company H-2 in the Texas A&M University Corps of Cadets.

H-34 (Sikorsky H-34). A piston-engine military helicopter originally designed as an antisubmarine warfare aircraft for the Navy. Army H-34s did not participate in the Vietnam War, but several were supplied to the ARVN.

H-53 (Military version of Sikorsy S-65). The largest, heaviest helicopter in the US military, the H-53 is designed to transport equipment, supplies, and personnel. The Marine Corps placed its initial order for the CH-53A Sea Stallion in 1962. Other versions include the HH-53 Super Jolly Green Giant for the Marine Corps, and the MH-53J Pave Low for Special Forces.

H&MS 11 (Headquarters and Maintenance Squadron 11). In 1954, Headquarters Squadron 11, the "Playboys," an aviation-logistics support unit of the Marine Corps, was designated Headquarters and Maintenance Squadron 11. In 1965, H&MS 11 relocated to Da Nang, Vietnam, and until 1971 supported attacks by Marine aircraft against VC forces. While in Vietnam, the squadron supported twelve aircraft types.

H&S (Headquarters and Service Company). A typical battalion H&S company usually includes the following key personnel and primary staff officers: Battalion Commander, a lieutenant colonel; Battalion Executive Officer, a major; Battalion Sergeant Major (the senior enlisted advisor to the Battalion Commander on enlisted personnel matters, especially those involving discipline and morale); Manpower officer (administration and personnel) with the title of "adjutant" (S-1), a 1st or 2nd lieutenant; Intelligence and counterintelligence officer (S-2), a captain; Operations and training officer (S-3), a major;

Logistics officer (S-4), a captain; and Communications and information officer (S-6), a 1st or 2nd lieutenant.

HA(L)-3 (Helicopter Attack Squadron [Light] 3 "Seawolves"). All-volunteer Navy squadron formed to support Naval Special Warfare and Mobile Riverine Forces during the Vietnam War.

HE High explosive.

HH-3E See Jolly Green Giant.

HH-43B (Kaman HH-43B Huskie). A helicopter with intermeshing rotors. The Air Force, the Navy, and the Marine Corps used it as a short-range overland search-and-rescue aircraft during the Vietnam War. Known by its call sign "Pedro," the Huskie flew more rescue missions than all other aircraft combined because of its unique hovering capability.

HH-53 (Super Jolly Green Giant). The first helicopter designed specifically for CSAR operations, it made its first flight in March 1967. Developed to replace the HH-3 Jolly Green Giant, it was equipped with armor plating, self-sealing fuel tanks, three 7.62-mm miniguns, and an external rescue hoist with 250 feet of cable and a 20,000-pound capacity. It could transport thirty-eight combat-equipped troops, twenty-two litter patients and four medical attendants, or 18,500 pounds of freight.

Hmomg An ethnic group from the mountainous regions of China, Laos, Thailand, and Vietnam. During the first and second Indochina Wars, France and the United States recruited thousands of Hmong people in Laos to fight against forces from North and South Vietnam and communist Pathet Lao insurgents. Hundreds of thousands of Hmong refugees fled to Thailand seeking political asylum.

Ho Chi Minh Communist revolutionary leader; prime minister and president of the Democratic Republic of Vietnam.

Hoi Chanh See Chieu Hoi Program.

Hooch A thatched hut or improvised living space (e.g., sand-bagged bunker or improved "foxhole")

Huey See UH-1 Iroquois.

Hump To walk, generally carrying a heavy rucksack

Huskie See HH-43B.

I-3 Company I-3 in Texas A&M University Corps of Cadets.

ID Intelligence Detachment.

IED (Improvised Explosive Device). Booby trap.

IFF (Identification Friend or Foe). An identification system developed during World War II that enables military-interrogation systems to identify aircraft, vehicles, or forces as friendly. IFF can identify only friendly targets. When an IFF interrogation receives an invalid reply or none, the object cannot be deemed friendly but is not positively identified as a foe.

In Country In Vietnam.

In the Clear Unencrypted.

IOBC Infantry Officer Basic Course.

IP Instructor Pilot.

JAG (Judge Advocate General's Corps). The branch or specialty of a military concerned with military justice and military law. Officers serving in a JAG Corps, called Judge Advocates, serve primarily as legal advisors to the command to which they are assigned. In this function, they also can serve as personal legal advisor to their commander. They are charged with both the defense and the prosecution of military law as provided in the *Uniform Code of Military Justice.*

Jolly Green Giant (Sikorsky S-61R). A twin-engine helicopter used in transport or search-and-rescue roles, it served in the Air Force as the HH-3E Jolly Green Giant.

JP (Jungle Penetrator). A wedge-shaped stand attached to a winch used to lift the wounded from the jungle floor to the hovering helicopter.

Jungle Rot (also tropical ulcer, Aden ulcer, Malabar ulcer, tropical phagedena). A skin lesion caused by microorganisms such as mycobacteria. Common in tropical climes, it is often a result of continuous exposure to damp, unsanitary conditions. The condition can affect any exposed part of the body but is more common in the lower limbs. If neglected, it can extend through the muscles and tendons, and even the bones.

JUSMAGTHAI Joint US Military Advisory Group Thailand.

Karst Terrain usually characterized by barren, rocky ground, caves, sinkholes, underground rivers, and the absence of surface streams and lakes.

KBA Killed by Air.

KC-135 (Boeing KC-135 Stratotanker). A military aerial-refueling aircraft that began service in 1957 and continues in service today.

Khmer Serei (Free Khmer). An anticommunist and antimonarchist guerrilla force whose primary objective was to overthrow the Cambodian leader King Norodom Sihanouk and become a permanent part of the Cambodian body politic. US Special Forces and its CIDG recruited the Khmer Serei into their ranks, where they participated in intelligence-gathering missions. Their knowledge of the border area and their ability to communicate with local populations enabled them to get intelligence about the Viet Cong.

KIA Killed in action.

Kill Zone The area of an ambush within which everyone is likely dead or wounded.

Knot Unit of speed equal to one nautical mile (approximately 1.15 miles) per hour.

KP Kitchen Patrol (also Kitchen Police.)

L-19 See O-1.

L-T Lieutenant.

LAW Light antitank weapon.

Loach See LOH.

LOH Light Observation Helicopter. See OH-6. When the OH-6 entered service in 1966, pilots dubbed it "Loach," a word based on LOH, the acronym of the program that spawned it.

Loran (Long Range Navigation). A radio-navigation system developed in the United States during World War II. First used for ship convoys crossing the Atlantic Ocean and then by long-range patrol aircraft, it found its main use on ships and aircraft operating in the Pacific Theatre.

LSD (Landing Ship, Dock). An amphibious-warfare ship of 9,000-plus tons with a well dock to transport and launch landing craft and amphibious vehicles. Some ships with well decks also have bow doors to enable them to deliver vehicles directly onto a beach (like an LST).

LST (Landing Ship, Tank). Vessel created during world War II to support amphibious operations by carrying vehicles, cargo, and troops directly onto an unimproved shore.

LZ Landing zone.

M-106 See also M-113. An M-113 modified to carry an M30 4.2-inch (107-mm) mortar.

M-113 A fully tracked armored personnel carrier first fielded by Army mechanized infantry units in Vietnam in 1962. The most widely used armored vehicle of the Army in Vietnam, it earned the nickname "Green Dragon" among the VC because it was used to break through heavy thickets to attack and overrun enemy positions. Its new aluminum armor was thick enough to protect the crew and passengers against small-arms fire but light enough that the vehicle was air transportable and moderately amphibious.

M-117 An air-dropped general-purpose 750-pound bomb first used by US military forces during the Korean War.

M-16 A select-fire 5.56-mm rifle with a twenty-round magazine that entered US military service in 1963 and was deployed for jungle warfare during the Vietnam War.

M-48 (M-48 Patton). A US medium battle tank first produced in 1952. The M-48A3, a modernized variant, first produced in 1963, served as the primary battle tank for the Army and the Marine Corps in Vietnam.

M-577 The Command Post variant of the M-113. It first entered service in 1962 and, because of its effective design, remained in service more than forty years.

M-60 Army machine gun firing 7.62-mm bullets at approximately 550 rounds per minute

M-72 The M72 LAW is a portable one-shot 66-mm unguided antitank weapon. In 1963 the Army and the Marines adopted it as their primary individual infantry antitank weapon.

M-79 A single-shot, shoulder-fired, break-action grenade launcher. First used during the Vietnam War, it can fire a variety of 40-mm rounds, including explosive, antipersonnel, smoke, buckshot, flechette (pointed steel projectiles), and illumination.

M129 ("Chunker"). A 40-mm automatic grenade launcher used in US aircraft.

MAAG Military Assistance Advisory Group.

MAC (Military Airlift Command). The primary strategic-airlift organization of the Air Force from 1966 to 1974, when tactical airlift units were merged into MAC to create a unified airlift organization.

Mach Number A measure of speed expressed in multiples of the speed of sound (about 768 miles per hour).

MACV (US Military Assistance Command, Vietnam). A joint-service command of the US Department of Defense created in 1962 in response to the increase in US military assistance to South Vietnam.

Mark 82 See Mk 82.

McGuire Rig Harness used in Vietnam to extract soldiers from areas without a suitable pick-up zone. It was simple, inexpensive, and did not require the soldier to carry special equipment. It did not allow extracted soldiers to be hoisted into the helicopter.

Medevac (also Medivac). Emergency medical-evacuation flight. The Radio call sign was "Dustoff."

MI Military Intelligence.

Mike Minute, Millimeter.

Mike Force (Mobile Strike Force Command). See also Nung. Army Special Forces in Vietnam who served with indigenous soldiers and were led by US and Australian personnel. A countrywide quick-reaction force for securing, reinforcing, and recapturing CIDG outposts, they also conducted reconnaissance, search-and-rescue, and search-and–destroy missions.

Military Region See Corps Tactical Zone.

Minigun (M134 Minigun). See also Gatling. A 7.62-mm NATO six-barrel machine gun with a high rate of fire (2,000 to 6,000 rounds per minute), it features Gatling-style rotating barrels with an external power source, normally an electric motor. “Mini” is used in the name because the M134 uses smaller shells than other guns with a similar firing mechanism.

Mk 82 (Mark 82). An unguided, low-drag, general-purpose 500-pound bomb. Among the smallest in service, it is also one of the most common air-dropped weapons in the world.

MSC Texas A&M University Memorial Student Center.

MTT (Mobile Training Team). Army unit assigned to train the Thai, Cambodian, Laotian, and Vietnamese Armies and to develop relationship with local populations.

NAD Naval Advisory Detachment.

NCO Noncommissioned Officer.

NCOIC Noncommissioned Officer in Charge.

NDP Night Defensive Position.

NILO Naval Intelligence Liaison Officer.

NKP Nakhom Phanom Royal Thai Air Force Base.

NLF (The National Liberation Front of South Vietnam). Viet Cong.

Nomex The trademark for a meta-aramid material, first marketed by DuPont in 1967, with excellent thermal, chemical, and radiation resistance.

Nung A Vietnamese minority group of ethnic Chinese descent with a reputation as fierce fighters. A Nung Security Platoon established in 1964 to guard the headquarters of the 5th Special Forces Group, in Nha Trang, soon grew to be three full companies. With the growth of the Mike Force concept, they took on countrywide reaction missions to assist units in trouble.

NVA North Vietnamese Army.

NVN North Vietnam.

O-1 (Cessna L-19/O-1 [Observation] Bird Dog). Because the O-1 has short takeoff and landing and low-altitude and low-airspeed capabilities, the Air Force used it in Vietnam as an FAC aircraft.

O-2A (Cessna O-2A Super Skymaster). An FAC aircraft delivered to the Air Force in 1966. It had two in-line 210 horsepower engines (one in front of and one behind the cabin). The Air Force added windows and wing hardpoints for 7.62-mm miniguns, bombs, rockets, and flares. It had a top speed of 205 mph and a ferry range of 1,400 miles.

O-6 (Officer 6). US Uniformed Services Pay Grade corresponding with the ranks of colonel and captain (Navy).

O&M Operations and Maintenance.

OBC (Officer Basic Course). A course in which officer candidates learn basic leadership skills and basic small-unit tactics.

OCS Officer Candidate School.

OH-6 (Hughes OH-6 Cayuse). See also LOH. A single-engine light helicopter with a four-bladed main rotor used for personnel transport, escort and attack missions, and observation.

OINC See also NCOIC. Officer in Charge.

OJT On-the-job training.

Operation Allen Brook A Marine Corps operation on Go Noi Island, fifteen miles south of Da Nang. The island was a VC and PAVN stronghold. Two companies of the 2nd Battalion 7th Marines, supported by tanks, arrived in May 1968. They leveled much of the island, but the VC and PAVN continued to resist. The operation concluded in August.

Operation Commando Hunt A covert Seventh Air Force and Navy Task Force 77 aerial interdiction campaign that began in November 1968 and ended in March 1972. Its objective was to prevent the transit of PAVN personnel and supplies on the Ho Chi Minh Trail.

Operation Homecoming In February 1973, following diplomatic negotiations, three C-141s flew to Hanoi and one C-9A went to Saigon to pick up released American POWs.

Operation Linebacker II An aerial bombing campaign conducted against targets in North Vietnam during the final period of US involvement in the Vietnam War. It was a "maximum-effort" bombing campaign to destroy major target complexes in the Hanoi and Haiphong areas. The attacks were conducted by B-52s rather than, as in Rolling Thunder and Linebacker I, by tactical aircraft.

Operation Market Time A program established by the US Joint Chiefs of Staff in 1965 to blockade the South Vietnamese coastline against North Vietnamese gun-running trawlers.

Operation Pegasus A combined Marine, Army, and South Vietnamese overland relief expedition launched in March 1968 that broke through to the Marines at Khe Sanh.

Operation Piranha A Marine Corps follow-up on Operation Starlite that took place 7–10 September 1965 on the Batangan Peninsula.

Operation Ranch Hand See Agent Orange.

Operation Rolling Thunder A gradual, sustained aerial bombardment conducted by the US 2nd Air Division, the Navy, and the Republic of Vietnam Air Force against North Vietnam from March 1965 to November 1968.

Operation Starlite The first regiment-sized action conducted by a purely US military unit in the Vietnam War. During August 18–24, 1965, 5,500 Marines assaulted a Viet Cong force of 1,500 men and several elite mortar units near Van Tuong. The VC regiment was not wiped out as expected, but the Americans judged the battle a success.

OPS Operations.

OV-10 (North American Rockwell OV-10 Bronco). A turboprop light attack and observation aircraft developed in the 1960s for counterinsurgency combat. One of its primary missions was as an FAC aircraft. It can carry up to three tons of external munitions and internal loads such as paratroops or stretchers and can stay aloft for three or more hours.

P-3 (Lockheed P-3 Orion). A four-engine turboprop antisubmarine and maritime-surveillance aircraft developed for the Navy in the 1960s and still in use today. Armed with air-to-surface missiles, the P-3 is capable of engaging ships directly.

PACAF Pacific Air Forces.

Palace Dog See Project 404.

Pathet Lao A Communist political movement and organization formed in Laos in the mid-twentieth century. During the Vietnam War they fought against anti-Communist forces.

PAVN (People's Army of Viet Nam). Regular North Vietnamese army.

PBR (Patrol Boat, River). A thirty-two-foot-long, fiberglass-hulled boat used in the Vietnam War to stop and search river traffic, insert and extract Navy SEALs, and assist the Army's 458th Transportation Company. Usually the boats had a four-member crew and operated in pairs. They drew only two feet of water fully loaded, and their dual diesel engines and water-jet drive enabled them to operate in shallow, weed-choked waters and to reach top speeds of 32 mph. Their armament included twin .50-caiber machine guns forward, a 7.62-mm light machine gun at the rear and one on each side, and a grenade launcher.

Peter Pilot An inexperienced copilot or any pilot in general.

PFC Private First Class.

Phoenix Program A CIA program designed to identify and neutralize the Viet Cong infrastructure.

Pink Team A combination of a White (Scout) Platoon and a Red (Aero Weapons) Platoon often supporting Blues (an Aero Rifle Platoon). The White Platoon used Light Observation Helicopters to skim low over terrain searching for signs of enemy activity and flying in tight circles to draw enemy fire. When the enemy was spotted, the Red Platoon used their gunships to protect the LOHs and attack the enemy. When the situation warranted, the Blues would be inserted to conduct ground reconnaissance and fix the enemy until a larger force could be committed.

PLAF People's Liberation Armed Forces of South Vietnam. See also VC.

Popular Force During the Vietnam War the South Vietnamese Popular Force and the South Vietnamese Regional Forces were forms of local militia. During the early 1960s they manned the countrywide outpost system and defended critical points such as bridges and ferries.

PRC-25 FM receiver/transmitter developed by the Radio Corporation of America in the 1950s. It had a range of 5–8 kilometers and was powered by a dry-cell battery with an average life of twenty hours. The "Prick 25" became the most widely used radio of the war.

Project 404 A covert Air Force advisory mission to Laos during the Vietnam War. Its purpose was to supply technicians needed to support and train the Royal Laotian Air Force. At the same time Raven FACs were brought in to supply pilot expertise and guidance for running a tactical air force. Together the two programs were named Palace Dog.

PT boat (Patrol Torpedo boat). A torpedo-armed fast-attack craft used by the Navy during World War II. It was small, fast, and inexpensive to build, valued for its maneuverability and speed, but hampered by ineffective torpedoes, limited armament, temperamental airplane engines, and comparatively fragile construction that limited it to coastal waters.

PT-76 A Soviet amphibious light tank introduced in the early 1950s that soon became the standard reconnaissance tank of the Soviet Army. Its full name is Plavayushchiy [Swimming] Tank-76. The number 76 is the caliber of the rifled tank gun.

Puff the Magic Dragon (Douglas AC-47 Spooky). The first gunship developed by the Air Force to provide close air support for ground troops during the Vietnam War. The military version of the DC-3, it was modified by mounting three 7.62-mm General Electric miniguns.

PX See BX.

Quan Canh ARVN Military Police.

R&A Research and analysis.

R&R Rest and recuperation (also recreation or relaxation).

Recondo (*Reconnaissance* and *Commando*). Highly specialized infantry training, or a Recondo School graduate who leads small, heavily armed long-range reconnaissance teams deep into enemy-held territory.

Red (Aero Weapons) Platoon See Pink Team.

REMF Rear-echelon motherfucker.

Rescap To fly over a downed pilot to keep the enemy away.

RF-4 An unarmed photographic reconnaissance version of the Air Force F-4C.

RLAF Royal Laotian Air Force.

RMT Radio-maintenance technician.

Roadrunners Teams of four to six Vietnamese nationals loyal to Saigon operating under the auspices of US Special Forces and posing as NVA soldiers while conducting intelligence-gathering missions in enemy-controlled territory.

Rockpile, The A 700-foot rocky outcrop dominating the surrounding terrain in northern Quang Tri Province. Marine observers on its top had a clear view of two strategic east-west arteries in the DMZ sector. About two thousand meters to the south was Fire Support Base Elliot, also called "the Rockpile" by those who served there.

ROK Republic of Korea.

Rome Plow Large, armored bulldozer used by the US military during the Vietnam War. Named after Rome, Georgia (home of the Rome Plow Company), the plow was equipped with a very sharp "stinger blade" weighing more than two tons that could cut down trees.

Ross Volunteers Named in honor of former governor and president of

Texas A&M University Lawrence S. Ross, the Texas A&M Ross Volunteer Company is the Honor Guard for the Governor of the State of Texas.

ROTC Reserve Officers' Training Corps.

RPG-7 (*Ruchnoy Protivotankovy Granatomyot* ["hand-held antitank grenade launcher"]). A portable, reusable, unguided, shoulder-fired, antitank rocket-propelled grenade launcher first delivered to the Soviet army in 1961. The term "rocket-propelled grenade" is a reverse acronym (the words are chosen to fit the letters) for "RPG." Its ruggedness, simplicity, low cost, and effectiveness have made it the most widely used anti-armor weapon in the world.

RR Radio research.

RTB Return to base.

RTO Radio-telephone operator.

RVN (Republic of Vietnam). South Vietnam.

RW Reconnaissance Wing.

S-1 through **S-6** See H&S.

S-5 (Plans and Strategy Office). Office responsible for civil/military operations strategy planning. At the unit level the S-5 is the primary adviser to the Commander on the civilian-to-military and military-to-civilian impact of the mission or operation within the host nation.

SA-7 A shoulder-fired, low-altitude surface-to-air missile system with a high-explosive warhead and passive infrared homing guidance. The first generation of Soviet man-portable SAMs entered service in 1968.

SAC (Strategic Air Command). Both a Department of Defense Specified Command and an Air Force Major Command, in control of two components of the US military strategic nuclear strike force: land-based strategic bomber aircraft and intercontinental ballistic missiles.

SAFAsia In Vietnam 1st Special Forces Group organized Special Action Force Asia to support theater-wide military training, civic-action, and disaster-relief operations. Augmenting 1st Group were the 97th Civil Affairs Group, the 156th Medical Detachment, the 400th Army Security Agency Detachment, the 441st Military Intelligence Detachment, and the 539th Engineer Detachment. In 1964, special operations in Vietnam shifted to the 5th Special Forces Group.

SAM Surface-to-air missile.

SAR Search and rescue.

SCONA Texas A&M University Student Council on National Affairs

Scout (White) Platoon See Pink Team.

SEA Southeast Asia.

SEAL (*Sea, Air, and Land*). The Navy's principal special-operations force. Its primary functions include small-unit maritime military operations that originate in and return to a river, an ocean, a swamp, a delta, or a coastline.

Seawolves See HA(L)-3.

SERE (*Survival, Evasion, Resistance, and Escape*) A program to train US military personnel in evading capture, survival, and the military code of conduct. Established by the Air Force during the Korean War, it was extended to the Army, the Navy, and the Marine Corps during the Vietnam War.

SF Special Forces.

Short Soldier near the end of his/her term of duty..

SKS (*Samozaryadnyj Karabin sistemy Simonova*, 1945 [Self-loading carbine of the Simonov System, 1945]) A semiautomatic carbine chambered for the 7.62-mm round. In the early 1950s the Soviets replaced it with the AK-47.

SLAR Side-Looking Radar.

Sling-out platform Area within which equipment is loaded into a sling for transport by a utility helicopter.

SOG Studies and Operations Group.

SOP Standard Operating Procedure.

SP (Sundries Pack) Box containing writing paper, envelopes, blue-ink pens, foot powder, toothbrushes and paste, chewing gum, M&Ms, bars of Hershey chocolate, and cartons of assorted cigarettes. One SP was intended to meet the requirements of 100 men for one day.

Sparrow (AIM-7 Sparrow) An American medium-range semiactive radar-homing air-to-air missile operated by the Air Force, the Navy, and the Marine Corps.

Standboard SAC crews have a saying, "Every flight a Standboard," meaning that they plan and fly every mission as though an inspector were looking over their shoulder.

Standboard Navigator Primary navigator, responsible for training and supervision of all unit navigators.

STRAC (Strategic Army Corps) A command active in the 1960s with a mission of high readiness. To be labeled STRAC was high praise. But the term also was applied to officers and NCOs who went *strictly according* to regulations, who seemed unable to think for themselves.

Stream A long, tight bomber formation, each aircraft being allotted a height band and a time slot to minimize the risk of in-flight collision.

SVN South Vietnam.

Swift Boat (also Patrol Craft Fast). Fifty-foot-long, shallow-draft aluminum vessel operated by the Navy during the Vietnam War to patrol coastal areas and, later, interior waterways to interdict VC movement of arms and munitions, transport Vietnamese forces, and insert SEAL teams for counterinsurgency operations.

T-54 A Soviet main battle tank that entered production in 1947. In Vietnam it was outperformed by the M48A3 Patton and even the M41 Walker Bulldog. The T-54/55 series became the most-produced tank in history.

TA-4 (Douglas TA-4F Skyhawk) Introduced by the 1st Marine Air Wing in 1967, the TA-4 was armed with two pods of 5-inch Zuni rockets (half smoke and half high explosive), and 20-mm guns. With its good low-level fuel specs, FM radio, and excellent rear-seat visibility, it proved a superb vehicle for Fast FAC operations.

TAC (Tactical Air Command, Tactical Officer) In 1947 the Air Force formed three command divisions: Strategic Air Command, Tactical Air Command, and Air Defense Command. Each had a specific responsibility. Tactical Air Command was to command, organize, equip, train, and administer forces and to plan for and participate in tactics for fighters, light bombers, and other aircraft. It developed the ability to deploy tactical striking forces anywhere in the world.

Tactical Zone See Corps Tactical Zone.

Tango (Armored Troop Carrier). LCM-6 landing craft modified for use by the Mobile Riverine Force of the Army in the Vietnam War. The 9th Infantry Division used Tangos early in the war. As they proved themselves, they were deployed elsewhere.

TASS Tactical Air Support Squadron.

TDMG Tentative Distinguished Military Graduate.

TDY Temporary Duty.

TFA (Task Force Alpha) The 553rd Reconnaissance Wing carried out a covert US joint military electronic-warfare operation during the Vietnam War. Using electronic sensors, computers, and communications-relay aircraft, the system directed strike aircraft to PAVN targets on the Ho Chi Minh Trail. From its creation the Infiltration Surveillance Center, at Nakhon Phanom, Thailand, and operations conducted from it were known as Task Force Alpha.

TFS Tactical Fighter Squadron.

Tip Tanks Fuel tank mounted on the wing tips of high-speed aircraft to increase fuel efficiency by reducing drag from wing-tip vortices and to distribute weight evenly across the wingspan.

TOC Tactical Operations Center.

TOW (Tube-launched, Optically tracked, Wire-guided) First produced in 1970, the BGM-71 TOW is one of the most widely used antitank guided missiles.

TPC Thailand Procurement Center.

Trigon Office of the Commandant Headquarters, Military Sciences Building, Texas A&M University.

U-21 (Beechcraft U-21A Ute) Military version of Beechcraft King Air 90. Low-wing twin turboprop with retractable tricycle landing gear. Capable of carrying two crewmembers and ten passengers. For command, control, and utility missions in combat zones.

UH-1 (Bell UH-1 Iroquois) A military helicopter powered by a single turboshaft engine with two-bladed main and tail rotors. The first combat operation of the UH-1 was in 1959 in the service of the Army during the Vietnam War. The original designation, "HU-1," led to the nickname "Huey." In 1962 the designation was changed to "UH-1," but the nickname remained.

Uncle Ho Ho Chi Minh, a Communist revolutionary leader who was prime minister and president of the Democratic Republic of Vietnam.

USAF United States Air Force.

USARV United States Army Vietnam.

USMACV See MACV.

USMC United States Marine Corps.

USO (United Service Organizations). In 1941, just before America entered World War II, President Franklin D. Roosevelt united several service associations into one organization, the USO, to lift the morale of our military and generate support on the home front.

VC (Viet Cong). The name given by Western forces to the National Liberation Front, a political organization established by North Vietnam in 1960 to foment insurgency in South Vietnam and Cambodia. Its army, PLAF, had guerrilla and regular units and a network of cadres who organized peasants in the territory it controlled.

VMCJ-1 Marine Composite Squadron One (VMC-1) was activated in 1952 and, after merging with Marine Photographic Squadron One

(VMJ-1), was designated VMCJ-1. During the Vietnam War, VMCJ-1 carried out many area-reconnaissance and electronic-warfare missions for MACV and flew combat missions as far north as Hanoi and Haiphong.

VNAF Republic of Vietnam Air Force.

VR/TACA Visual Reconnaissance/Tactical Air Coordination (Airborne). See Fast FAC.

White (Scout) Platoon See Pink Team.

WO1 Warrant Officer Class 1.

WP White phosphorus.

XO Executive Officer.

Zero Dark Hundred An unspecified hour in the early morning (implying an unpleasant time to be awake). The term is derived from military time, in which hours before 10:00 am are prefixed with a zero (read as "zero" or "oh") and 00 minutes (read as "hundred")—as in "zero five hundred," meaning 5:00 am.

Zippo Boat See also PBR. Riverine boat with a flamethrower. Its 1,350 gallons of compressed napalm could be fired for just over three and one-half minutes to a distance of 300 meters when clearing VC bunkers and concealed fighting positions from the riverbanks of the Mekong.

About the Editor

Michael Lee Lanning is the author of twenty-one nonfiction books on military history, sports, and health. More than 1.1 million copies of his books are in print in fifteen countries, and selected editions have been translated into twelve languages. He has appeared on major television networks and the History Channel as an expert on the individual soldier on both sides of the Vietnam War.

The New York Times Book Review declared Lanning's *Vietnam 1969–1970: A Company Commander's Journal* to be "one of the most honest and horrifying accounts of a combat soldier's life to come out of the Vietnam War." *The London Sunday Times* devoted an entire page to its review of his *The Military 100: A Ranking of the Most Influential Military Leaders of All Time*. According to the *San Francisco Journal*, Lanning's *Inside the VC and NVA* is "a well-researched, groundbreaking work that fills a huge gap in the historiography of the Vietnam War."

A veteran of more than twenty years in the US Army, Lanning is a retired lieutenant colonel. During the Vietnam War he served as an infantry platoon leader, reconnaissance platoon leader, and an infantry company commander. In addition to having earned the Combat Infantryman's Badge and Bronze Star with "V" device with two oak leaf clusters, Lanning is Ranger-qualified and a senior parachutist.

Lanning was born in Sweetwater, Texas, and is a 1968 graduate of Texas A&M University. He currently resides on the Bolivar Peninsula of Texas.

Index